INVIS

Books by Ivan T. Sanderson

Animal Treasure

Caribbean Treasure

Living Treasure

Animal Tales

How to Know
the North American Mammals

The Silver Mink

Living Mammals of the World

Follow the Whale

The Monkey Kingdom

Abominable Snowmen

The Continent We Live On

The Dynasty of Abu

Book of Great Jungles

This Treasured Land

Uninvited Visitors

"Things"

More "Things"

Invisible Residents

A gold artifact (one and a quarter inches long) from the Colombian
national collection, housed in the *Banco de la Republica*. It is obviously
a trinket and an artist's conception of something he had seen. However, it
is *not* a representation of any kind of animal; but it looks just like a
very modern, delta-winged, steep-climbing jet-fighter. Yet, it has been
dated as being 1000 years old!

INVISIBLE RESIDENTS

THE REALITY OF UNDERWATER UFOS

IVAN T. SANDERSON

INTRODUCTION BY
DAVID HATCHER CHILDRESS

Invisible Residents

Published by
Adventures Unlimited Press
Kempton, Illinois 60946 USA

www.adventuresunlimitedpress.com

ISBN 1-931882-20-7

Printed on acid free paper in the United States of America

10 9 8 7 6 5 4 3 2 1

INVISIBLE
RESIDENTS

ADVENTURES UNLIMITED PRESS

FOREWORD

BY
DAVID HATCHER CHILDRESS

A 1935 illustration of a spacecraft suddenly coming out of the water, foreshadowing the modern phenomena of underwater UFOs, or USOs. From *Weekly Illustrated* (Mary Evans Picture Library).

Ivan T. Sanderson's book *Invisible Residents* is a unique contribution to the study of the UFO enigma. Originally published over 30 years ago, it still remains an important book in the study of this enduring puzzle.

Ivan T. Sanderson was born in 1911 and before he died in 1973 he wrote over 18 books. *Invisible Residents* was one of his last books, first published in 1970. Sanderson was a biologist who was fascinated by the unexplained and wrote on such topics as mystery animals (including Bigfoot and the Yeti), lost civilizations, UFOs and "Ooparts," or "Out-of-Place-Artifacts."

In *Invisible Residents* he put forward the curious theory that "OINTS"— Other Intelligences—live under the oceans. This underwater, parallel, civilization may be twice as old as Homo sapiens, he proposed, and may have "developed what we call space flight." In the book Sanderson proposed that the OINTS are behind many UFO or USO (Unidentified Submarine Object) sightings as well as the mysterious disappearances of aircraft and ships in the Bermuda Triangle.

In the years since his book was first published, Sanderson's theory has largely been deemed a crackpot theory, though Hollywood managed to pick up on the idea and make several movies along his hypothesis, including *Cocoon* and *The Abyss*, among others.

Sanderson's original book is long out of print, but his original theory remains, in whole and in part. In whole, it is the rather outrageous theory that an underwater humanoid civilization—with advanced technology, no less—is inhabiting the deep oceans of our watery planet. In part, he is giving evidence, and attempting to explain, the often bizarre UFO-USO sightings that involve metallic craft exiting or entering a large body of water, typically the ocean (though in some cases rivers and lakes).

Sanderson subtitled his original book: "A Disquisition upon Certain Matters Maritime, and the Possibility of Intelligent Life under the Waters of This Earth." However, the most important part of Sanderson's work on this subject seems to be the enduring enigma of the UFO phenomena and the very real possibility that some UFOs are able to travel underwater, and the related possibility that some theoretical "UFO Bases" are actually underwater, rather than underground or in space as advanced by the typical "Moon as a Space Base" theory.

Above: An artist's depiction of an underwater base built into a guyot, or some other seamount. Here you can see locks for small submarines (and other craft) plus a drilling derrick on top of the mount at the upper right. The long, tubular array on top of the mount could serve as a long-wave radio transmitter (ELF) or as as a water desalinization plant or even an oxygen-generating mechanism. From *Underwater and Underground Bases* by Richard Sauder (2001, Adventures Unlimited Press). **Opposite**: The illustration from the cover of the second issue of *FATE* magazine, Summer, 1948, which shows spheres rising from the water in the Crow River UFO case.

A 1958 photograph of a UFO over Kaizuka, Japan. Japan has experienced many UFO flaps starting in the late 1940s, many of them involving underwater UFO stories or of UFOs picking up water as they hovered.

Indeed, how fascinating a theory for the UFO investigator, that bases for these craft may well actually be underwater. What better place to have an impenetrable base than deep within the oceans of the planet? Yet, if UFOs, or at least some of them, are coming from beneath the oceans or lakes of our planet, does it necessarily mean that there is another civilization besides our own that is responsible? In fact, could it be that since WWII a number of underwater UFO bases have been constructed on the planet by the very human governments of our planet? We know that many of our governments, on nearly every continent in the world, have constructed submarine bases that are hidden in oceanside cliffs or even entirely underwater. Could some of these underwater bases house UFO-type craft that are capable of moving through the water and through the air as well? Evidence is pointing in this direction. On the other hand, as Sanderson and others have conjectured, extraterrestrials may also be using our oceans for space bases. The enigma endures.

Statistically, UFOs are most commonly seen around 1) military bases, 2) electrical power lines, and 3) bodies of fresh water. UFOs coming out of the Earth's oceans are, generally, in a category unto themselves.

UFOs don't necessarily have to come out of the water to be around water. A number of UFOs have been noted hovering over bodies of water and apparently lowering a tube down to the water and "sucking it up." These so-called "thirsty UFOs" may be using water to power their craft, may simply need to replenish the on-board water supply much as a commercial jetliner, or, it has been speculated, may be taking water to UFO bases on the Moon.

One famous encounter occurred three years after *Invisible Residents* was published. On May 22, 1973, Japanese student Masaaki Kudou had taken a summer job as a security guard at Tomakomai, on the island of Hokkaido (Japan), at a timber yard near the sea. After a routine patrol around the site that clear, starry night he parked his patrol car, turned off its lights and looked over the lumberyard and the bay beyond.

What seemed at first to be a shooting star coming down toward the bay, suddenly stopped in its tracks, vanished, reappeared, and began to gyrate slowly down over the bay. It stopped about 70 feet (21m) above the water and then lowered a transparent tube toward the water with a soft sound (described as "min-min-min").

When the tube reached the water, it began to glow. The tube was withdrawn, and the UFO moved to hover over Kudou's car. Everything around the car was lit up like day. Kudou was afraid the UFO would attack or even kill him.

Leaning over to watch through his windshield, Kudou saw that the UFO was perfectly smooth and glowing white, with windows around it. Through one he could see the shape of a humanoid figure; two smaller figures were visible through another of the windows. Three or four more brightly-lit UFOs now joined the first, and with them a large, brown cylinder. The spheres maneuvered and vanished into the cylinder, which then sped away to the north. Kudou, who felt as if he had been bound hand and foot, regained his senses. His car radio was making a meaningless static noise and he had a severe headache. The entire event lasted about 12 minutes. "Experts," as usual, were baffled by the case, especially the fact that high tech "aliens" would need to slurp up sea water in a Japanese bay. Why do aliens, or their craft, need something so plentiful and "cheap" as water? Could their craft actually be powered by water? It is an astonishing thought!

Another thirsty UFO popped up on September 30, 1980 at the White Acres ranch, near Rosedale, Victoria, Australia. The White Acres Ranch is a cattle station of about 600 acres with several large water tanks. On that night, George Blackwell, a station hand and caretaker of the ranch, awoke at about 1:00 am to the sound of the farm's cattle going wild. Blackwell could hear a "strange screeching whistling" as well, and got up to investigate. The moon was out on that night and there was no wind at all.

Blackwell saw a domed object about 15 feet (4.5m) tall and 25 feet (7.5m) broad with a white top and blue and orange lights. For a while it hovered over a water tank made of concrete about 450 yards from the house. It then came to rest on the ground 20 yards further on. Blackwell drove a motorcycle to within 50 feet of the craft. There was no effect on his motorcycle, but the whistling from the UFO suddenly rose to deafening heights, and suddenly there was a loud bang and the craft lifted off. At the same time, a blast of hot air nearly knocked Blackwell over. The UFO dropped some debris as it flew away eastward at the low altitude of only about 100 feet (30m).

Blackwell examined the site early the next day and found a ring of blackened grass, flattened in a counter-clockwise direction. Inside the ring was green grass, but the flowers that had been growing there had disappeared. In a line to the east outside the ring was a trail of debris which

Left: A photograph of a curious Saturn-like UFO over Hanover, Pennsylvania taken in the late 1950s and given to Project Blue Book to examine (no specific date given by Project Blue Book). **Below**: An odd Saturn-like UFO photographed over a field at Acton, Texas on November 19, 1968. From Project Blue Book (US Air Force).

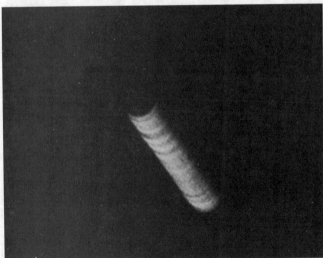

Above: This tubular UFO, similar to the cigar-shaped, submarine-like objects often reported to come from under water and then fly in the air—was photographed over New York City on March 20, 1950. The photographer's name was deleted from Project Blue Book's files—as were most names—when the material was released, including these two photographs. **Left**: A close-up of the amazing UFO. Would it be capable of travelling underwater, as some witnesses claim?

comprised some small rocks, weeds and cow dung.

For days afterward Blackwell suffered headaches and nausea, and his watch refused to work normally. Most importantly, Blackwell had discovered the water tank that the UFO had been hovering over had been completely emptied of the 10,000 gallons (45,000 liters) of water that it had originally held!

UFOs sucking up water—for whatever purpose—is just one aspect of our tale of UFOs-USOs and their relation to water. It is the UFOs that actually dive in and out of water that are of critical interest here. During the last 30 years, new sightings have occurred and new information on old sightings has come forth through the Freedom of Information Acts in the USA, Britain and Australia.

The government of Australia released 600 pages of UFO-related documents to the Australian UFO Research Association of North Adelaide in 2003. Debbie Payne of the Association reported on their findings from these documents in an article in *Nexus* magazine (Vol. 12, No. 1; Dec. 2004). Payne said that the Australian military had reported a number of UFOs around the top secret Woomera rocket range in the vast desert of south central Australia, including a flying disc seen during the launch of a test rocket in April of 1967.

Many years earlier at Woomera, on October 27, 1952, a dark cigar-shaped object with two portholes was seen to fly rapidly across a clear sky by four witnesses, two of them army officers. Payne suggests that the Woomera facility in Australia, which covers an area the size of England—270,000 square kilometers—is the equivalent of Nevada's Area 51 and may be involved in the manufacture of highly advanced aircraft that observers would call UFOs.

Do some of these UFOs—extraterrestrial or man-made—have the ability to go underwater as well, as Sanderson asks us? Payne in her article mentions that UFOs are commonly seen coming out of the water in the Milne Bay area of Papua New Guinea. Says Payne, "Milne Bay is on the easternmost tip of Papua New Guinea, bordered by the Solomon Sea above and the Coral Sea below. The surrounding islands and seas were rife with reports of all kinds of weird and wonderful sightings. I believe there may well be an underwater base in this area, because of the number of sightings over such a great period of time and also because the survey map indicates that the ocean is very deep in this area. The sea beds around these islands are littered with underwater caverns."

The long-time British UFO researcher Jenny Randles reports in the February 2005 issue of *Fortean Times* that the British government has continued to deny any involvement with the famous 1979 "Pennine Mystery Light Case" as she calls it. Randles reports that during a 48-hour period during February 22-24, 1979, a low-flying military exercise took place over the UK, and several major UFO encounters were reported during this period, possibly related to the military activity. These included three landings in the area known as the Pennine Mountains which run down the center of northern England.

Randles tells the very interesting story of a security guard on the Central Pier in nearby Blackpool who saw a roaring orange UFO moving low across the Irish Sea at 2:45 am on the night of the UFO flap. Half an hour later that night the same security guard saw something else which stunned him. "Climbing up from the cold waters of the sea was a spiraling mass of white lights that swirled upwards like a corkscrew and vanished quickly into the dark sky."

These curious incidents, during officially announced military maneuvers raise the question of whether the British, and naturally, the Americans, have underwater military bases—bases which are capable of launching, shall we say, UFOs?

The American researcher Richard Sauder has used the Freedom of Information Act to obtain thousands of documents on underground and underwater military bases. In his books *Underground Bases: What Is the Government Trying to Hide?*, and the sequel, *Underwater and Underground Bases*, Sauder details an astonishing amount of technology and activity in this pursuit.

Sauder documents current tunneling technology, and discloses actual designs for underground and underwater military bases. On the subject of underwater bases he shows how flat-topped seamounts, or guyots, whose mesa-like tops may be several hundred feet below the surface, may serve as underwater bases that include airlocks for submarines that enter an oxygen-rich, rock-cut harbor inside the subsurface mountains. Other underwater installations are located near coastlines, and the tunneling under the seafloor can begin at a coastal military base which is on dry land.

Either way, Sauder concludes that underwater bases have been built by various governments around the world—and they are Top Secret! Also,

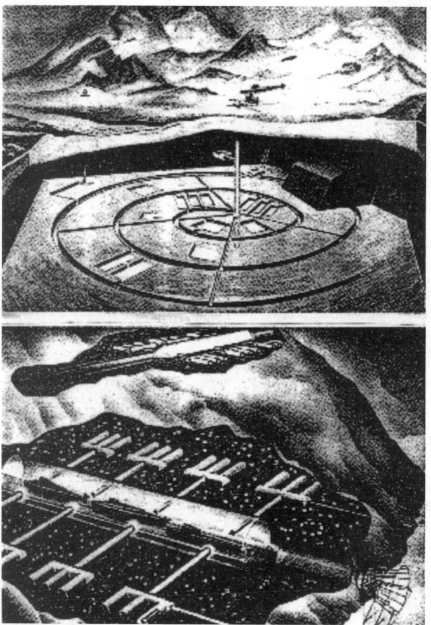

Two conceptual designs for undersea bases from the US Navy. The top is the radial design and the bottom a typical rock-site with large airlocks and dock inside. From *Underwater and Underground Bases* by Richard Sauder (2001, Adventures Unlimited Press).

he suspects that some sort of craft that is both a USO and a UFO can be launched from these underwater bases.

Articles on UFOs-USOs appear consistently in newspapers and magazines around the world. On March 28, 2005, the *India Daily* ran a story entitled "Reverse Engineering ET Deep Underwater Craft." Quoting the article (which contains some deviations from usual American-English usage): "Oceanographers and Naval engineers are investigating certain phenomena that show evidence of the presence of extra-terrestrial deep underwater crafts—the floating versions of UFOs. These crafts are capable of sharp and efficient maneuvering, has the implacable stealth to avoid detection, can hover in the deepest parts of the oceans and are capable of going deep into the tectonic plate levels under the ocean."

The article went on to say that, "scientists and engineers are finding solid evidences that these crafts are present in many numbers under our oceans though undetected and invisible in regular human eyes… There are not many sightings of these crafts as very few people really dive into the depths of the ocean, which is really unexplored. A computer model has recently revealed the possible propulsion systems. The same anti-gravity principles apply though the model becomes much more complex due to buoyancy and other aquatic issues.

"Some divers in different parts of the world have reported sightings of strange underwater objects that propagate on its own but there is no real evidence that these are really extra-terrestrial crafts. Some believe, there are countries who have the knowledge of these crafts and are trying to reverse engineer their next generation submarines and underwater crafts from these."

The article concluded, "The biggest problem of reverse-engineering these underwatercrafts is their stealth. As such deep underwater part of the oceans is seldom explored. The super stealth around these vehicles makes them further difficult for detection. According to some UFO researchers, these extra-terrestrial crafts are busy changing the under ocean landscapes. The underwater accidents of submarines due to collision with unknown underwater ridges and mountains have increased steadily over the last five years. The navies of many countries have reported these accidents regularly."

So sit back and read Sanderson's classic book on USOs in a brand new light. The knowledge that has been gained from the decades of research since it was written gives us a whole new perspective on USOs and the continuing reality of this phenomenon. Indeed, it is startling to think that UFOs are real nuts-and-bolts craft using some form of electro anti-gravity—hence the bright lights associated with most craft—which can dive into the water at any time and presumably dock in underwater installations that have been built, possibly, all over the world!

How intriguing a hypothesis, used in a number of Hollywood movies, that the ultimate docking stations for some of the UFOs seen constantly around the world are deep within our oceans. These underwater docking bases may have been built by humans in our distant past (and are still operational to this day), or built by extraterrestrials, or by the current post-war governments of Earth—or even a combination of the three!

A depiction of the incredible event of a rocket-like object bursting out of an ice pack in Antarctica in 1965. During Operation Deepfreeze, Dr. Rubens J. Villela and two other witnesses observed this rocket-like object burst through the thick ice (at least 37 feet) and ascend rapidly. Sanderson begins his book with this curious incident.

Perhaps the only photograph of an "underwater UFO." Terry Rose described the glowing underwater object that way after he took this photograph from a Seattle, Washington, pier in January of 1966. Rose commented on his submission of this photograph to the US Air Force, "I wasn't a believer in flying saucers." Photograph from Project Blue Book (US Air Force).

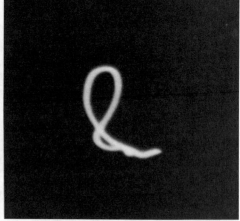

On the night of December 30-31, 1978, the crew
members of a New Zealand cargo plane were flying
off the coast near Kaikoura when they saw strange
lighted objects appearing around their aircraft. At
one point they encountered a gigantic lighted orb
which flew along with the plane for nearly a quarter
of an hour. Other orbs sometimes tracked the plane,
and some turned their lights on and off. A television
crew was on board the plane and at one point filmed
a UFO making a spectacular loop in the night sky.
The loop appears in *one frame* of the film, meaning
the whole movement was accomplished in less than
1/10th of a second. From the book *The Kaikoura
UFOs* (Hodder & Stoughton Ltd., 1980).

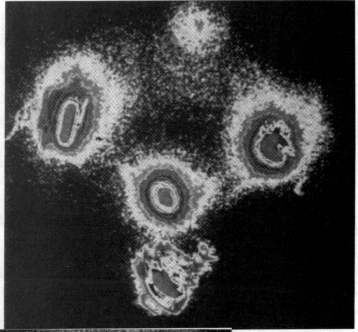

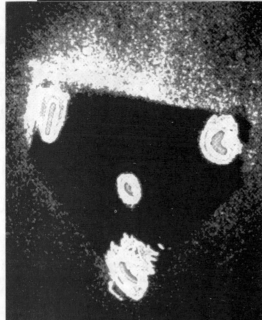

Above: Photograph of the triangular UFO that flew over Belgium on the night of 30-31 March, 1990. This UFO was reported by Belgian police officers and then chased by F-16 interceptors of the Belgian Air Force. **Left**: An enhancement of the photograph showing its clear triangular shape.

A triangular UFO seen by hundreds of observers, and photographed a number of times, on the night of September 4, 1968. Triangular UFOs, cylindrical UFOs and discoid UFOs have all been seen going into, and coming out of, large bodies of water.

CONTENTS

ACKNOWLEDGMENTS

Material reprinted from other sources includes the following:

"What Lights the Mystery 'Wheels'?" by Wallace L. Minto, reprinted by special permission from *Fate Magazine,* © Clark Publishing Company, 1964.

"Unexplained Phenomenon of the Sea," by J. R. Bodler, reprinted from *Proceedings* by permission; copyright © 1952 U.S. Naval Institute.

Material from "Submarine Craft in Australian Waters" is reprinted with the kind permission of Henk J. Hinfelaar, of Henderson, N.Z., director of New Zealand Scientific Space Research and editor of its quarterly journal, *Spaceview.*

I am also indebted to the Aerial Phenomena Research Organization, Inc. (APRO), 3910 E. Kleindale Road, Tucson, Arizona 85712, for material from *The A.P.R.O. Bulletin*; and to the National Investigations Committee on Aerial Phenomena (NICAP), 1536 Connecticut Avenue N.W., Washington, D.C. 20036, for material from *The U.F.O. Investigator.*

Special thanks are due the editors of *Flying Saucer Review,* 21 Cecil Court, Charing Cross Road, London, W.C. 2, England, for use of material from their splendid journal.

I also wish to acknowledge the help and assistance that I have received from:

Many members of the Society for the Investigation of the Unexplained, of which I am administrative director.

My personal associates: Miss Marion L. Fawcett, Michael R. Freedman, and my wife.

Certain individuals, and most particularly Vincent Gaddis, Desmond Leslie, Arthur Young, Jack A. Ullrich, and June Larson.

IVAN T. SANDERSON

PART I

1 · THE MYSTERY

One evening in the Antarctic, a Brazilian scientist by the name of Dr. Rubens J. Villela, seconded to the U.S. Navy's "Operation Deep Freeze" and aboard an icebreaker, was literally jolted almost out of both his body and his mind by a "something" that suddenly came roaring up out of the sea through no less than 37 feet of ice, and went on up into the sky like a vast silvery bullet. The ship was in Admiralty Bay, which faces the South Atlantic Ocean. The only other witnesses were the officer on watch and the helmsman, as it was an extremely cold day and all other personnel were below decks. Further, these witnesses saw only the tag end of the performance because they were busy with charts; but what they did witness was quite enough. Enormous blocks of ice had been hurled high into the air and came cascading down all around the hole burst through the thick ice-sheet, and the water was rolling, and apparently boiling, while masses of steam issued from both the hole and the descending ice.[1] From Dr. Villela's description, the spectators were apparently "not amused." Nor are we.

First of all, this is the kind of report that aggravates everybody, and notably reporters—and for sundry reasons that I will take up in a moment. Second, it infuriates scientists and technologists, and possibly even the Navy, since the story was never officially confirmed. Finally, it unnerves the general public, and particularly the better-informed and those of enquiring mind. In fact, it is an all-round and damned nuisance to everybody.

To begin with, this report was issued quite formally by the U.S. Navy, but only to the Brazilian press, as far as I can ascertain. When the latter published it, and the European wire services picked it up, it was promptly denied in official quarters. However, the Spanish-speaking Latin-American newspapers reproduced it, notably in Chile, and from these airings the North American wire services ran it merely as a "filler"—and only once. Then, everything returned to abnormal. To get at even these facts has taken us years, and the net result has proved to be remarkably bipartisan. One party simply shrugs and says "cover-up"; the other, in this case officialdom, says just as simply "rubbish." Neither attitude gets us anywhere; yet I not only contend, but insist, that reports such as this should not, and cannot, just be left lying around in newspaper morgues. The validity of the facts stated constitutes only one aspect of the matter. The report, once made, constitutes a fact in itself, and in this case it cries out for explanation.

The average citizen just simply does not know how many such seemingly out-of-this-world reports are published somewhere and almost every day and from all over the world. Sometimes they come over the air, but very often, as in this case, only once. Other times, they appear only once in some local newspapers though, in recent years, sometimes even in the larger and more widely read newspapers. Still more lie around elsewhere until some magazine writer gathers a bunch together and presents a sort of historical commentary. Later, these gleanings sometimes become so massive that somebody publishes a book on the subject; and we admit, and unashamedly, that this is just what we are doing in this book. At the same time, an ever-increasing number of such reports are finding their way [quietly] into scientific and technical journals. The point that I would like to make here is therefore as follows.

We really know very little about our world or its environmental setup. What is more, the world that we *do* know, or think we know, is extremely limited, as will become abundantly apparent in the next chapter. We have only the vaguest notion of what lies more than a hundred feet under *our* feet, on land, though geologists are doing pretty well, at least in general terms, down to a few miles. We are fairly good under water down to about five hundred feet around the periphery of the continental land masses and islands, but we know practically nothing of the great body of what Caidin[2] has so aptly named "hydrospace," which includes all seas and oceans from the surfaces down to their bottoms. We're a bit better informed about our atmosphere, but most of its several major aspects still baffle us, and there seem to be things going on in it that are presently quite beyond our comprehension.

This disposes of the extent of our knowledge, or lack of it, of our physical environment; but this is not all that we don't know. Just what is *physical,* and what are the parameters and perimeters of this estate? Does the purely physical run out when it becomes invisible? Obviously not, as we cannot see electricity, for instance. Does it run out when it becomes undetectable by our senses and/or by our instruments? Apparently not either, since we are constantly and with ever-increasing frequency stumbling upon other realities that have physical properties beyond the ranges of our (hitherto) most sensitive instruments. Then again, our minds, with their little computers that we call brains, seem to be sensitive to all manner of things that don't show up on our instruments. This last is very aggravating. Therefore, it would seem, to me at least, to be most extremely incautious to deny the possibility of anything; and just as extremely stupid *not* to investigate anything that does not seem to have at least a physical basis. Dr. Villela's observation falls squarely into the category of the most desirable for such a pursuit. The matter was observed, or was alleged to have been observed; it was a potentially tangible item; and it was witnessed, at least in part, by others. It was officially permitted to be published. It did (does) not fit the pattern of our world as we have put that together. What pattern, therefore, *does* it, or could it, fit?

This is a nasty question, but it has to be asked. Have we any guidelines? The answer is a very definite *yes*. Dr. Villela's report is neither unique nor isolated, and it fits rather alarmingly into a very extensive and clear pattern—albeit into one that has so far been more or less totally ignored. So let us examine this pattern.

We feel almost diffident in bringing up this issue because it has recently become such a whipping-post by all and sundry. Nonetheless, it is the very pith of the matter, and it must therefore be given a good airing forthwith. The plain truth of the matter is that, whatever anybody says, we still have a problem on our hands. I refer to what have come to be called UFOs.

Now, it is quite useless for anybody to declare that this whole business is merely some form of subjective manifestation of human perception. It is equally useless for anybody to declare that those aspects of it which have been declared objective are all cases of mistaken identity or attributable to "natural" (so-called) physical phenomena that we don't as yet understand, because many of these reports are of purely physical or of potentially tangible items. That they are not what we call "natural" does not mean that they are in any way "unnatural"; and for the very simple reason that anything that exists must be *natural*.

The real problem, on which just about everybody seems to have gagged, is the clear demonstration that these things as observed are of great, if not infinite, variety. Thus, while *some* of them may be unknown meteorological phenomena, others may be sort of "living" entities, and still others constructions, which is to say what we call "machines" made by other entities.[3] In the last instance, said other entities would necessarily appear to be what we call "intelligent." Therefore, we can but ask: What entities and what intelligences?

Now, UFOs—which include such things as "flying saucers"—are commonly and popularly conceived of as being aerial phenomena; and to this end, they have been the purlieu of air forces, meteorologists, and astronomers. Unhappily, far too much has been written upon this subject, ending with the publication in early 1969 of a massive report by a committee set up by the University of Colorado under the chairmanship of Dr. Edward U. Condon, and under contract to the Office of Scientific and Technical Research of the United States Air Force.[4] This outfit spent two years and some $600,000 of Air Force appropriation to conduct an in-depth study of this UFO problem. The conduct of this organization and its report were a farce, and its final over-all recommendations were completely null and void.[5] It said, "Our general conclusion is that nothing has come from the study of UFOs in the past 21 years that has added to scientific knowledge. Careful consideration of the record as it is available to us leads us to onclude that further extensive study of UFOs probably [*sic*] cannot be justified in the expectation that science will be advanced thereby." This may be so, but this study neither investigated the subject in depth as instructed, nor did it even so much as mention the aspect of the problem of which we now write. In fact, this committee seems either never to have even heard of this or, if they did, to have totally ignored it.

I will not bore you with a reiteration of the so-called "flying-saucer" nonsense, as it is now extant in more books and papers than I would care to enumerate. If you are interested, go to any library and ask what they have under the heading of UFOs or "Flying Saucers." You will probably find it listed under something as inappropriate as "The Occult," spiritualism, or psychology; but do not blame the librarians, as this reflects only the present level of our abysmal lack of understanding of reality. By this, I mean simply that anything that is not in the published textbooks is automatically classified as either science fiction or kooky. Nonetheless, there is a small body of UFO literature that is worth reading. This is by some people with proper scientific training, and sometimes even with official backing. In these works you will learn, probably to your considerable surprise, just how very real, tangible, and factual the whole matter actually is.[6] Despite what anybody may have told you—be they the working press, the "experts," the run-of-the-mill scientists and technologists, or even officialdom—don't be put off or misled. Read for yourself what hard facts there are on record, and then draw your own conclusions.

The term "flying saucer" is an abomination, preposterously facetious, false, and irrelevant. First of all, just about the only shape of these things that has never been reported is that of a saucer, either right way up or upside down. Second, they don't "fly" even in the sense that rockets may be said to do. The now popular term UFO, or "Unidentified Flying Object," is not much better. That they are unidentified, either as a whole or in part, must for the moment be accepted, but that they "fly," as we know flight, is rubbish. But the allegation that they are objects, per se, is the really sticky one.

What precisely *is* an object? The dictionary defines it as something that "gets in your way," with the implication that it is *tangible*. As a result of this somewhat indefinite definition, the USAF some time back divided "UFOs" into two distinct categories—UAPs, or Unexplained Aerial Phenomena; and UAOs, or Unidentified Aerial Objects. These have been the accepted definitions for a decade, but even the buffs seem never to have cottoned onto this fact. And, as a matter of fact and to be thoroughly facetious, there is an awful lot onto which the buffs, let alone the press, the scientists, and the public have not yet cottoned.

For instance, it may come as somewhat of a shock to all of these good people to learn that, by actual count, over 50 percent of all so-called "sightings" of UFOs have occurred over, coming from, going away over, or plunging into or coming out of water. That this fact is known to officialdom is manifest from their official publications, but they seem to have left this aquatic factor out of their statistical analyses. In other words, they have been keeping damned quiet about this business; and probably, as I will endeavor to demonstrate, for very good reasons indeed.

The reason most commonly given or suggested for official "silence," or what many people assert is a deliberate "cover-up" by officialdom, is fear of panic on the part of the general public; and to this end the stupid uproar caused by Orson Welles' famous broadcast of 1938 is brought up *ad nauseam*. However, the public has come a long way into the path of reality since 1938, what with buzz-bombs, H-bombs, flights to the moon, and passes at Mars and Venus. Also, they have become quite used to both UAPs and UAOs, and they are quite prepared for the disclosure that there are intelligencies superior to ours loose in the universe; and to accept the fact that these could have visited and still do visit us. The armed services, if not the political establishment, know this perfectly well. What they don't know, or like, is something quite else.

This is that they might give the impression that they believe, or have satisfactory proof, that such superior intelligencies do exist; that they are *here* all the time, and always have been; that they can control our brains and patrol our minds; and that we are powerless to act on our own initiative should our intent be at variance with the "wishes" of such superior intelligencies. If you will read the literature carefully and watch the press reports you will note that nobody—including people like Dr. Condon—could care less about funny lights in the sky, apparently solid bodies maneuvering therein in daylight, or even any form of UAP, however grotesque and enormous. But watch out when a UAO is said to have swooped down close to the earth's surface or actually to have landed and produced physical effects on our electrical circuitry. All types of officialdom then just pop up out of seemingly nowhere, and within hours or even minutes; whole areas are cordoned off; police officers suddenly go silent or change the stories they have already told their local and trusted newsmen; and a *real* panic is on—not on the part of the public but on that of officialdom! And I am speaking not only of the United States but of just about every country in the world—with the possible exceptions of Brazil and India.

Further, if a human being or even a domestic animal is alleged to have been harmed or to have shown any signs of physical "interference" in conjunction with such a low-fly, touch-down, or landing of a UAO, activity becomes even more furious, and the "regulations" much more stringent. But when any kind of *mental* interference is so much as alleged, officialdom seems to become well-nigh hysterical. Evidence of this will be provided in subsequent chapters, and notably when we get down to the core of our theme, to which we had now best direct our attention. Simply stated, this is as follows.

It was mentioned above that by actual count more than 50 percent of all so-called UAOs have been recorded as coming out of, going into, appearing from over, or disappearing over water. Does this not have any significance? Nearly three-quarters of the surface of our planet is covered with water; but, despite airplanes now flying over the oceans, and boating going on all about, we have only a minute portion of this vast aqueous area under regular surveillance. Our shipping lanes across oceans are only on an average about twenty miles wide, and our airlanes not much more. So what really goes on *on* the oceans, and even on their peripheral seas, is really quite unknown to us; and what goes on *under* them is even less known. As a matter of fact, we are not so hot on lakes either, especially big ones, and it is really quite extraordinary how little we know about what goes on under the surface of even rivers—especially if they are turbid. Some of the things I have personally fished out of some large tropical rivers gave even the local people the willies; *vide*, an enormous stingray from the upper reaches of a rather modest West African river.[7]

Turning, then, to another aspect of this business, let us consider the matter of our astronauts' performances. They are shot into the upper atmosphere or inner space; and when they come back, where do they land? They "splash down" in an ocean. Only the Russians have not taken up this behavior. Why? Even though water is just as solid as rock if you bash into it at a high enough speed, it does at least have a comparatively non-bumpy surface, and it does "give way" to a certain extent.

So, if an ET—and we had better get used to this term, and its corollary, ETI, for Extraterrestrial Intelligence, as coined by the lamentable Condon Committee—comes into our atmosphere, what more natural than that he (it) should either land upon, splash down on the surface of, or go right on down into water? If only people, and notably the UFO buffs, would wake up to the facts, and do a little homework, they would perceive that this is just what they often *do* do; though, of course, we must not neglect the now famous admonition of Gordon Creighton: to wit, that we should preface all our remarks and statements about UAOs with the classic: "Bearing in mind that these things don't [officially] exist . . ." [8]

The next aspect of this matter that has been even more sorely overlooked or buried is the coming out of water by UAOs— and some other unpleasantnesses, incidentally, as we shall see later. A fine example is the report of the somewhat gallant Dr. Villela with which we opened this Pandora's box. This leads by simple logic to the consideration of what is going on *below* said water, and it is here that officialdom—let alone "science-dom," if it ever seriously considered the matter—becomes quite hysterical. After very prolonged consideration and contemplation of this aspect of the affair, and after listening to many people (like Art Ford[9]) who have spent years investigating the matter, I have been forced to agree with such investigators that the reason for this is simply that officialdom—and I use this expression collectively—knows no more about the business than the buffs or anybody else, and that they are just plain scared. There is nothing that officialdom dreads more than having to admit that it *doesn't* know what is going on, or what everything or anything is all about; and, more especially, having to admit that they have no answers or remedies.

The structure of modern societies, communities, and nations is not really understood, in that the average person just dubs everything to do with government "The Establishment," and then equates that with all other establishments or established organized bodies like science, religion, business, and so forth.

The truth is, that all states are of a pyramidal structure, with a body politic forming the apex. This, however, is but the facing of the pyramid. Its true functions are prosecuted behind and underneath this façade, and usually by a permanent bureaucracy that seldom if ever surfaces. This, in turn, may or may not be aided by, or be at loggerheads with, one or more autonomous or semiautonomous outfits such as a judiciary or a religious (i.e., mystical) hierarchy. In olden times this often *was* the bureaucracy.

Bureaucracy consists in the administrators, and they actually set and guide all policy. Legislatures are merely public relations and publicity outlets for these policies. Then come the ranks of executors. These are the technical departments, which almost everywhere and throughout history have been the same: defense, meaning offense, or the department of war; internal security; and money. All others are dependent upon these.

This all worked splendidly until about fifty years ago, when a new factor surfaced. This was science, with its handmaiden technology. This started in outfield, and it first very swiftly demolished established religion as a power source and then moved in on the law. Next, it so interfered with the basis of everything —i.e., money, to be crude—that over-all authority had to wed it or at least try to take it in. But technological science proved to be a more stubborn hegemony than any religion had ever been, so that we ended up with "government" wooing it. Science complied, but on its own terms; so that, today, it really runs the whole shooting-match. What head of state, or politician, or jurist understands how an H-Bomb is put together, or even how to explode one? How many of the executives really know? They are given little keys and colored buttons to push; but when to push them still remains the prerogative of the technicians. And here we come to another lot—the computer boys. Today even the basic scientists, and a great majority of the technologists, haven't the foggiest notion what *they* are up to, or even know just what *they* can do. Now we're getting down to basics.

I only bring all this up because we, the general and benighted public, absolutely *must* realize that we are now really quite powerless to do *anything*. Further, and what is of much more importance to our particular theme, officialdom doesn't know, any more than we do, what is really going on. "Sciencedom" may do so, but it is in such a position that it can only denigrate anything that does not fit in with its current theories or objectives. Technologists still do more or less what they are told, but they are strictly "yes-no" or "black-or-white" boys. They constantly assert that they don't have the time to explore any "gray," or other possibilities, of any problem. Yet, it is interesting to note, within recent years they have developed a jargon that even the basic scientists don't understand! This I personally find rather delicious.

So when it comes to something like underwater UAOs, we find that *nobody* really has a clue as to what is going on. Let us not forget that the poor so-called armed services—the armies, navies, and air forces—are only "junior" executives with very specific terms of reference. They are not scientists or even technologists, except as regards military matters. Yet the poor fellows were tossed just about the most abstruse cosmological problem of all time in the form of UAOs and UAPs—or UFOs if you will—and were then expected to come up with an explanation of these, within limits that conform to our current scientific principles, and that are agreeable to technologists! This is absolutely preposterous. And, what is more, they have been expected to provide public relations material to the administrative bureaucracy and for the information of the poor politicians who have to try to satisfy the public.

Meantime, however, there is a fourth force in operation— at least in the western world, or in what are perhaps rather euphemistically called the democratic countries, as opposed to the "Peoples' Democratic Republics." This is the press. Here we strike something quite else, and it is in this sphere of activity that we begin to get down to some real facts.

In the United States, the army is called the "Silent Service." (More or less everywhere else it is the navy, if the country has one, that is so called.) This service has not surfaced in the world of UAOs until very recently.[10] The poor air forces have been given the ball and, although they have carried it for two decades, said "ball" is now a rather damp, limp, wet pulp. The navies, on the other hand, have come through in quite another manner. They were no more impelled to pronounce upon this matter than were the armies, but, it now transpires, they really got with it. Meantime, the air forces had to carry the brunt of the affair, and without any real help from anybody. This is not an apology for that service, but I have watched all this for thirty years and, whatever their shenanigans may have been, my heart really bleeds for these honest souls who are supposedly paid simply to guard us in peacetime, and both defend us and bash our enemies in wartime, *in the air*.

As you will see if you read on, even the navies, knowing what they do—and I know that they do—are just as bewildered as everybody else. Take the case of the so-called "Bermuda Triangle" (which it isn't) and the missing planes therein, which we will come to in a later chapter. The Navy put on a fine front of obfuscation or bland indifference, and they pulled down a perfectly legitimate security curtain on this; but, I repeat, they too seem not to have the foggiest notion what this is all about or how to interpret that which they themselves have on record. How can the commander of a ship on antisubmarine exercises accept the statements of even *all* his radar operators in his fleet to the effect that they have tracked, and are locked onto a submarine "construction" traveling at 150 knots at a depth of 20,-000 feet, if he has never even been told of the probabilities, let alone the possibilities, of such a reality?

So let us not blame anybody for not understanding possibilities, and especially service executives. What mere air force man would ever have conceived of the Van Allen Belt only a few years ago, and why should he have done so? Why should a Navy man know that a ridge 50 miles long by 15 miles wide rose 2¼ miles overnight in the South Atlantic in 1924?[11] Ridiculous! This was of concern only to the cable companies.

Why the scientists shouldn't know, and more especially when they were the ones who said so in the first place, is another matter. So let us see just what this congerie of "experts" *has* got to say.

2 · A SECOND MYSTERY
Oceanic UAOs

The following extraordinary reports have been published by those identified in the bibliography through the reference numbers in this text. When I first read these stories I must admit that I indulged in the standard howl of the professional skeptic; but then I started inquiring into the status of those who had published these statements. A few "pen names" turned up, but it did not take us long to ascertain to whom these applied. Then there was the usual run-of-the-mill news item (so called), without by-line and often even without date or reference. These too we tracked down for the most part. Then, having gathered together this material, I tottered off to Washington and spent a rather dreary week going from department to department, and steadily up the line to the topmost personages, asking a series of simple journalistic questions—to wit: (1) Have you ever seen these reports? (2) If so, do you know anything about them? (3) Are they true, or are they pipe dreams? (4) If they are all, or in part, nonsense, why have they never been denied? The answers I got—and they were few enough—were most enlightening.

It is useless to present the reports themselves until this little history has been placed on record, because it is almost as bizarre as they are. I was privileged to meet and be granted interviews by the heads of five departments of the Navy and of four other outfits concerned with underwater affairs. I do not give the individuals' names nor list their departments, because the former change constantly and the latter are engaged in what are termed rather sensitive fields; but they are known to my publishers. These (literally) topnotch executives included high-ranking service personnel and civilians of very high scientific standing; one and all were most understanding and cooperative. However, one and all gave the same answers to my questions. These were, without exception, as follows:

To Question No. 1, "No." To No. 2, "No." To No. 3, "They sound like nonsense to me." To No. 4, "I have no idea; it's not my department."

But then came some most surprising requests by these people. One and all asked—almost begged—of me to send them reports on, or transcripts or copies of, said items! And it was the absolute head of the most highly technical department of our underwater research who first so requested; and this after I had shown him reports from official Navy documents giving the project numbers of the grants-in-aid made to the scientists concerned to undertake the particular investigation and research. This gentleman had very courteously offered me ten minutes of his more than valuable time one morning, but kept me enthralled for an hour and a half drawing charts and writing out statistics on a large blackboard in his office, while a number of admirals and lesser lights cooled their heels in the highly secured outer office. I was somewhat embarrassed, and several times made a move to get out of his hair, but he would have none of it until he had done the best he could to get into my dumb reporter's head just what his department *is* trying to do. But it was his parting shot that really got me. "Please," he said, "get me copies of this stuff, especially those with Navy grant numbers on them. There is so much to read I never get to see these things, and the others in the department who are supposed to put things on my desk probably think this whole thing is a lot of nonsense."

I finally worked my way up to an old personal friend, now in charge of publicity for one of the most vital aspects of our underwater research by the Navy. Here I encountered just about the same thing. At first he wasn't really listening, but then some remark I made seemed to get through to him, and he put down his telephone, his pen, and, in a manner of speaking, his secretary by telling her to take all calls including those from the Admiral. He then swiveled around and stared at me for quite a long time. "What on earth are you talking about?" he asked. I repeated what I had just said and flipped one of the reports onto his desk. This he read very carefully and taking a very long time. Then he just stared ahead. "Well, I think it's all nonsense," he said, "but there's only one place to go to and that's Intelligence; but, confound it, they've just got a new man there whom I don't know." With this he rang for his secretary, and I was subjected to one of the most amazing charades that I have ever witnessed; and I was in government service myself, and in a navy to boot, for many years!

"Who's the new chief of O.N.I.?" he barked.

"Sorry, Commander, I don't know."

"Well look him up."

"But he's not listed yet."

"Well ring 'em up."

Pause for station identification, while the secretary made two calls on the frightfully inside line and the Commander pondered. Then said secretary hung up, sighed, took a deep breath and said:

"I'm sorry, Commander, but they won't tell me."

There was a splendid, professional, naval explosion, and that was that. And this, mind you, indulged in by the official and ultimate arbiter of all publicity, public relations, and information on behalf of that department of our Navy that is concerned with certain suboceanic and sub-seas research and development!

Utterly frustrated, my friend gathered up copies of all the

material I had brought and promised to send it on to this new person in charge of intelligence. He also vowed to find out who this gink was and to stuff it under his nose and get a plain answer. That was a year ago, as of the time of writing this, and I haven't heard a word since; though I have had half a dozen delightful chats with this chap's secretary—herself most highly secured, I should add!

I then wandered over to various other security agencies, but now with a single and simple question—namely, "Can I publish all this, or would you prefer that—despite the fact that most of it has already been published—I just forget it?" And, here I ran into another set of indifferences. The first reaction of all of them was, perhaps naturally, that I was some sort of screwball; but, in view of my credentials and more so the names of those people who had kindly rung up to vouch for me and make appointments, they most graciously, though obviously more than reluctantly, spared me some of their time. At first they simply didn't listen. Busy officials never do: their minds are necessarily on other more important matters such as their particular, current official crisis, their wife's health, or the exigencies of the departmental pecking order. However, in each case I eventually managed to say something so shocking that they came out of their dreams and cast glassy orbs upon whatever I shoved under their noses. The first reaction of one and all was the same—to wit, "What do you want me to do about it?"

In such circumstances I always come back with my initial, simple question—in this case: "May I publish on this or would you prefer that, for security or any other reasons, I refrain from doing so?" Any such direct question invariably produces bewilderment. It did. But when the poor boys—and some gals —finally digested the essential substance of my request, I invariably got the same answer. This was simply: "I don't know." None of this helped very much, so I was left just as frustrated as before and had to come to my own decision. This is to present to you the facts, alleged facts, and what has been published, and then get on with some analysis and speculation. You will have to make up your own minds as to the validity of all this, and you may then put your own interpretations upon it. I very much fancy that your reactions will be just the same as those of the officials of whom I wrote above. Nonetheless!

I am going to start in the middle of this survey, thereby breaking all precedent, since I was admonished in my youth by one of the most awesome personalities I have ever met, one Chief Ekumaw of the Assumbo people of the northern Camerun, in West Africa, to remember always that the proper place to begin a story is at the beginning. Nonetheless, this commencement here concerns affairs that are alleged to have happened as late as 1963. This is a compendium of statements published on the matter by quite a number of people.[12] These were the reports that finally "awoke" my official contacts, as mentioned above, from their departmental reveries; but they are the ones that have proved least susceptible of confirmation. The accounts, as published, constitute classics of obfuscation; yet diligent inquiry brought to light the following.

Sometime in 1963 the U.S. Navy conducted some exercises to train personnel in the detection and tracking of underwater craft. The maneuvers were conducted off Puerto Rico in the Atlantic some five hundred miles southeast of the continental United States. All reports seem to agree that there were five "small" naval vessels concerned, but in more than one account the aircraft carrier *Wasp* is stated to have been the command ship. There appear also to have been a number of submarines engaged in these exercises, and all vessels were intimately linked by advanced electronic communications systems. There were also aircraft, at least one of which trailed a detection device a little below the surface of the ocean from a line, while flying at very low altitude. The submarines are said to have been "fixed" for what is somewhat mysteriously called "silent running," a performance that cries out for further exposition.

There then occurred a rather special and particular uproar which, at least as far as I have been able to ascertain, was initiated as follows. A sonar operator on one of the small vessels, otherwise listed as a destroyer, reported to his bridge that one of the submarines had broken formation and gone off in what appeared to be pursuit of some unknown object. This operator did not, of course, know if this was a "plant," since the maneuvers they were engaged in were exercises designed to train personnel in detection of enemy craft, and in such exercises decoys must of course always be employed. However, this operator's report was not at all within the limits of any such simulation. Trouble was that said unidentified subaqueous object was traveling at "over 150 knots"!

The deck officer on watch immediately reported to the skipper, said to have been a lieutenant commander, and this officer was not amused. Nonetheless, after calling his communications boys on the intercom, he got in touch with the command vessel, the *Wasp,* but was further frustrated to find that their radio intake was virtually jammed with similar reports coming in from all the other ships and from the sonde-trailing aircraft. Then comes a curious note from more than one of the reports that I have. This is to the effect that no less than thirteen craft (including submersibles and aircraft, one must suppose) noted in their official logs that their underwater tracking devices had latched onto said high-speed submersible. All of which is said to have immediately been reported to C.O.M.L.A.N.T. in Norfolk, Va. At this point, all the reports become somewhat vague and obscure. Various numbers of people, in various numbers of ships, are alleged to have observed or heard the sonar blips caught by their own operators, and all to have concurred in the fact that this object was being driven *by a single propeller at more than 150 knots.*

The world record for a propeller-driven *surface* craft is 200.42 mph, but this was with a Rolls-Royce-engined hydroplane. The record for a diesel-engined surface craft is 60.21 mph. The all-time high was achieved by Sir Malcolm Campbell in his turbojet-engined *Bluebird K.7,* at 328 mph. The fastest speeds for submerged submarines have been achieved by the Skipjack class of tear-drop-shaped nuclear vessels of the United

States Navy. The semiofficial record is 45 knots (51.8 mph).[13] Thus, the object recorded above beat anything that we can do at the present stage of our technological development, by nearly four times in speed.

But that was not the whole story. It is said that the technicians kept track of this thing *for four days*, and that it maneuvered round about, and down to depths of 27,000 feet. The record dive for a standard submarine is 6,250 feet, achieved by the *U.S. Aluminaut* on the 12th of November, 1967, twenty miles off the west coast of Grand Abaco Island in the Bahamas. The record for mere submersion is, however, the descent to 35,-800 feet made by the little *Trieste* in the Pacific in 1960.[14] However, this craft could hardly move along at all, while the Skipjacks cannot go down to more than a sixth of that depth. In other words, this thing was literally out of our world. What was it?

Perhaps a more pertinent question is, Are these reports true? As I have said, I have been unable to obtain any confirmation of them. The authors who originally wrote of them are known and are respectable writers of factual matters, and they have specialized in underwater investigations, and apparently with much help and advice from naval authorities. This is thus, at least as far as I am able to state as of the time of writing, a dead end. We are then presented with the corollary question as to how *possible* and/or *probable* any such things as the item described above might be. Here we enter a really extraordinary world that, except in a very few abstruse quarters, has not up till now been brought to the attention of the general public.

First, it transpires that this is by no means a unique case. Not only do the authors identified above constantly state that there have been numerous other reports of a similar nature by and to our Navy since that date, but that still others have been reported by several other navies. Second, there have been equally surprising reports made by both naval and commercial ship's officers, mostly giving names and dates, and going back more than a hundred years. Moreover, of those incidents which have occurred *since* this classic, several are outstanding and are very properly documented.

The log of the Norwegian ship *T.T. Jawesta* records that, on the 6th of July, 1965, at 2152 hours (9:52 P.M.) GMT, and at 24° 40′ N., 15° W., while in passage between Venezuela and the Canary Islands, the lookout on the bridge reported a bright object in the sky moving in a northerly direction. The captain, H. A. Trovik, was alerted by ship telephone, and later submitted a report to the Geophysical Institute in Bergen, Norway, because his chief mate, Torgrim Lien, stated: "I can say with complete certainty that it was no question of an aircraft of conventional type, or rocket, or meteor, or ball lightning." The object is described in very considerable detail as issuing tongues of flame and making sudden turns, and the report then goes on to state that: "Its speed was tremendous, and it was visible for about 30 to 40 seconds. It was moving at the time, in a N–S direction, its approximate course being 180°. Despite its enormous speed and the closeness of its passage, we could not hear the least sound from it. The look-out on the port side, seaman Hernandez Ambrosio, maintained that it seemed *as though the object had come up out of the sea*, and that it was traveling northwards, and then suddenly changed course toward us. The helmsman, ordinary seaman Narciso Guillen, saw the object just after it had passed over the ship. And on the poop, fitter Juan Hernandez and mess-hand Ignacio Suarez also saw it. Their accounts tally with mine."[15]

It must be understood that we are trying to deal in this chapter with *oceanic* items; and it must be further, and even more clearly, understood that there is a world of difference between *oceans* and *seas*. This will be taken up in more detail in a later chapter.

The importance of this case is, therefore, that it is both a truly oceanic one and also of a "something" coming up out of an ocean, just as Dr. Villela's thing did. The other recent significant case was reported on the 20th of July, 1967, in the log of the Argentinian ship *Naviero*, belonging to the Argentine

Shipping Lines Company. This occurred some 120 miles off the coast of Brazil, opposite Cape Santa Marta Grande (Lat. 28° 48′ S., Long. 46° 43′ W.); the time was about 6:15 P.M. Argentine time (10:15 GMT); and the *Naviero* was running at 17 knots.

The officers and crew were at their evening meal at the time. The Master, Captain Julian Lucas Ardanza, received a call on the intercom system from one of his officers, Jorge Montoya, to the effect that there was something strange near the ship. Arriving at once on deck, Captain Ardanza beheld a shining object in the sea no more than about 50 feet away on the starboard side. It was cigar-shaped and he estimated its length at about 105 to 110 feet. It had a powerful blue and white glow, made no noise whatsoever, and left no wake in the water. There was no sign of any periscope, or railing, or tower, or superstructure; in other words, no external control surfaces or protruding parts. The mystery craft paced the *Naviero* for 15 minutes. Captain Ardanza estimated its speed at up to 25 knots, as against the 17 of his own vessel (an old Liberty-type ship built in the U.S.A.). The next development, however, was disconcerting to say the least. The mystery craft suddenly dived and passed right under the *Naviero* and vanished rapidly in the depths at great speed. As it went it glowed brightly beneath the water. The *Naviero* was carrying explosives and gun powder, and in order to stave off any panic among the crew should they get the idea into their heads that they were being "pursued" because of this type of cargo, Captain Ardanza and his officers judged it prudent to asemble the crew and tell them what had been seen. In the subsequent interviews with reporters from the Argentine press, the Captain said that during his twenty years at sea he had never seen anything like that before. Chief Officer Carlos Lasca described the object as "a submergible UFO with its own illumination." The possibility that the object seen was a whale or a conventional type of submarine is ruled out. The witnesses were firm in their insistence that the "luminous cigar" looked totally different from a submarine or a whale and could not possibly have been either of these things. The case has been classified by the Argentine maritime authorities as an "Unidentified Submarine Object."[16]

The normal reaction of so-called authorities of all kinds to such reports is not printable. Lloyd's of London, however, calmly engulfs or ingests them for the simple reason that, if registered vessels' logs cannot be relied upon, Lloyd's might as well give up; and this estimable organization has determinedly clung to such reports throughout the ages. (It had better do so unless all marine insurance also goes flooey.) So let us reverse ourselves and start again, going backward into maritime history. Such history is virtually clogged with reports of this nature; but we will pick out only a few that offer truly factual data.

The first that is of significance, prior to the uproar over the U.S. Navy's antisubmarine maneuvers off Puerto Rico, is the very strange mention in Thor Heyerdahl's classic *Kon-Tiki* which states simply: "On several occasions we glided past a large dark mass, the size of the floor of a room, that lay motionless under the surface of the water like a hidden reef, which it couldn't be, since the raft was in the middle of the Pacific, between the Peruvian harbour of El Callao and the island of Raroia, with many hundreds of fathoms under her. It was presumably the giant ray of evil repute but it never moved, and we never went close enough to make out its shape clearly. Then again, about two o'clock on a cloudy night, when the man at the helm had difficulty distinguishing black water from black sky, he caught sight of a faint illumination down in the water which slowly took the shape of a large animal. It was impossible to say whether it was plankton shining on its body, or whether the animal itself had a phosphorescent surface, but the glimmer down in the black water gave the ghostly creature obscure, wavering outlines. Sometimes it was roundish, sometimes oval, or triangular, and suddenly it split into two parts which swam to and fro under the raft independently of each other. Finally there were three of these large shining phantoms wandering round in slow circles under us. They were real monsters, for the visible parts alone were some five fathoms long. Mysterious and noiseless, our shining companions kept a good way beneath the surface. The glimmer of light on their backs revealed that the *beasts* were bigger than elephants but they were not whales, for they never came up to breathe."[17]

Heyerdahl is a perfectly splendid fellow with remarkable insight and a truly pioneering spirit, both intellectual and practical, but he clings to an outmoded orthodoxy in a manner that is incomprehensible. For instance, after his brilliant investigations of the present and past cultures of Easter Island, and after asserting that the tall invaders of that island with Semitic features and red hair came from mainland South America, and having correlated these with the people of similar physiognomy and culture who he says came up out of the Amazonian basin to organize the montane Amerinds of the High Andes, he still steadfastly refuses to equate these with the Phoenician colonists and miners of the Amazon,[18] and he ridicules Ramos.[19] This we find rather strange. Also, he is not a zoologist, otherwise he would not publish such a ridiculous statement as that one of the large dark masses he passed over was "the giant ray of evil repute." Said selachian fishes are not open-ocean denizens and, although in some cases they are almost as large as a small room in a small apartment, they are of an extremely mild disposition, being gentle munchers of clams in comparatively shallow waters. Heyerdahl also attributed the "large glowing objects" to some form of animal life. Perhaps some forty-foot whale sharks or such can be infested with a thick layer of luminous bacteria on their backs; but then, how come the changes of shape and the division into, first, two and then three separate entities?

Lest you get the impression that all this has cropped up only in our modern age, let me assure you that any such is an entirely false notion. An old personal friend of ours, Livingston Gearhart of Buffalo, N.Y., dug this one out of the records. It goes as follows:

This is the full report, as it appeared. I have checked it against the original on microfilm. And further research has shown that the S.S. *St. Andrew* was listed in the "due-to-arrive" columns of preceding days. The *New York Times* story bore this head: "A Shower of Meteors around the *St. Andrew.*" This is the story that was published, on the front page:

"When the Phoenix Line Steamship *St. Andrew* arrived from Antwerp yesterday, Captain Fitzgerald reported that the steamer had passed through a meteoric shower at 4:30 o'clock on Tuesday [October 30, 1906] about 600 miles northeast of Cape Race. The largest meteor observed fell into the sea less than a mile away. Had it struck the *St. Andrew* all hands would have perished. Yesterday afternoon Chief Officer V. E. Spencer, who was on the bridge when the meteors appeared, told what he saw there. 'On Tuesday afternoon,' said Mr. Spencer, 'the weather was clear and bright, although there was little sunshine. Just after one bell, 4:30 o'clock, I saw three meteors fall into the water dead ahead of the ship one after another at a distance of about five miles. Although it was daylight, they left a red streak in the air from zenith to the horizon. Simultaneously the third engineer shouted to me. I then saw a huge meteor on the port beam falling *in a zig-zag manner* less than a mile away to the southward. We could distinctly hear the hissing of water as it touched. It fell *with a rocking motion* leaving a broad red streak in its wake. The meteor must have weighed several tons, and appeared to be 10 to 15 feet in diameter. *It was saucer shaped* [all italics ours] which probably accounted for the peculiar rocking motion. When the mass of metal struck the water the spray and steam rose to a height of at least 40 feet, and for a few moments looked like the mouth of a crater. If it had been night, the meteor would have illuminated the sea for 50 or 60 miles. The hissing sound, like escaping steam, when it struck the water was so loud that the chief engineer turned out of his berth and came on deck, thinking the sound came from the engine room. I have seen meteors all over the world, but never such a large one as this.' "[20]

Mr. Gearhart goes on: "It is interesting to note that Charles Fort reports that an enormous object was seen to *rise* out of the sea off Cape Race on November 12, 1887."[21]

This report states: "An object, described as a large ball of fire was seen to *rise* from the sea near Cape Race. We are told that it rose to a height of fifty feet, and then advanced close to the ship, then moving away, remaining visible about five minutes."[22] (As reported by Flammarion "It was enormous."[23]) Details in the *American Meteorological Journal* recount that the British steamer, the *S.S. Siberian*, Captain Moore in command, had observed this phenomenon, and that the object had moved against the wind. Captain Moore also stated that "about the same place I have seen such appearances before."[24]

Meantime on the 28th of October 1902, at 3:05 A.M., one of the most startling reports of all came to hand. This occurred in the Gulf of Guinea, which is to say in the great bight to the west of West Africa in the South Atlantic. The log of the *S.S. Fort Salisbury* states: "Course due north, sea calm, sky clear." Then, according to Vince Gaddis: "The lookout observed a huge, dark object several hundred feet off to starboard. He called Second Officer A. H. Raymer, who hurried on deck and joined the lookout and the helmsman. 'It was a little frightening,' Raymer said later. 'We couldn't see too much detail in the darkness, but it was between five and six hundred feet in length. It had two lights, one at each end. A mechanism of some kind—or fins, maybe—was making a commotion in the water.' The officer reported that the object seemed to be slowly sinking. He didn't believe it was a vessel that had turned turtle. Its surface was not smooth, but 'appeared to be scaled.' "[25]

Reverting to 1887 once again, we find a neat one from the log of the Dutch (Hollandsche) barque, the *J.P.A.*, Captain C. D. Sweet, that when at 37° 39′ N. and 57° W., "in a fierce storm; two objects were sighted in the air above the ship, one luminous the other dark. They fell into the sea with a loud noise." [26] And so these reports go on, backward in time unto the first records of true oceanic navigation. And they come from all over, such as the following nice little historical ditty which is reproduced from the *UFO Investigator*, the journal of the National Investigations Committee on Aerial Phenomena, of

Washington, D.C. This tells us that in *The Diary of Andrew Bloxam*, published in 1925 by the Bernice P. Bishop Museum, of Honolulu, there appeared the following entry: "About half past 3 o'clock this morning [the 12th of August, 1825] the middle watch on deck was astonished to find everything around them suddenly illuminated. Turning their eyes to the eastward they beheld a large, round, luminous body *rising up* about seven degrees from the water to the clouds, and falling again out of sight, and a second time rising and falling. It was the color of a red-hot [cannon] shot and appeared about the size of the sun. It gave so great a light that a pin might be picked up on deck." [27]

I append this purely historical record to the matter-of-fact extracts from ships' logs because not all diarists prior to a hundred years ago were mere weavers of so-called "travelers' tales." In fact, the majority of the accounts were written by the then most serious-minded reporters, and to the best of their ability and current knowledge. Why should this estimable Andrew Bloxam, Esq., indulge in such nonsensical reportage unless it was intended as a true account of a happening? One does not wish to be grossly impertinent, but one is constrained to ask just what the heck is the matter with all the classes of skeptics, stuffed shirts, and other experts? How can they continue to attempt to deny the validity of all these reports when they are taken from such serious documents as ships' logs? Their contention is that all of them are either lies or cases of mistaken identity. Mistaken for what? And what do these self-appointed experts make of the corollary evidence of some form of highly technical civilization occupying the bottoms of the oceans? These two items are highly obnoxious to just about everybody, quite apart from the professional skeptics and other assorted clowns.

The following is taken from an article by Ed Hyde in *Man's Illustrated* and reads: "O.N.R. scientists began a series of long-range underwater communication tests. They were quite aware that long-distance communication beneath the sea had been tried—and failed. However, one scientist came up with a completely new theory and decided to try it out. He set up a mile-long antenna to prove his point. The antenna was laid along the continental shelf, which stretches out 100 miles from the east coast of the U.S. before dropping into the very deepest areas of the Atlantic. Far out to sea was an O.N.R. research ship with instruments lowered close to the bottom to pick up the signals. Transmission of the signals got underway. What startled the men aboard the research ship was the reception of the signal, and then a *repeat of the signal followed by a strange code which the computers are still trying to break*. What happened, according to a later naval report, was that the signals in the experiment were picked up and mimicked by 'something unknown,' and then this 'something' began transmitting its own signals on the same wavelengths used by the Navy scientists. 'Something strange was definitely down there,' the Navy report stated. Alert O.N.R. scientists had even tracked the source of the alien signal and discovered that it appeared to emanate from one of the deepest areas of the Atlantic—a spot with depths measured at 29,000 feet."[28]

If anybody wants to deny this one, they are perfectly at liberty to do so, but let them go and have a quiet chat with Mr. Hyde. Either there *is* something going on down there or there is not; and it's about time everybody made up their minds one way or the other.

3 · A THIRD MYSTERY

UAOs into and out of the Seas

We will now move one stage closer to home. We remarked in the last chapter that we were then assiduously confining our reports to items recorded from oceans, and we asked that the difference between these and *seas* be accepted, if not fully appreciated, at that stage. Once again, however, we are going to put off the exposition of the difference, as it will be taken up in detail in Chapter 12. Meantime, I would ask you just to accept that there are good reasons for separating those oceanic reports which were recorded above, from those that come next; namely, those from what I call the shallows. This is a comparative term, meaning marine or salt waters that are other than the true oceanic basins but that include both the continental shelves, the seas upon these, and certain infra-oceanic-type areas, like the Gulf of Mexico and the Mediterranean, but *not* the true inland seas like the Caspian. The reason for this division will not become fully apparent for some time yet, but I would ask you to believe me when I say that it is not purely arbitrary.

We have seen that reports of "somethings," and apparently of some forms of constructions in the oceans have been submitted for over a century, and alleged from many centuries before. The same applies to the seas and continental shelves. Moreover, the reports from these are very much more massive and much better documented. In dealing with the oceans, we took an arbitrary starting point (1963) and then worked, first forward to the present, and then backward to the beginning of the nineteenth century. This time, we are going to start at that point, though this also is not by any means "the beginning," and then work forward chronologically. The reason for this, which will become manifest as we go along, is, of course, primarily that this record clearly demonstrates that it has nothing to do with the development of submersible craft by us. But first a rather charming little historical note.

A.D. 1067—from Geoffrey Gaimar's *Lestoire des Englis*: "In this year people saw a fire that flamed and burned fiercely in the sky. It came near the earth and for a little time brilliantly lit it up. Afterwards, it revolved, ascended on high, and then *descended into the sea*. In several places it burned woods and plains, and in the County of Northumberland this fire showed itself in two seasons of the year." [29] We don't quite get the bit about its appearing in two seasons, but the implication is clear: simply that the British Isles were twice visited by some annoying form of UFO, circa 1066, which seems to have been on a rampage and which eventually went down into the sea. They had their troubles even then. Similar affairs exercised the clergy and other authorities, and the common people, throughout the following centuries.

Then a most remarkable fellow—and a "Fellow" of the Geological Society of Great Britain—published in 1860 a 58-page report to the British Association, entitled *Meteorites and Fireballs; from A.D. 2 to A.D. 1860*. His name was R. P. Greg, and the preamble to his paper reads: "This Catalogue is intended partly as a sequel to the Reports on Luminous Meteors, now continued for a series of years in the volumes of the British

Association Reports, and partly as a continuation, in a corrected and extended form, of a Catalogue of Meteorites published by the author, in two papers on the same subject in the Numbers of the Philosophical Magazine and Journal of Science for November and December 1854." [30] This is one of the most remarkable papers ever published and should be read by just about everybody, from astronomers to UFO buffs—and *before* any of them start pontificating. Here are over two thousand reports of tangible objects that maneuvered in the sky, fell from it, blew up, killed people, dropped all manner of junk, from "stones" to metal objects, and great blobs of jelly-like substances; and which on occasion appeared out of, or plunged into, the sea. (Yet, that even stones fell from the sky was absolutely denied until 1803!) What is more, this report is only an aside to a whole series of others on the same subject which, as Mr. Greg tells us, catalogue "Luminous Meteors." These go on for page after page and year after year.

Now, Charles Fort took the year A.D. 1800 as his starting point, and he burrowed most diligently into American, British, and French scientific literature and newspaper morgues. Fort's works did not offer bibliographies, because he included all his references in the body of his text. We have extracted these to the best of our ability, but Fort developed his own method, and this is most confusing and often obscure to the point of incomprehensibility; and so far, we have not found any evidence that he made use of Greg's work. Nevertheless, he dredged up quite a number of the same reports, and among these several of goings-into and comings-out-of the sea by unidentified objects that appeared to be constructions, and intelligently controlled in that they maneuvered and otherwise performed in a manner that meteors and bolides cannot do. (Be it noted that what has come to be called ball lightning does perform all manner of gyrations and maneuvers just as if it had intelligence, but this is a phenomenon of quite another ilk.) The only case that Fort unearthed in the period 1800–1860 that Greg missed appears to be the following.

> *Report of the British Association, 1861-30:*
> That upon June 18, 1845, according to the *Malta Times*, from the Brig *Victoria*, about 900 miles east [sic] of Adalia, Asia Minor (36° 40′ 56″ N. Lat.: 13° 44′ 36″ E. Long.) three luminous bodies were seen to *issue from the sea*, at about half a mile from the vessel. They were visible about ten minutes.[31]

Further reports stated that these objects were about five times the diameter of the moon and appeared to be connected by some kind of glowing streamers. The same objects appear to have been observed at the same time from as far away as the Syrian coast.

There is only one thing wrong with this report; namely that the word "east" is an obvious typographical error and should read *west*; 900 miles east of Adalia, on the south coast of Turkey, would put the location at the junction of Turkey, Iraq, and Iran somewhat southwest of the Caspian Sea, but that distance *west* places it exactly at the coordinates given in the report; and this is west-of-south of, and not too many miles from, the island of Malta.

Reports of objects, mostly luminous, luminescent, or displaying lights, or emitting beams of light, coming out of and going into the sea are so numerous that one has to resort to a mere listing, as did the estimable Mr. Greg for aerial phenomena of this nature and for "falls" of stuff from them and from the sky generally. This list, while very impressive, is frankly a crashing bore, being endlessly repetitious, and is not for inclusion in a popular work such as this. Nonetheless, there are a few items that we will quote so that we may comment on the business as a whole—and in order to bridge the gap from that wonderful, though all too brief, period of enlightenment, circa 1860, of which we will hear a lot more—and our modern post-W.W. II age. I take two items from Jacques Vallee's splendid work *Anatomy of a Phenomenon*. They go as follows:

> Second of November, 1885: M. Mavrogordato of Constantinople: at dawn, a very luminous flame, first bluish, then

greenish, and moving at a height of five to six meters, made a series of turns around the ferryboat pier at Scutari. Its blinding luminosity lighted the street and flooded the inside of the houses with light. The meteor was visible for one minute and a half and finally *fell into the sea.* No noise was heard when the immersion took place.

Sixteenth of June, 1909: M. Beljonne, at Phu-Lien Observatory, Tonkin, sends us peculiar bolide observations. The first one, especially remarkable, was made at Dong Hoi, Annam, by M. Delingette, Inspector in the Civil Guard, head of the meteorological station. At Dong Hoi, on June 16 at 4:10 A.M., a bolide of an elongated shape, truncated at both ends, flew over the city on a west-east course, casting luminosity. The witnesses—Hoang Nic, of Dong Hoi; Tran Ninh, of Sa-Dong-Dahn; Quyen, of Dong-Duong-Hoi; and Danh Lui, of the same village—who were fishing at sea, reported that the phenomenon lasted from eight to ten minutes, between the time the object appeared and the time it *fell into the sea,* at about six kilometers from shore.[32]

In 1968, NICAP brought to light an extraordinary case from the northeast Pacific that occurred in 1945. It reads: "The most detailed of these cases [of submerging or 'emerging' UFOs] involved a large UFO seen in 1945 by crew members of the U.S. Army Transport 'Delarof,' which had been hauling munitions and supplies to Alaska. The reporting witness, recently interviewed, was Robert S. Crawford, now a consulting geologist with the Indiana Soil Testing Laboratory, Griffith, Ind. Crawford is a graduate of the university of North Dakota, and while at the college he reported the sighting to Prof. N. N. Kohanowski, Dept. of Geology, who is a NICAP adviser. . . . The Delarof incident occurred in the summer of 1945, while Crawford was serving as one of the Army radiomen aboard. The ship, heading back to Seattle, was in the open sea past Adak. It was about sunset, and Crawford was on the port side, near the radio room, when he heard shouts from some of the crew. He turned and saw a large round object which had just *emerged from the sea.*

(Several crewmen saw the UFO actually appear from under-water, an estimated mile or so from the 'Delarof.') The un-known craft, showing darkly against the setting sun, climbed almost straight up for a few moments, then it arced into level flight, and began to circle the ship. All the observers were con-vinced it was a large object. Comparing it with the width of a finger held out at arm's length, Crawford estimated the UFO to be 150 to 250 feet in diameter. As it circled the Delarof, the flying object was in easy range of the ship's guns. But the gun crews held their fire, though on the alert for any sign of hostility. The UFO circled the vessel two or three times, moving smoothly and with no audible sound. All the witnesses felt it was self-propelled; otherwise, the strong winds would have visibly af-fected its movements. After several minutes, the flying object disappeared to the south or south-southwest. Suddenly the crew saw three flashes of light from the area where it had vanished. The Delarof captain posted an extra watch as the ship moved through that sector later, but nothing was seen."[33]

Such goings-into and comings-out-of had continued unabated for centuries and were still going strong at the dawn of the modern space age—which, incidentally, coincides with the initia-tion of both "saucermania" and ufology in America—to wit, the year 1947. In that year, we had a "something" off southern California that much upset the populace. This occurred on the 20th of September of that year, and was reported by the U.S. Coast Guard as "A flaming object [which] *fell into the sea* off the coast; no planes missing; observatory at Griffith Park did not think it was any kind of meteor." [34] Odd indeed, since it sounded very much like a meteor, and this is normally ortho-doxy's first line of defense in such a case. However, further in-quiry elicited the fact that the damned thing maneuvered, and for some time, and had thereby considerably peeved the Coast Guard. Similar occurrences continued.

In December, 1950 the American seaplane tender *Gardiners Bay* was steaming up the channel from Inchon, Korea, when her personnel sighted two mysterious smoke-trailing objects which *struck the water* at tremendous speed. Two huge columns of water rose to about 100 feet in height at the point of contact. No aircraft could be sighted overhead, either visually or by radar, and the Navy announced, "Identification remains a great mystery." [35]

On the 1st of April, 1952, an object resembling an airplane *fell into the Gulf of Mexico* some two hundred miles south of Lake Charles City, La. This was reported to the authorities by the *S.S. Esso Bermuda*, and a search was instituted. Nothing was found, and no aircraft were missing. [36]

In late 1952 the *Sunday Times* of Cape Town, South Africa, reported that a "rocket" had been seen over Table Bay. It was said to have gone straight up and then down again, but it was not clear if it came out or went into the water. A police launch searched the area since it was believed to have been a distress rocket—but there were no ships in the area. [37] (There are dozens of similar reports of "distress rockets," "flares," and the like seen off many coasts.)

In March 1954, *Fate Magazine* reported that "A couple of months ago San Francisco Bay area police were swamped with telephone calls reporting that 'hundreds of boats' were gathering just off shore." [38] A search by the Coast Guard revealed nothing. Other callers reported that there were hundreds of red and orange lights bobbing in the ocean just south of Golden Gate Park. Investigation here also revealed nothing.

In late summer of 1954 the *Groote Beer*, a Netherlands Government ship, arrived in New York with a report that eighty miles out the crew had seen a strange, flat, moonlike object *rise out of the ocean*. Captain Jan P. Boshoff was called to the bridge as soon as it was sighted and observed it through binoculars. He stated that at first it was grayish but then turned brighter on the lower part; it also had bright spots resembling lights around the edges. The ship's third officer, Cornelius Kooey, reported that the object made an angle of 60° to the southwest with the recently set sun. Measuring its altitude with a sextant at 8:15 P.M., he discovered that its speed was about 32 minutes of arc in 1½ minutes of time. [39]

Undated, but apparently about the same time, the Honduran

freighter *Aliki P.* sent a message, picked up by the Long Beach Coast Guard, as follows: "Observed ball of fire moving *in and out of water* without being extinguished. Trailing white smoke. Moving in erratic course, finally disappeared." [40]

In late 1954, the Navy Hydrographic Office reported that the American tanker *Dynafuel*, sailing in the Gulf of Mexico not far from New Orleans, saw smoke on the water. The ship's master said, "The smoke appeared to come from *under water* and resembled smoke from bombs dropped during target practice. It lasted 10 minutes." The NHO had no explanation. [41]

In February, 1955, Annabell Culverwell of Jerome, Ariz., was on the beach at Ocean Beach near San Diego. She reported that she saw "a huge geyser of water with the rear end of what looked like a space ship protruding from the top. . . . The geyser subsided [and] at the place where the geyser disappeared was a ring of what looked like woolly clouds. They did not move although a strong wind was blowing." [42]

On the 22nd of July, 1955, witnesses in Santa Maria, Calif., reported that a long silvery object *emerged from the water*. [43]

And then there is the "washtub" off Pusan, Korea, seen on the 15th of January, 1956. "The object was described to military authorities as being 'about the size of a large washtub and emitting a blue-gray glow. It was seen *falling into the water* about 50 yards off-shore near Heunde. It was early enough in the evening to attract the attention of a large number of Korean townsfolk. They reported that the glow continued for about an hour and a half before the object 'apparently sank into the sea.' By this time Korean National Police arrived at the scene and they, in turn, alerted U.S. Military Police. Cpl. Ben Elliot, an M.P. on patrol duty that night, was on the scene quickly enough to observe the object floating in the water for almost an hour. He described its glow as being similar to the flames from burning alcohol or benzine. The glow, he said, appeared to be about the size of a large washtub but the object itself could not be seen on the surface of the water. None of the witnesses expressed any desire to row out to the object for a closer look. As a result, it eventually sank out of sight into the sea's depths without being inspected. At this writing, no further reports concerning the object have been made. It was thought that Pusan University staff members might arrange for divers to attempt to recover remains of the object. If they did their findings remain as much a mystery as the object itself." [44]

On the 13th of December, 1956, a Swedish ship radioed the harbor control at La Guaira, Venezuela, that a cone-shaped object was falling vertically into the sea off the Venezuelan coast. It was very brilliant and gave off "strange glares. When the object *hit the water* an explosion was heard, then the sea where the object fell became brilliantly colored. After the colors subsided the sea became very disturbed with a 'boiling motion,' which continued for some time." [45]

On the 19th of April, 1957, crew members aboard the *Kitsukawa Maru*, a Japanese fishing boat, spotted two metallic silvery objects descending from the sky *into the sea*. The objects, estimated to be ten meters long, were without wings of any kind. As they hit the water, they created a violent turbulence. The exact location was reported as 31° 15′ N. and 143° 30′ E. [46]

On the 22nd of June of that same year two patrolmen at Rye, N.Y., watched a large object with two white lights and one red light *plunge into* Long Island Sound. [47]

And on the 24th of August the trawler *Eros*, proceeding through the Ahu Passage near Ninigo Island in the Bismarck Archipelago off New Guinea, reported a large yellow "star" which turned red, then green, then crimson. It hovered about twenty minutes and then turned from crimson back to green and *appeared to enter the sea*. [48]

On the 1st of September, 1956, police at Porthcawl, Glamorgan, Wales, saw a blood-red object with a jagged black streak across its center *rise from the sea*. It was described as being a "good deal larger than a full-sized harvest moon" and as having headed out toward the Atlantic. [49]

On the 21st of November, 1956, Customs officer Mr. Ueda

and the Maritime Safety Station officer Mr. Kume were walking along No. 1 Pier, Port of Kobe, Japan, when they heard the sound of an explosion at 8:23 P.M. They saw something resembling fireworks on the bay and watched as two balls of fire whirled and eventually *submerged*.[50]

In March of 1959, on the coast of Poland near Kolobrzeg, Polish soldiers saw the sea suddenly become agitated. A triangular object, each side measuring about four meters, *came out of the water* and started to fly in circles over the barracks, then sped away and vanished.[51]

A UPI report published on the eleventh of February, 1960, stated that at noon, EST, an object (presumed to be a Russian missile, but later denied) was spotted by U.S. Navy planes in the Russian impact area of the Pacific. The object went *down into the sea*.[52]

Two truck drivers, separately, about twenty-five miles east of Port Angeles, Washington, on the ninth of March, 1960, informed police that they had watched a large flaming object "half the size of a barrel" *going down* in the Strait of Juan de Fuca. The fiery object, thought to be a plane, was not found, and no planes were reported missing or down in or near the area.[53]

On February 27, 1961, the steamer *Boston Gannet* was plying between Lewis and Harris in the outer Hebrides, when its officers and crew witnessed a strange object twisting and turning and *falling into the sea*. Several ships raced to the spot at the mouth of Loch Seaforth, but found nothing; no aeroplanes were missing from airfields, and certainly no aircraft were reported missing from flights over Scotland. The mystery remained unsolved.[54]

Bailey's Beach, Long Island, the twenty-ninth of April, 1961: A contractor working on the beach saw what he at first thought was the head of a red-faced man out for a swim—a spherical object bobbing on the waves two hundred yards from shore and drifting out to sea; but it suddenly *rose to sixty feet above the water* and took off in a straight line out to sea at an estimated 100 mph.[55]

The *London Daily Mail* on the 7th of July, 1961, reported that the crew of a pilot cutter had signaled that an aircraft had *crashed into the North Sea* some twenty miles out from Walton-on-the-Naze, Essex, and eight miles from them. A thorough search revealed nothing, and no planes were missing.[56]

The 18th of September, 1961: Fourth Officer G. Gendall of the vessel *Queensland Star,* in the Indian Ocean, reported sighting a UFO through a cloud formation. White in color, it vanished into the clouds and then reappeared, dropping toward the sea. The object apparently *entered the sea*, as the water in the surrounding area grew intensely bright where the object had fallen. Particles of white matter continued to fall to the sea after the object had disappeared, and the sky and the water in the immediate vicinity were illuminated for several minutes.[57]

According to the Honolulu *Advertiser* of the 13th of March, 1963, residents in Windward Oahu "observed a light in the sky north of the island at about 6:30 P.M. yesterday. One resident said it was 'very bright' and appeared to descend slowly *into the sea* in a series of movements." It was reddish and was visible for five or six seconds.[58]

The 22nd of November, 1963, the North Sea, near Aberdeen, Scotland: The Aberdeen collier *Thrift* arrived in Blyth at noon yesterday, eight hours overdue after an unsuccessful search off Girdle Nest for a mystery object which *disappeared into the sea* 3 miles astern of the ship. The *Thrift* was heading south for Blyth when shortly before 6 P.M. on Wednesday evening 4 members of her crew including the skipper, Capt. J. Murray, saw a "flashing red light" which passed within a mile of her port side, 15–20 feet above sea level, and suddenly disappeared 3 miles astern. Capt. Murray alerted Stonehaven radio, put his vessel about and made for the spot where the light had vanished. The collier had two radar contacts on her screens, but when she reached within a quarter of a mile of them, they disappeared. The *Thrift* searched for 3 hours, circling the area several times and was joined by lifeboats from Aberdeen and Gourdon, a Shackleton from RAF Kinross, which dropped flares on to the surface, and a B.P. transporter. They recovered no traces of wreckage. The *Thrift* gave up the search at 8:50 P.M. and went to Blyth, being further delayed by bad weather. "We could not make out what the light was," said Capt. Murray. "It passed about three-quarters of a mile off our port side, flashing brilliantly until it disappeared. It made no noise at all, yet we could hear the Shackleton when it was miles away. Judging by the way the radar contacts disappeared from our screens it seems that whatever was there must have sunk before we could get to it. We found no trace of wreckage during our search, but something definitely fell into the water." [59]

The 20th of August, 1964: Two boys, Pat and Cliff Irwin of Richland, Washington, reported to the Coast Guard that a red-and-white plane had crashed *in the sea* off Oysterville, leaving a red-and-white smoke trail. The Coast Guard duly checked but found nothing; no planes were missing.[60]

On the 15th of December, 1964, an unidentified "aircraft" crashed *into the sea* off Rhyl, England. No aircraft were missing, and a sea and air search revealed nothing.[61]

The *Seaside* (Oregon) *Signal* on the 12th of January, 1965, noted that Mrs. Paul Zimmerman Gearhart and her two sons saw a triangular UAO which came slowly out of the southeast and then "suddenly *plunged into the sea* some miles off shore" at Tillamook Head. It left two trails of fire behind.[62]

On the 29th of January, in Monterey, Calif., Mayor George Clemens and his family spotted a very bright light performing "acrobatics" in the northern sky. It hovered a while, then shot straight up at high speed for about five hundred feet, then faded and dropped down and hovered again. Then it dropped further *down toward the water and disappeared.* This was also seen by a local flyer in the air at the time. The Coast Guard investigated but found nothing and had no explanation.[63]

England again, on the 15th of February, 1965, where a "ghost plane" *crashed in the Bristol Channel one mile offshore* at Minehead. This "unusual aircraft" was apparently seen by many people before it reached the Channel; it was said that there was "something abnormal about it. It did not seem to be distinct, but had a misty appearance about it." There was no mist or fog about. One witness stated that it came from behind some trees and "disappeared before our eyes." It made no sound at any time. Air-sea search found, as usual, nothing.[64]

On the evening of the 3rd of August, 1965, the Barking Sand tracking station on Kauai Island, Hawaii, reported a rocket-type object that *crashed into the ocean* about ten miles south of the island. Other islanders reported the object to have fallen "like a rock," while United Air Lines pilot L. L. Jones described it as yellow-green with an "overgrown falling star" appearance. It disintegrated just above the water. Navy officials on duty said, "Officially we don't know what it was." [65]

In Melbourne, Australia, a number of strange lights were seen in the western sky on the night of the 29th of August; but one witness said that an object shaped like a half-moon flashed across the western sky and then *disappeared into* Port Phillip Bay.[66]

On the afternoon of the 2nd of December, 1965, Mrs. Irwin Cohen of San Pedro, Calif., reported that she and her son took pictures of a glowing red-orange object that *went into the ocean.* She said that steam rose from the object as it hit. They thought it was probably a Navy missile; the Navy does not seem to have commented on the incident.[67]

And at 5:45 P.M. on the 16th of March, 1966, a white ovoid object *"crashed into the Atlantic* close to Cagarras Island [Brazil], after a violent explosion." It was watched by people on Arpoador beach, who said the object had a white contrail. Two witnesses reported that "a smaller parachute-like object was dropped from it just a few seconds before the crash." Other witnesses stated that more than one "parachute" was dropped. The Brazilian Coast Guard (CMS) and Air Force Life Saving Service (SAR) searched till 7:15 P.M. but found nothing.[68]

On the 4th of August, 1967, Dr. Hugo Sierra Yepez was fishing in the Gulf north of Arrecife, Venezuela, when he felt a vibration and the sea "began to boil in big bubbles, in a circle about 6 meters in diameter." A gray-blue, flat globe [*sic*] *emerged*, hovered close to the surface, dripping water, ascended in a curve, and then shot upward into space. The craft was described as having a "revolving section with triangular windows." [69]

At Catia La Mar, Venezuela, on the 25th of August, one Ruben Norato was on the beach when he saw "precipitous movement" of the water. Then three huge plate-shaped disks *appeared out of the water* and streaked out of sight.[70]

And during the first week of May, 1968, five UAOs were observed *diving into the ocean* off the coast at Arrecife, Venezuela.[71]

But perhaps the best-documented and most-publicized case of all is the UFO that dived into Shag Harbour, Nova Scotia, on the 4th of October, 1967. The story was reported in detail in the Yarmouth, N.S., *Light Herald*:

> The object was first seen at 11:30 P.M. Wednesday night in the area of Shag Harbour, Shelburne County, near Bon Portage Island. David Kendricks, who was driving in the area from Cape Sable Island to Shag Harbour with a friend, Norman Smith, spotted a bright reddish-orange light in the sky over Bear Point. He described the lights as pin-point sources, which appeared in a row, and came off and on one at a time. The lights were at an angle of 45 degrees, dipping to the right, and the lights came on in order from bottom to top. At approximately the same time, Laurie Wiggins, 19, sighted the object while driving with a group of four other people at Woods Harbour. He described the lights as four lights in a row which went on and off in order and tilted from level to a 45 degree

angle and disappeared slowly into the water. As they got out of the car, they saw the lights change to a single white light and bob in the water an estimated half mile off-shore. Wiggins then called the Wood's Harbour R.C.M.P. who arrived at the scene within 20 minutes. Const. Ron O'Brien of the Barrington detachment of the R.C.M.P. with two other officers saw the light floating on the water about half a mile off shore, and reported that it was carried out to sea by the tide and disappeared before they could get a boat to it. In the meantime, a large number of other witnesses reported seeing the lights at the same time and in the same area. The R.C.M.P. immediately called the Canadian Coast Guard Station at Clark's Harbour, and lifeboat No. 101 plus eight local fishing boats began searching the area. Within an hour the boats had arrived in the area where the object had disappeared, and reported finding a very large patch of bubbling water and foam. One fisherman described the froth as 80 feet wide and yellowish in color and said that he had never seen anything like it before in the area.[72]

Seven Navy divers searched the area for two and a half days but found nothing, and the search was abandoned. The possibility that it was an airplane was discounted by Canadian officials; no planes were missing.

Had enough? Well, hang onto your metaphorical hats, because there is much worse to come.

The above is merely a sampling of one aspect of this subject: to wit, unidentified things going into and/or coming out of the sea. And I would ask you to note the high percentage of these that emanated from what can only be called official sources, such as the Coast Guard and the police. There is a world of difference between some funny lights said to have been observed in the sky, and manifestly solid objects going into or coming out of the seas and oceans—*and* lakes and rivers, as we shall see in a moment. These things are altogether more "concrete," in the general meaning of that word.

4 · A FOURTH MYSTERY

Inshore UAOs

Since time immemorial man has contemplated going under water and staying there for protracted periods and preferably for as long as he might wish. There were initially several approaches to this effort, notably the "submarine," but it was not until A.D. 1620 that anybody seems to have achieved any success in this department. (The other principal line of endeavor will be mentioned later on, and almost at the end of this exercise, as it is of a purely biological nature.) In that year a Hollander by the name of Cornelius van Drebel built a sealed-in boat that was propelled by six pairs of oarsmen at a depth of about fifteen feet in the Thames River in England for several hours. This demonstration was put on for, and paid for by, King James I of England, and it was a complete success. However, although a number of others fiddled around with the idea and developed a lot of designs, nothing practical happened until 1776, when an American by the name of David Bushnell built a man-powered submarine which he named the *Turtle* and with which he attempted to sink the British man-of-war, the *Eagle*, which was anchored off New York. He tried to attach a time bomb to the *Eagle*'s bottom but couldn't penetrate her copper sheathing, so the sub rowed away and let off the bomb harmlessly. Nothing much developed during the next four decades; but then we find the *Housatonic*, which was blockading Charleston, being sunk by a "torpedo" attached to the end of a boom projecting from a sub. The *Housatonic* sank, but a hatch of the sub blew, and she also sank with all hands. This was in 1864.

The history of submarines then builds up slowly. The two countries in the lead were France and America. In 1888, the French launched the first naval submarine, named the *Gymnote*, a 30-ton vessel propelled by a single screw driven by an electric motor. Ten years later the French launched a 270-ton submarine which was christened the *Gustave Zedé*. Meantime in the United States, John Holland and Simon Lake conducted continuing researches; and Holland launched his first sub in 1875. However, it was not until 1898 that one of his designs was accepted by the Navy, and 1900 before the first was launched. The Italians had successfully employed a sub designed by one Pullino in 1892, and another, larger one, of 95 tons displacement, in 1894. The Germans had launched a 200-ton submersible in 1890 but did not really go into production until 1905.

We may see, therefore, that we did not have submersibles until the turn of the century, and until W.W. I there were very few of them. But *much more important*, we didn't have aircraft either, though balloons had been floating around in limited numbers for over a century. The significance of this seems to have been lost. The point is that, except in very exceptional circumstances, you can't see anything of what is even immediately under the surface of oceans, seas, lakes, or even rivers *from their surfaces*. On the other hand, it is often truly astonishing how much you can see from the air. Very few of the early balloons drifted over water, and early airplanes avoided sea passages and transoceanic flights as much as possible, except as stunts or as pioneering flights like that of Lindbergh. It was, in fact, not until W.W. II that transoceanic and transmarine flight became common, regular, and thus capable of having the surface layers of the seas at least under anything like a continuous surveillance. And as both military and commercial flights increased in number globally, so did reports of UAOs mount—and, be it noted, this means "Unidentified Aquatic Objects" in this case. As we have seen, however, what appeared to be submersible craft or constructions coming up from below *ocean* surfaces, had nonetheless been reported throughout the ages.

The same have been reported from what I call the shallows; but it was not until the end of the 1950s that this bit burst upon us—and burst it did. This succession was kicked off by a report of an incident off Bodega Bay, California, on the 13th of March, 1958, which stated simply that "an undersea 'object' which refused to identify itself was spotted by Navy pilots 50 miles northwest of San Francisco. Nearby naval air and sea craft, including 11 destroyers from San Diego [mark you] were rushed to the area, but nothing was found."[73] Among unsatisfactory reports this takes a pretty high place. Destroyers dashing five hundred miles just to look into such an incident would appear to be a rather exaggerated procedure; but then again, the details of the report may well have been garbled.

It was just about this time that the Americans were getting really nervous about the Russians. It was known that the latter had the largest fleet of submarines in the world, and there had been funny reports about small pyramidal objects that gave off beeps, being deposited all down our eastern seaboard at the edge of the continental shelf, from Newfoundland to the Bahamas, and which were assessed as direction finders for potential subaqueous marauders and thus to have been planted by the Russians. Russian submarines were latched onto and tracked, tracking our submarines; so we started tagging theirs. (I often wonder what the "OINTs," if they exist, think of this childish nonsense; but you'll have to wait until the last chapter to find out what I think.) Moreover, said "Rooskies" were said to have turned up also on our Pacific coast, and to have become very bold in their approach to our shores. Thus, everybody was in a constant state of alert. However, the Russians appear to have developed a similar case of jitters, and about the same time, and we very nearly came to blows over the business more than once. But then both parties were jolted back into reality by a number of reports that put an entirely different complexion on the whole matter. These began with the Golfo Nuevo case in February of 1960.

For two weeks the Argentine Navy did everything in its power to track down two unidentified submarines detected in the Golfo Nuevo, which measures about twenty by forty miles. They had the assistance of U.S. Navy experts and sub-hunting equipment, but despite this, and apparently uncounted tons of explosives, the mystery subs eventually just went away, still unidentified. They were able to stay submerged for several days and could outrun the surface ships. Initially there was only one sub, the second showing up several days later. All nations owning submarines denied emphatically that the subs were theirs. In view of the general mystery, wild rumors—such as the suggestion that they (or it) were German submarines which had been cruising around since 1945—spread unchecked, but the Navy, general loss of face notwithstanding, took the matter seriously.[74]

With this report we come to the next stage in this distressing business, because it displays several features of a (then) very novel nature. We must get it clear that reports of submersibles in both the oceans and seas, and going into and coming out of them prior to the last turn of a century, fall into one category simply because, not having such craft ourselves, we could not blame them on that old standby, "mistaken identity." For the first half of this century, however, they could all be very readily and most safely so described—provided they stayed *in the water*. At first, all were attributed to what the general public still then considered to be the near miracle of submersibles that actually worked, but of which that public obtained the quite mistaken notion that they could do all manner of things of which they were in no way capable.

At the same time, anything that fell into the sea, despite whatever fantastic gyrations it performed before doing so, could be almost as safely attributed to meteors, meteorites, bolides, or ball lightning by the experts, because the general public had not the foggiest notion just what such natural phenomena can and/ or can*not* do. When it came to things coming up out of the water and going on up into the sky, what I designate as "public relations" became intensely strained. Not only did we not then have any such thing, but no known natural phenomenon could perform thus. What made it much worse for all "experts," and the military outfits to boot, was that by this time saucermania had broken out and the public was in full cry. The amazing thing to me is that the saucer boys, while yelling "UFO" at each of these cases, never seem to have latched onto the fact that they *did* come out of water, or to have realized the significance of this fact.

At this point I am going to take the liberty of jumping ahead by two steps to point out that, during the past year, as of writing this, we have entered the final stage in this revolving circus in that we now *do* have a working plane—not just on a drafting board—that can go into and come back out of water. This is going to change everything all over again in that the press and all the other skeptics may attempt to lull the public once again by saying of all the new "into-and-out-ofs" that they are observations of these wondrous devices that *we* have invented. But, until a year or so ago, no such argument was raised, and in the absence of any such ready-made suggestion all the experts were absolutely stymied and had to fall back on the same old ridiculous, so-called explanations that they had thought up for aerial UFOs; items like hot-air inversions, mirages, mass hallucination, balloons, naughty little boys, and drunken housewives.

The significances of the Golfo Nuevo case are, however, manifold. First, it created a major incident of some considerable duration that was observed by tens of thousands of people, both civilian and military. Second, nobody, and least of all the military, dared try to deny it or explain it away. Third, there was international cooperation, and as the reports state, untold thousands of tons of explosives were dropped within an area of less than eight-hundred square miles without any apparent effect whatsoever upon these mysterious visitors. Fourth, the Russians got as bad a case of the jitters as did everybody else and were almost as quick to deny that they had anything to do with this as they were later to discredit any notion that they had anything to do with the assassination of President Kennedy. The Russians are not fools, and they don't want a major war any more than we do, despite all their saber-rattling. And every nation owning so much as one submarine could well deny any complicity, because they all knew perfectly well that none of theirs could withstand the pounding these things did; and also, that every other nation knew this. So everybody kept as quiet as they could about the matter.

But the poor authorities didn't get much of a chance, because only a year later the underwater boys really swung into action. It started up with a report on the thirteenth of February, 1961, when an unidentified submarine was seen off the coast of Natal at Tongest and Umhloti between 3 and 4 A.M. Witnesses said the sea was lit by a strange light which disclosed a ship with a conning tower and people on deck.[75] Then the reports came thick and fast.

In July of 1961 the *Ruby H*, a 67-foot shrimp boat owned by Ira Pete, was cruising off Port Aransas in the Gulf of Mexico when she "hooked into 'something' that ripped the vessel's stern right off." Pete and his two crewmen were rescued by another fishing boat. They were totally unable to say what the "something" was.[76] Again 1961, the 14th of November, Australian and New Zealand warships engaging in maneuvers off Sydney Head "detected and pursued a large underwater object that interrupted their maneuvers." There was no visual sighting of the object. The Sydney *Sun* stated that "the speed and ease with which the mystery craft eluded the fleet suggests it was nuclear-powered." The official Navy report called it an "unidentified object," though Senator Gorton, Minister for the Navy, had suggested that it was an "ocean-going submarine"! No American or British submarines were in the area.[77]

Now here is this Mr. Gorton again. My life seems to have

been plagued by him, as he was the most senior official in charge of the investigation of the famous "Globster" that lay about on a beach on the west side of Tasmania for two years and caused the most appalling uproar. Senator Gorton was listed then as the Commonwealth's Minister of the Navy, and he just happened to be on an inspection tour of something or other in a tiny town on the north of Tasmania, and immediately took charge of this case, ordering all newsmen to keep out of the area where this thing lay, and even preventing a representative of the National Geographic Society of America, who had chartered a helicopter to go there, from proceeding. This case would perhaps not be considered to be in any way connected with the subject at hand, but here is a curious point. Nobody, except a few biologists—originally identified as having doctorates but in due course being reduced to the status of "amateur naturalists" or "college students"—did anything about this thing, which was twenty feet in diameter and which could not be cut with an ax but withdrew its flesh from a newsman's cigarette lighter flame, for two years or until somebody wrote the leading newspaper in Hobart, the capital, and stated that several other like things had turned up on beaches over the years; *and that they had come down from the sky and not up from the depths of the sea.*

On the 24th of August, 1962, a "mystery sub" was detected off the island of Gottland, Sweden. It was ordered to surface but did not respond to either "polite requests" or depth charges and finally left the area, apparently in its own good time.[78]

On the 8th of April, 1963, the New Bedford dragger *Sunapee* was fishing sixty miles south of Montauk Point, L.I., when she started to move backward. Captain Nelson Ostman, skipper of the 74-footer, said the crew had seen a submarine in the vicinity earlier and realized immediately that they had caught onto the sub. He tried to swing the vessel around so that the net would pull free, but the maneuvering was unsuccessful and the *Sunapee* lost her nets, lines, and drags, valued at $3,000. The Navy at Boston said it knew nothing of the incident and was investigating.[79] On the ninth of August, 1963, the 90-foot dragger *Resolute*, fishing off Portland, Maine, nearly capsized when an unidentified underwater object became tangled in her nets. Captain John Larson stated that he and his crew had had to cut thousands of dollars' worth of nets to save the boat, which had been towed backward and nearly submerged by the object. They also stated that they thought the object was either a submarine or a huge whale. The Navy said they had no subs in the area at that time.[80] In both these cases it could have been a sub or a whale, but we record them for reasons that we shall see later.

On the 5th of February, 1964, a 105-foot converted PT boat, the *Hattie D.*, chartered by one R. W. Rutherford, struck an unidentified object twenty-five miles off Cape Mendocino, California, and sank. Said Rutherford, "We struck an unseen object, It was not a log. It was like metal. It hit the bow first and then took away our rudder. I wouldn't want to say anything for publication as to what it was, but it definitely was a strange object."[81] In another report of this incident he is quoted as saying, "What holed us was steel and a long piece." [82]

W. S. Robertson, writing in *Flying Saucer Review,* says, "I now wonder if a new sea-sighting wave is beginning, when we read of the first case of 1965 in the *Daily Mail* of February 5. . . . The trawler *Star of Freedom* (70 tons) from Fleetwood, Lancashire, struck an unidentified object in the early hours of the morning of February 3. She was steaming at the time at nine knots in 80 fathoms, 15 miles E.S.E. of Barra [Scotland]. The crash lifted her bows from the water. A distress call was sent out, and the crew manned the pumps. Eventually the badly holed trawler was beached in Castlebay harbour. Skipper George Wood is convinced that he hit a surfacing submarine, but both British and American naval authorities denied that any of their submarines was responsible, and refused to comment on the possibility that a foreign vessel had been involved. It is beginning to look like just another UFO in the sea mystery." [83] Might we suggest that this *was* a "foreign" sub?

Actually, the first case that year seems to have occurred on the 12th of January. As reported in *Flying Saucer Review,* it went:

USO [*i.e.*, UAO] in Kaipara Harbour, New Zealand. On January 12, 1965, Captain K.,* an airline pilot, carried out a "positioning" flight (no passengers) from Whenuapai (Auckland's airport) to Kaitaia, north of Auckland. The crew comprised Captain K., a first officer, and an operations officer. They left Whenuapai at 11 A.M., and were to reach Kaitaia by 12:10 P.M. Captain K decided to fly visually, following the coast line at low altitude. On approaching the southern end of Kaipara Harbour (just north of Helensville) he dropped 500 feet to have a closer look at anything on his flight path. The plane was a DC3. The tide in the harbour was well out and the water over the estuaries and mudflats quite shallow. When about one third of the way across the harbour, he spotted in an estuary what, at first glance, he took to be a stranded grey-white whale. He veered the aircraft slightly to port in order to fly more directly over the object, and on approaching it, he saw that what he had mistaken for a whale was a metallic structure of some sort. He observed the following details:

1. It was perfectly streamlined and symmetrical in shape.
2. It had no external control surfaces or protrusions.
3. It appeared metallic and there was a suggestion of a hatch on top, streamlined in shape, not quite halfway along the body as measured from the nose.
4. It was resting on the bottom of the estuary and headed towards the south as suggested by the streamlined shape.
5. The shape was not that of a normal submarine.
6. Captain K. estimated its length at 100 feet, with a diameter of 15 feet at the widest part.
7. The object rested in no more than 30 feet of water and the craft was very clearly defined.

Captain K. did not alert the other two crew members, *having been ridiculed over the years for various other reports* [?]. However, in May he reported to Navy Intelligence, who confirmed that due to inaccessibility of the estuaries, the craft sighted could not possibly have been a conventional submarine.[85]

---

*Although identified here as Captain K., this would seem to be Captain Bruce Cathie, a National Airways Corporation pilot, who saw such an object in that harbour.[84]

On April 11, 1965, two men had gone to the beach at Wonthaggi, 82 miles from Melbourne, Australia, to inspect a wrecked fishing boat. While on the cliffs they saw two objects about half a mile off shore and watched them for 15 minutes. One of the men, Mr. R. Banks, said, "We saw two strange craft, half a mile off shore and about 100 yards apart. Their strange appearance had us baffled, so we sat down and watched them. They turned away from one another and headed out to sea. While they were going away they disappeared, and then we realized that they were submarines and only their conning-towers had been showing." The sighting was reported to the Navy and a naval spokesman commented as follows: "A preliminary investigation of the report suggests, in view of the locality and configuration of the coastline, that the objects are unlikely to have been submarines." It was also stated that the objects could not have been either British or American submarines, as the Royal Navy submarines operating in Australia were in Sydney, and that any movements of American craft in or near Australian waters were generally reported to the Royal Australian Navy.[86]

There were three sightings of submarines north of Brisbane, Australia, in a period of five days. On the 15th of April, two boys saw a cylindrical or oval object about three-quarters of a mile off Coolum. On the 18th of April, two fishermen reported that they were chased by a large vessel off Mooloolaba. They estimated its length at 100 feet and said it had a small bridge and a cabin or cowling on its stern. And a former Air Force pilot flying in the area between Coolum and Noosa Heads reported seeing an object resembling a crash-diving submarine. The Australian Navy investigated all three cases but had no comment.[87]

And on the 6th of June:

Private aircraft pilot, Mr. C. Adams, and a television cameraman Mr. Les Hendy, reported seeing four or five "mysterious objects" floating in the sea 3 miles east of Fraser Island, 150 miles north of Brisbane, at about 11:30 A.M. Mr. Adams first noticed two of the objects from a distance of about 8 miles while flying over Fraser Island. The weather was clear and the objects appeared to resemble two big dark-coloured logs. They were narrow and up to 100 feet long. As he steered toward them, two or three similar but smaller objects appeared near the other two. They did not appear to move, but seemed to "sort of submerge" when the plane was about one mile away from them. From the air they appeared to be lying just below the surface and when "submerging" from sight seemed to do so without disturbing the surface. Mr. Adams was certain that the objects were too big to be fish or sharks, and the wrong shape to be whales. Mr. Hendy regretted that they were too far away from him to film them. Several experts got their heads together and decided that the objects sighted were migrating whales. However, their explanation was soon squashed when part-owner of the Seabrae Hotel—Mr. G. Sampson— and Mrs. V. Grady reported that they had sighted a similar object on the very same day, half-a-mile out between Redcliffe Pier and Redcliffe Point. They watched it for 10 minutes. It was long and black and there appeared to be a black balloon suspended over it. A Fisheries Dept. spokesman commented that it was unlikely to be a whale, because they very seldom come into Morton Bay.[88]

On to New Zealand: On the 13th of November, two fishermen, Mr. R. D. Hanning, 41, skipper of the *Eleoneai*, and a Mr. W. J. Johnson, set out from Bluff, the port of Invercargill,

to tend cray pots in the area of Stewart Island, the southernmost part of New Zealand. At 11:30 A.M. they were about half a mile off Rugged Islands, the northwestern point of Stewart Island, when they saw a strange craft come out of the water. Its tapered structure rose about 15 feet above the surface, and measured about 5 feet high [*sic*] at the top and 12 feet at the water line. Then, about 30 feet away from it, there was another object, box-shaped, about 10 feet long and 5 feet high. There was no sign of any periscope or railing, and nothing but the "tower" and "box" were visible. The water was smooth, and the object was in clear view only about 300 yards away.

(The object's position was only 500 yards off Rugged Islands.) The men had it in sight for 10 to 11 seconds, when suddenly there was a great surging of water like a tide boil and both objects disappeared. Both men were rather startled at this display and in fact were somewhat frightened by it. They hung around for a few minutes, decided not to investigate, and steamed off. The water—at the spot from which they made the sighting— was about 30 fathoms deep to a sandy bottom, although the coast near Rugged Islands is rocky and rugged.

They later reported this to the Navy and were emphatic that it was not a whale and did not resemble any other submarines they had seen. They said it was black or brown without any markings. A Navy spokesman stated that "it was most unlikely that the object—whatever it might have been—was a submarine, because it would have been operating in an area where there were rocks, a definite submarine hazard. Besides, there was no logical reason for any submarine to be in that area."[89]

To return closer to home, on the 5th of July, 1965, as reported by AP, Dr. Dmitri Rebikoff was conducting one-man submarine operations off Fort Pierce, Florida, at depths of 90 to 100 feet collecting data for Dr. Jacques Piccard's projected cruise under the Gulf Stream. Capt. L. Jacques Nicholas, coordinator of the project, reported that Rebikoff told him, "Beneath the various schools of fish moving at approximately the same speed as the stream (3½ knots) there loomed a pear-shaped object. At first from its size we thought it to be some form of shark. However, its direction and speed were too constant. It may have been running on a robot pilot. We received no signal (from it) and therefore do not know what it was." Rebikoff reportedly took photographs but, according to the AP report, "The film was not processed immediately."[90] And we are prepared to bet that even if it was it will never be released.

At 4 P.M. on the 18th of March, 1966, on a stretch of deserted beach ten miles north of Deseade (south of the Gulf of

San Jorge, Argentina *), Carlos Corosan, a 35-year-old farmer, saw a large cigar-shaped craft with no wings. He said it was less than 35 yards away and estimated its length at 65 to 70 feet, describing it as metallic in appearance, reflecting the rays of the setting sun. It was gray-black and apparently smooth, with no visible markings or windows or any kind of appendages. However, gray smoke was coming from the tail section. Corosan said it was "just chugging along," sounding rather like an automobile with engine difficulties. Then, "the mysterious craft stopped and emitted a short, muffled blast of smoke [*sic*]," whereupon the smoke became "very dark black." Corosan, having decided that this was no ordinary craft, now ran for cover. At this point the object was hovering about 40 feet above the water and maintained this position for a few minutes. It then began to hum and "vibrate all over as though it were coming apart." The humming noise was followed by another short blast, and the craft began to rise slowly, taking a north-northeast course, with the same erratic chugging motion. Corosan now started to leave his hiding place, intending to report to the authorities, but heard a much louder explosion, followed by a decrease in the humming sound. He turned around just in time to see the object "crash" into the sea. "It did not float at all. It just hit the water with a huge splash and went down quickly." There was no geyser or any sign that the object had filled with water. After thirty minutes of watching for any sign of survivors, he reported to the local authorities. The Argentine Goverment has neither confirmed nor denied Corosan's sighting, though the latter claims to have seen Navy ships in the area and an unidentified official is said to have indicated that they are looking for the "lost object" though it is thought that the Falkland current may "have swept the object away." [91]

On the 27th of September, 1966, two divers from the Naval

---

*In the original article the incident is placed *in* the Gulf of San Jorge; however, Deseade is actually about 45 miles south of the Gulf on the Atlantic coast.

Ordnance Laboratory Test Facility accompanied Martin Meylach, an amateur treasure hunter, who had discovered a rocket-like object in 40 feet of water off the coast of Miami, Fla. He had found it while searching for sunken Spanish treasure with a magnetometer four miles offshore and reported it to Homestead AFB, which turned the matter over to the Navy. Officials at Homestead said they had no idea where the mechanism came from and discounted theories that it was some sort of missile dropped by craft from a nearby base.[92]

There's a lot about all this that I just plain don't like. In the infamous good old days, fish lived in water and men on land, and while all the other types of animals divided up the two elements one way or another between themselves, nothing lived in the air—at least permanently—though spores and birds called swifts seemed to spend most of their time therein. Beyond the air was a rather soothing thing called Space, which meant simply "nothing." Thus, it is rather peeving to have to conceive of life forms indigenous to space and maybe to our and other atmospheres; but to have to contemplate intelligent living entities, and especially metallurgical experts of a most advanced competence, and even of humanoid form, living in our waters or hydrosphere becomes actually annoying. On the other hand, it more than just tickles my sense of humor, and not only because my greatest delight is teasing stuffed-shirted experts, nor even because I have been waiting nearly thirty years to say "I told you so"; but because it is just another wormhole in our coffin of egocentric, anthropocentric, and terracentric obtuseness. And that these underwater chaps can bat it out at 200 mph at 20,000 feet down when we can't even get going at that depth is absolutely delicious!

But I'm not through yet: not by a long chalk! First, we have to clear up what would at first appear to be a minor matter but might have even greater significance than all that has gone before. Then we will have to tackle the ever present matter of "reality" before we can get down to the really dirty aspects of this whole deal. So to a review of the nasty little items; to wit, what I call "the water babies."

5 · A FIFTH MYSTERY

UAOs into and
Out of Fresh Waters

It may have struck you, as it has me, that
all these inshore marine affairs appear to
come to a dead stop at the end of 1966. At
first I thought that this might be due to our
having become bored with the whole UFO
bit at that time—and indeed we personally
did—and so have done a sloppy job of reading the cascade of material that descends
upon us month after month. So we ran a new
check on all the clippings, which we file
chronologically by year and month, and we
then combed all the serious-minded journals,
but—absolutely nothing. Doubtless the moment the buffs read this, if any of them do,
there will be an inundation of reports for
1967, 1968, and 1969. Nonetheless, I cannot refrain from commenting: and more especially because *oceanic* affairs and the next
lot that we are going to tackle in this chapter have both gone evenly on until the time
of writing.

Please note that, since the Cuban confron-
tation, there had been a mounting frenzy
over Russian fishing fleets just off international limits and over their submarines pene-

trating the limited inshore waters claimed by countries (variously) as national domain. Our loyal "enemies" knew all about our capabilities of detection, but they really didn't give a damn, knowing that we didn't want to start anything. Our computers had told us to go ahead on the Cuban business, and we did; and if you dig back into the morgues of reliable newspapers like *The New York Times* of that period you will find some almost hilarious reports; notably one about our tagging an "enemy" sub for days around Caribbean waters and even "talking" to it, to the positive fury of its commander.

Now, if the majority of the unidentified submarine objects reported, as listed in the last chapter, were Russian probes, that's perfectly all right by me. What a relief!—though it would not cause me to deviate one iota from the general contention which I propose to develop as we go along. Nonetheless, it might explain the sudden cessation of such reports in 1966 in that the Russians then decided to be a bit more discreet or a bit more efficient, while the UAOs, having been discreet for millennia, might well have thenceforth been ignored even by the buffs. I have had plenty of "stories," as diametrically opposed to reports, of such things during the past three years, but the sources from which these have come are not suitable for discussion here.

The other curious aspect of this cutoff of inshore reports is, as I have said, that there has been no pause in reports of the "water babies," by which I mean goings-into, comings-out-of, or lurkings-in *fresh waters*. In a later chapter you will be able to see at a glance the true significance of this; namely, the truly minute area of fresh waters, compared with that of salt waters. We must, of course, counterbalance this with the fact that human beings actually inhabit an equally minute portion of the *land* surface; while shipping lanes and transoceanic flight patterns are confined to very narrow limits indeed. Yet, of all the UFOs (i.e., aerial oddities), an astonishing number are reported to have entered, come out of, or been seen in lakes and rivers. What the exact statistics are I do not know, as there is no proper catalogue of UFOs and what has been listed has not been computerized and properly analyzed. Furthermore, the business seems to be regional, in that certain lakes and rivers appear to be veritable hotbeds of UFO–UAO activity. The best example is Lake Erie.

Is this all due to the fact that there are an awful lot of lakes, ponds, rivers, and creeks on the land areas that *are* inhabited by human beings; or does it have any other significance? Also, one wonders what goes on in all the millions of lakes around which no people live and which, in the majority of cases, they never even visit. Just look at the map of Canada! And this goes for all the other vast forested areas of the land surfaces of our earth. And you should note that these, though greatly exceeded in area in the aggregate by deserts, prairies, and other drier areas, are still of positively vast extent. I could name two dozen waters within a ten-mile radius of where I sit writing this (at least according to the U.S. Geological Survey 1:24,000 map) into which hundreds of UFOs could dart without a single soul noticing them; and I'm less than eighty miles from New York City.

The history of the water babies runs almost exactly parallel to that of the marine UAOs. There are a great number of hints of them in ancient literature—Indian, Mesopotamian, Egyptian, Greek, and especially Roman. However, these are for the most part overlaid with a thick smear of allegory. Also, the ancients, when confronted with an enigmatic natural phenomenon that was not well known, tended to become a bit muddled. Not having machines—at least any developed on this planet—they normally attributed things like UAOs to the department of "monstrosity," by which I mean that of unusual, unknown, or monstrous animals. Therefore I do not presume to review these items at this time. Experts now say that there is a great deal of factual history to be gleaned from a proper analysis of myth, legend, and folklore. This may be so, but I will be perfectly frank and say that I doubt a great deal of what even the real experts say on this score, not because I doubt their erudition but because I have yet to come across one who in making his assessments has ever taken into account the kind of things we are talking about in this book. Why should they? After all, the very idea of supersubs and suboceanic civilizations (or labs, or what-have-you) is preposterous enough, but to ask anybody to interpret certain passages in Vedic scripts as implying or trying to describe such is really quite beyond the pale and altogether too much to ask any serious-minded scholar to countenance or to take into consideration. Nonetheless, these implications are there for any who may be cognizant of such suggestions to interpret as they will.

Once again, therefore, we will start with the dawn of what I call the modern age; to wit, the end of W.W. II. But first, just one charming little ditty of almost two centuries ago, just to show that our immediate ancestors were cognizant of this business. This was reported in the *Annual Register* (published in England) for 1767 and reads as follows:

> On the water, at Isla near Cowper Angus, a thick dark smoke rose and then dispelled to reveal a large luminous body like a house on fire. It presently took a pyramidal form and rolled forwards with impetuosity till it came to the water of Erick. It rushed up this river with great speed and disappeared a little above Blairgowrie. It caused an extraordinary effect! In its passage it carried away a large cart, and bore it many yards over a field of grass. A man riding on the high road was carried from his horse and stunned. He remained senseless for a long time. It destroyed half a house, but left the other half behind, undermined. It also destroyed an arch of a new bridge at Blairgowrie, immediately before it vanished. As few appearances of this kind ever were attended with like consequences, various conjectures have been formed concerning it.[93]

The first real break in under-*fresh*-water affairs began with the outburst of "flying boxcars" and suchlike over Sweden in 1946. For those not familiar with this business, I must explain that literally hundreds of (from a mechanical point of view) obscene objects were reported by tens of thousands of people in that country to have been observed meandering, dashing or darting about, and maneuvering in their skies, both by night and by day. At that time the stupid moniker "flying saucer" had not been coined and nobody had thought of the equally stupid designation "UFO." Thus, the stolid, pragmatic Swedes very realistically assumed that these horrible things were some leftovers from the Nazi rocket experimental base of Peenemunde or that they were devices taken from that place by the Russians and developed during the year or so since the cessation of W.W. II in their country. (The fact that the Westerners got Peenemunde was gaily ignored.) The record of these things is really very aggravating, because there was absolute proof that they were not meteors or any other such so-called natural phenomena, while half the total population of the country appears to have observed them, and they came from all directions and went in all directions. Further, a very high proportion fell down! But, as both official releases and press reports stated at the time: *"Unfortunately it has been impossible to get hold of any of them because all of them have fallen into the lakes."*

Now, one has to acknowledge the fact that there are an awful lot of lakes in Sweden. In fact, according to the Swedish Information Service, no less than 10 percent of its land surface is under fresh water. Yet is it not rather odd that *all* of these "flying boxcars," or "V-1s," or whatever else they were described as being at the time, were said to have fallen into lakes? If this was not so, why did anybody say that it *was* so? The old cliché had it that 40 million Frenchmen could not be wrong. This was proved to be baloney in 1940; but that even two of the 7.5 million Swedes could all be hallucinated, and for several months, seems to me to be stretching credibility a bit too far. The bloody things apparently turned up in their skies and a lot of these things fell down; but all that did so fell into lakes. Why? So let us proceed from this somewhat ridiculous little historical interlude to a chronicle of like affairs elsewhere.

We have compiled some enormous sheets of references, with a round dozen columns for specific features of each, covering this business of the water babies going into, coming out of, or being observed in fresh waters. We were searching for any pattern therein which might indicate a regional incidence, or a date, time of day, or other such factor, but none such emerged. Nor were the descriptions of the objects consistent; in fact, they varied just as much as do descriptions of straight UAOs. Yet, after pruning this mass of data down, we found that we had a sort of latter-day Greg chart (see Chapter 3). So extraordinary is the result that we present a sampling in the tables, pages 226–229.

The first case in this condensed list that calls for further elaboration is that of the Bordes on Titicus Reservoir, in northern Westchester County, New York, on the night of the 16th to the 17th of September, 1955. I take this account directly and verbatim from the journal of an organization in New York entitled C.S.I., which was a most serious-minded outfit but which was most unfortunately disbanded some ten years ago. Its operatives were very good reporters and extremely cautious in their investigations, and it is for this reason that I prefer to present their report in full. It goes as follows:

The couple arrived at the lake, to troll for bass, shortly before midnight. At about 1:30 they were in a small cove on the north side of the lake, which is about three miles in length with the long axis east to west. Mrs. Bordes was rowing while her husband was busy untangling fishlines. For the first time in their experience they had not taken a single fish. It was pitch dark; there was no moon, and the stars were hidden by overcast. At this moment Mrs. Bordes saw a strange object rise out of the water on the shoreward side of the boat, no more than a few yards away. It was a rose-colored, luminous sphere—at least, it appeared spherical as seen from the top—about the size of a basketball, with darker areas on it. It rose about a foot into the air and then fell back into the water with a resounding splash. Mr. Bordes, standing in the stern with his back to it, thought a big fish had jumped.

Mrs. Bordes is a more than usually intrepid young woman, who enjoys hunting and fishing at night, but this sight was so unnatural that it alarmed her; she took up the oars and rowed straight for shore. Her husband, still intent on his task, expostulated, until suddenly he, too, caught sight of something. "Quiet!" he whispered. "I think I see a phenomenon!" Mrs. Bordes, petrified, then saw the "phenomenon" too. Some two hundred yards to the southeast of them, toward the center of the lake, and apparently floating on it, glowed two parallel lights, like bluish-white fluorescent tubes. They were of a sinuous wavy shape (see drawing) but rigid; they did not undulate. Their length seemed to be about twice that of a 15-foot rowboat. Above these "serpents" was a round light of lesser brilliance, more yellowish-white in hue. Considerably smaller than a full moon, and dimmer than a car headlight, it appeared the size of a basketball or "pawnbroker's ball" at a distance of a few hundred feet. It was not hovering in midair, but was apparently fixed to a solid body, which was only intermittently visible as a dim grey shape against the blackness (dotted lines in sketch). As they watched, they perceived that this round light was regularly eclipsed from one side and then opened up again, giving a very definite impression of a rotating spotlight; and although it projected no visible beam, they could see each other's face when the light was shining toward them. Mr. Bordes, who felt more curiosity than fear, wished to row closer to the object; but his wife, in near-hysterical fright, threatened to jump overboard if he did any such thing. He therefore put her ashore, and started off in the boat to investigate by himself. As he attempted to approach the lights, without any sound they began moving off to his left (eastward). Mr. Bordes emphasized that they were moving into a rather stiff breeze at a rate much too fast for any rowboat. (No boats other than rowboats are permitted on the reservoir.) Then they stopped, and came toward him slightly. At this point he returned to the north shore to pick up his wife, and they rowed westward to the boat mooring, nearly a mile. During the whole return trip, the object appeared to be following them at roughly its original distance; the boat was illuminated the whole time by the light, and Mrs. Bordes was weeping with distress. When they left the boat and drove off in their car, the luminous object was still visible on the water, though by now it was moving off to the east again. These motions were so definite, according to Mr. Bordes, that any optical phenomenon of the mirage order seemed to be out of the question. Besides, no natural source of such brilliant light could be found.[145]

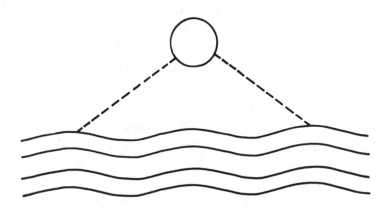

As a matter of fact, there seems to be a curious emphasis on reservoirs among the cases of freshwater babies. At first one might suppose that this could be due to these bodies of water being man-made and thus under better surveillance than natural waters. On the other hand, fewer people live around reservoirs or go out upon them than onto natural lakes, simply because there are usually considerable restrictions as to swimming, boating, and fishing in same, while the surrounding watershed is usually fenced off and unavailable for homesites. Then again, even if there are large populations around such artificial waters, some other most odd factors appear to come into play. Let me tell you of a case that I investigated personally. This is a bit complicated but seems to me to be of considerable significance. It came about this way.

To start at the beginning: In October of 1966, the local press in the greater New York area burst out in a rash of what appeared to be rather wild reports of "flying saucers" over and around a large reservoir in northeastern New Jersey named Lake Wanaque, which is the main feeder for the Jersey City water supply. Instead of just dying away as these scares usually do, however, this thing was picked up by the wire services and ballooned into the most extraordinary affair. Moreover, it trickled on for almost two years. Wanaque is well within an hour's drive of New York City and only a few miles off the major highway west from Manhattan, namely good old Route 46. The lower end of the reservoir, which was built some forty-five years ago, abuts onto and penetrates an area of rather high population. This peters out to the north along a road that follows the east side of the reservoir. The resultant lake meanders on north for about six miles, is surrounded by woodlands, and is a most beautiful location.

When the initial "flying saucer" scare got started, literally thousands, if not tens of thousands, of citizens poured into the area night after night to watch for (and often observe) the mysterious lighted objects over the water. Among these interlopers were hordes of pressmen, ranging from hardnosed skeptics to several of the better science reporters, and a number of professionals who had long since decided that UFOs were not a laughing matter. Also, a whole spectrum of working scientists turned up with, I learned only recently, yard-long credentials that they disclosed to the local officials. Then came the military, though as a matter of fact, it now turns out that they were there first, and for very good reasons. This is that Wanaque is a most highly secured area owing to its vital part in the water supply not only for civilian Jersey City but for its ambient complex of industry and essential services. During W.W. II it was one of the most tightly secured areas on the eastern seaboard, and the police forces securing it had top priority lines to the military at all times. Then again, just about the time of this scare, certain groups of irresponsible idiots had threatened to sabotage the dam and thus flood out the locals and paralyze that large industrial area.

Armed Services representatives were there from the instant some non-officials reported these UFOs to the press, and they stayed there. However, a most curious and then rather novel factor was interjected—or was alleged to have been so. This was the arrival in the area of a number of persons, some of whom are said to have been wearing military uniforms, of both Army and Air Force, and of various ranks, who did not identify themselves but went around interviewing local people who had stated for the record that they had seen these things; and doing so almost to the point of harassment. And simultaneously came the self-appointed ufologists. These, we were told, caused almost more embarrassment than the previously mentioned lot. Reports from these people were almost as wild as those issued by the working press; and, it now transpires three years later and on proper investigation, both were pure bunkum. The facts are quite different, as I shall now explain. But first I must explain why I was asked to investigate this matter at so late a date.*

A member of the society of which I am administrative director wrote to me on the 9th of April of 1969 and asked if I could go to the Wanaque area and ascertain whether there might be any grounds for a certain report made by a rather prominent New Yorker to a mutual friend of ours who holds a position of considerable eminence in the official field of the UFO problem. I replied to the effect that I would be happy to do so, provided I was given the necessary facts. A few days later I received another letter giving me just such facts as I might need, and a

*The following may sound disreputably "cloak-and-daggerish" and infuriate the stuffed shirts, who, quite rightly, of course, suspect anyone indulging in esoteric investigations, who will not divulge names, of being "secretive." This is not the case on this occasion; I merely went to Wanaque as a reporter and at the request of certain parties who have at least semiofficial connections. Further, as a reporter, I gave my solemn promise that I would not publish the names of my informants without specific permission so to do in writing. I have asked for this, but it has not been granted. Said sources are known to my publishers, and it must be their decision whether they should disclose them, and to whom. Since all of the persons whom I quote are themselves officials, their stories are of course known to the appropriate authorities.

few days later still, my assistant and I drove down to Wanaque. There we went about our business in the manner that has become customary to us over the years. By this I mean that I went first to the appropriate authorities, presented my credentials, told them why I was there and what I wanted to investigate, asked if they had any objections, and sought their guidance. As always, I was received with the greatest courtesy and given all kinds of cooperation, time after time, far exceeding any requests that I had made. Thus, we were passed on from one department to another and, in the case of the various police forces, by prior appointment made by one with the other.

The main story that we had been asked to look into was a little bizarre, to say the least, and since we found no evidence for its authenticity and since it really has nothing but purely corollary connection with the business at hand, I prefer not to go into it. However, it was initially linked to the UFO–UAO business, and that was the field that we ended up in. When we got to Wanaque itself we called upon an official who has been in charge of certain aspects of security for the dam and reservoir for over thirty years. This meeting had been arranged by the New Jersey State Police. When I meet a man of this caliber and background I feel very foolish trying, however tactfully, to come around to the subject of anything like UAOs. But, taking the proverbial ungulate by its frontal protuberances, I plunged right in after the usual exchange of pleasantries. And I have never got a greater shock in my life. I am not writing a scenario, so I will get on with the facts.

This gentleman gave us a blow-by-blow account of the happenings of 1966 and 1967, with details of the events. He named many of the pressmen, scientists, officials, ufologists, saucerians, nuts, screwballs, publicity men, kooks, krooks, and krakpots who turned up to plague him, the various police forces, and other departments. We recognized the names of a very high percentage of these. Apparently affairs had got very nearly out of hand several times, as thousands of people swarmed into the area, clogging the single main road along the east side of the reservoir, gawking and gaping all night with field glasses, telescopes, and all manner of other devices known and unknown. The local police had to call in the State Police to clear the road; and this went on, our informant said, for night after night. Then he dropped a series of bombshells, as follows: (1) These mysterious lights, *and lighted solid objects*, have been seen in the area for half a century. (2) *None* of those seen during the 1966 outbreak were over any part of the lake (reservoir). (3) All were, as they have always been, seen over the small mountain range or range of large hills that runs up the west side of the lake. (4) Though those seen by the crowds maneuvered, they in no case performed at that time as either the press or the ufological publications said they did. (We were shown reports of just what they *did* do.) But, as if this were not enough, our informant, who—if anybody—should know what he was talking about, further informed us of certain other aspects of this matter.

First, after stating that said objects had been seen there since his father's time—and his father had held his position before him—he told us of the great troubles they had caused during W.W. II, when all authorities in any way connected with the protection of the reservoir were under stringent orders to report anything suspicious to the military, immediately. Sort of wagging his head, he told us of incident after incident when his department was obliged to send out an alert and the military came pouring in; but of course to no avail, for what could Army command make out of UFO reports in the early 1940s? The resultant frustration appears to have been almost overwhelming. But then our informant moved on to other things.

Next, he told us the details of an incident when the senior officer on duty had called him at eleven o'clock one night at his home and asked him to get out into his garden with his binoculars immediately, and look above his house. Said officer had called from his post about two miles away. When our friend ran out and looked up, there was a large, glowing, spindle-shaped object hovering at what appeared to be no more than five hundred feet directly above him. Focusing on this and feeling assured that it was a *solid* object, and not just a light, he ran back into the house and grabbed the telephone to give the official alert. By the time he ran out again the object had vanished.

Perhaps because he could see by our expressions that we were not smirking, he then sort of took a deep breath and said rather simply: "There have been other things, and on several occasions witnessed by my men also, but which I will never talk about, even when I have retired and am no longer under regulations." I could see that he was not only sincere but really considerably worried, so I did not press the point. And perhaps because I did not do so he volunteered the observation that these incidents all concerned some things going into, coming out of, or having been investigated actually *in the reservoir*. What I ask is, why were none of these basic facts extracted by the working press, the UFO buffs, or anybody else? This I just don't get.

Turning now from reservoirs, which I am forced to do by lack of space if not simply to try and avoid boredom by repetition, let me introduce still another strange aspect of the water babies. This will doubtless at first sound rather abtruse, but I think it should be taken into account. It would seem to fall into class (b) of the contemplation of unknowns; i.e., misidentification or "they didn't know how to interpret what they saw," so beloved of the skeptics, and the second line of defense of the stuffed shirts.

Either freshwater UAOs exist or they don't. The same must be postulated of large unknown animals, or "monsters" that are reported from fresh waters. If both do exist, one is constrained to ask how many of the one are mistaken for the other, both being sort of unlikely and outrageous to the average person. Items like the famous Loch Ness Monsters, and the other Longnecks reported from other lakes in Scotland, Ireland, Scandinavia, Russia, Siberia, Canada, and the United States, would most definitely appear to be animals as we know them, because of their conformation, their movements, and their general behavior; but there are others of an entirely different nature that have been reported almost as often. These have been said to look more like gigantic fish or whales; in other words, to have been spindle-shaped and to have exhibited either no external excrescences or what appeared to be fixed fins. These have usually been attributed to giant sturgeon, the best-reported case being that from Lake Seton in British Columbia.

There has been a tradition of very large specimens of these fish in this lake since before the arrival of the white man, and they have reportedly been observed at close quarters for two decades by summer visitors and other persons fishing on the lake. The lake itself is a bit odd in that it is pale greenish in color and never freezes. In 1964 one Paul Polischuk and his wife reported that when out on the lake on a clear Sunday morning, just cruising about in a 25-foot boat, they came alongside one of these giant fish, which was swimming quietly along. Mr. Polischuk later stated that it was about ten feet longer than his boat. The local chamber of commerce is said to have offered $1,000 to anybody who could land this monster.[146] Everybody, including some educated, indigenous Amerinds brought up at the lake, asserted that the thing was one of their giant sturgeon. And there is nothing outlandish about this, since the record sturgeon that was caught in the Volga River in Russia measured no less than 28 feet.

This is one side of the coin; the other is exemplified by the really monstrous things seen in what is called Lake Iliamna—almost an inland sea—in Alaska. These have also been known to the local Amerinds and to the Eskimos since ever, and they have been seen from the air by quite a number of people, including U.S. Navy fliers. They are spindle-shaped and run up to the length of the larger whales. In this instance, however, the indigenous people do not claim them as fish or any other animals—and Amerindians and inland Eskimos know their local animals if anybody does—but give them strange names that imply otherworldliness. This I find most interesting, as I have the utmost respect for the ideas of indigenous peoples about their local fauna and, at the same time, the utmost disrespect for the

opinions of settlers, colonists, and other outsiders and interlopers. The latter bring their prejudices and preconceived no-
tions with them, and they almost always sneer at the locals'
opinions, imagining as they invariably do that they are inferior
persons. (You should hear the opinions of the indigenes on the
newcomers!) The point is: why should people with old and even
ancient knowledge of these mysteries clearly differentiate between known animals on the one hand and things they feel are
not any kind of animal on the other? I think that this is a point
that both ufologists and monster-hunters should bear in mind.

Turning another metaphorical page, I would like to devote
what space I have for this subject to the most remarkable case
that I know of. It is of quite another nature, but it is as near
"watertight" (and no pun is here intended) as any I know of
from various points of view, and most notably the established
prerequisites of Dr. J. Allen Hynek, for twenty years consultant
to the U.S. Air Force on UFOs, regarding witnesses. This is a
case of an obviously material object plunging into a river in
Brazil in 1963. The case has been reported, and re-reported, and
written up, and paraphrased ever since, but there is only one
truly reliable account that I know of, and I have asked permission of the author of this to herewith republish it in full. Said
author is Mrs. James (Coral) Lorenzen, who with her husband
initiated a private citizens' organization named the Aerial Phenomenon Research Organization in 1952 and which has published since then a splendid journal entitled *The A.P.R.O. Bulletin*. The Lorenzens and their devoted associates are, in my
opinion, the best reporters on the whole spectrum of ufology;
they have maintained throughout the years a pragmatic and
balanced attitude to the subject and have always conformed to
established scientific principles. This husband-and-wife team
have also published three most excellent books on the subject.[147] The account of this incident as they gave it in their
journal goes as follows:

On the 31st of October, 1963, Rute de Souza, 8-year-old
daughter of Elidia de Souza who lives near Iguape, Brazil,

heard a strange and increasing roar and on looking to see where it came from, was terrified to observe a silvery object coming toward the river near her house. The object soared over her house, then above her, struck a palm tree near the top and began to "writhe" and struggle in the air above the river. Then it fell into the Peropava River near the opposite shore. Rute began to run to her house to tell her Mother, and met her Mother coming out. Mrs. de Souza had also heard the roar and ran to investigate. Shortly Raul de Souza, Rute's uncle, came upon the scene. He, too, had heard the roar where he was working about 300 feet from the house. All three stood in amazement as they watched the water "boil up" in the spot where the disc had fallen. The water continued to surge up, followed by an eruption of muddy water and then mud. On the opposite shore of the river fishermen including Japanese Tetsuo Ioshigawa had witnessed the event and it was from Ioshigawa that investigators and reporters obtained sufficient description that led to the estimation of size of the object—about 25 feet in diameter. All described the disc as like polished aluminum and shaped like a "wash basin." The object appeared to be at about 20 feet altitude when it hit the tree. It was in level flight until that time and after it struck it began its gyrations which led to the conclusion of the witnesses that it was experiencing trouble of some sort.

During the ensuing weeks, divers of various sorts began to attempt a salvage operation. At first, divers using only face masks tried but failed, to be followed by Scuba divers and eventually a professional deep sea diver with full diving suit and air compressor came to attempt to locate the disc. At last report, nothing had been found and all the divers complained of the hampering effect of the mud at the bottom of the river. The Peropava is 12 feet deep at the point where the disc sank and has a muddy bottom comprised of about 15 feet of mud and clay. If the disc sank through the water and in turn the mud, as the boiling up of water and then mud seems to indicate, it may have proceeded through the muddy river bed to solid rock underneath.

In order to fully assess the meaning of this incident which is pretty well established as having occurred, we must take into consideration all of the factors. Although mine detectors were used and the Brazilian equivalent of the Civil Engineers attempted finding and salvaging the disc, reports do not indicate any success of any kind, not even the location of the disc. We must consider the possibility that the disc, after settling to the bottom, either proceeded through locomotion of some sort away from its initial resting place and is not now in the original spot. If so, it could be anywhere in that river. Also, the size indicates that it may have been manned and if so perhaps repairs could be effected under water and escape from the river and the mud accomplished during the night hours, at some spot more isolated than where it originally sank.[148]

I have talked to a great many people about this business, and the outcome has proved to be a very fine exercise in plain, simple logic. At first sight, the suggestion that UAOs have a preference for water appears to everybody, and even to the buffs, to be fallacious. But then, when the fact is demonstrated that this *is* the case, their second reaction is just the contrary; namely, that it is obvious! But then, as several have pointed out to me, we must not overlook another factor. This is the equally obvious one that I mentioned at the outset; to wit, that (a) aerial and aquatic UAOs may be the same things, and (b) any truly extraterrestrial things would naturally land on water and take up residence on the bottoms of bodies of water. Looked at this way, one may perceive that, since human beings don't live *on* the seas and oceans, and since they inhabit only about 2 percent of the land surface of this earth, the chances of anybody seeing a UAO going into or coming out of water are reduced almost to zero. Further, when we consider the areas upon which human beings do dwell, it hardly needs to be said that these are necessarily the most fertile and therefore indubitably around or near water. Thus, there should automatically be a higher rate of reports of goings-into and comings-out-of fresh waters. Then there is another thing.

Let us take rivers first. If you were a UAO pilot scheduled to get back to home base at the bottom of some marineland by a certain time and you ran into a radar beam, or had some mechanical trouble or any other annoyance, what would you do? If I were he, I would duck into the nearest pond or lake or river, and more particularly a river down which I could get to the sea. And don't overlook the fact that UAOs could just as well be filled with a liquid as with a gas. If we lived in water we would fill our space capsules with that substance. So, in the event of mechanical or other failure the pilot would dart into the nearest water, so he could open his hatch, catch his "breath," and get started on repairs or call for help. And a not inconsiderable percentage of those reported to have gone into fresh waters gave every appearance of being in distress.

This is particularly apparent when we come to the North American Great Lakes. In fact, one might almost be permitted to suggest that they have a sort of service station on the bottom of Lake Erie—or rather, *below* its bottom. If we may assume that there is what can only be called for convenience' sake a subaqueous civilization, it would most logically be at the bottom of the oceans; but only creatures of very low intelligence would build domes *on the surface* thereof. It is only creatures of our still rather limited intelligence who would ever even consider building things like domed-in cities and suchlike on the surface of the moon. Ninety-nine percent of all animal life that lives on the land of this planet actually lives *under* the surface. Anything using the moon as a way-station or what-have-you, and having the intelligence to get to that dreary hunk of rock, would naturally dig down. We would suggest that, on this score, you read a book entitled *The Moon Is a Harsh Mistress*, by Robert A. Heinlein.[149] Then consider this.

In their book on that most remarkable genius Nikola Tesla, Inez Hunt and Winetta Draper state:

> Tesla philosophized concerning man's inadequate conception of existence, declaring that even a crystal was a form of life. He carried the idea to dizzier heights when he said that there might be intelligent beings on other planets which, because of varying conditions, could subsist in a form unknown to us.

Then, in a statement wholly unintelligible in 1900, but not so easily scorned sixty years later, he declared: "We cannot even with positive assurance assert that some of them might not be present here, in this our world, in the very midst of us, for their constitution and life manifestations may be such that we are unable to perceive them." [150]

Tesla was quoted as saying that in the solar system there seemed to be only two planets capable of sustaining life such as ours, but that there could well be other forms of life on them, that perhaps there might be a form of existence which did not require nourishment such as we know it.

"Organic life might undergo . . . modifications, leading to forms which, according to our present ideas of life, are impossible. Changes could be gradual . . . So I think it is quite possible that in a frozen planet, such as our moon is supposed to be, *intelligent beings may still dwell in its interior, if not on its surface.*" [151]

In the first quote above, Tesla is of course speaking of what we have come to call "The Invisibles" or, facetiously, "OINTs," meaning "Other Intelligencies"—than ours, that is. There is ever-mounting evidence that at least some of the occupants of UAOs may be thus described, and there is now a very distinct suspicion that some of these may be able to "flash on and off," as it were. We will come to consider this matter in more detail later on, but the mere possibility must be borne in mind. Until our discovery of infrared and ultraviolet photography or scanning, such entities need not have bothered about the possibility of detection by us. But when organized technological investigations started to turn up some evidence, the OINTs would be confronted with two major alternatives; namely, either to let themselves be discovered and identified, or to change their rules. Such things as "visions" or encounters with individuals of the nature that have been called "contactees" did not bother them because, despite the enormous prestige of organized religion, nobody except the faithful ever really believed that they actually occurred—outside the human mind.

Almost the same may be said of these OINTs' attitude to hardware and other more material matters. Thus, it is perfectly legitimate to assume that until our modern technological age, UAOs need not have bothered to do more than sink into water, shallow or deep, and then have just gone about their business; but when we, little men, started probing both the shallows and the depths, the whole picture changed. It would seem that whatever entities have been using the bottoms of our oceans, seas, lakes, and, in emergencies, rivers, do not wish their presence to be known to us, but until very recently did not have to bother with us. However, now that we have TV cameras that we can tow back and forth to photograph the ocean bottom—as we did in the great search for the *Scorpion*—we might well be considered pests, if not potential menaces. Our getting under water, as in submarines, would not really disturb such creatures, because there is an awful lot of water; we have very few submarines, even when you add all those of all nations together; and we can't get down very far; while the tiny probes we have made to really great depths are far less than needle-points in the immensity of their environment.

There remains but one comment to make on freshwater UAOs. This is that, if you read all the endless reports upon the subject, you will find that very few indeed are of large objects. "Bearing in mind that these things don't exist," in the classic words of Gordon Creighton, but assuming for the moment that all these reports do indicate some reality, one is forced first to speculate and then to make some assumptions. Why this discrepancy in the dimensions of freshwater and marine UAOs?

Crippled or not, large constructions would obviously do everything possible to avoid splashing down in a small body of water. Only in very large lakes—*vide* Lake Erie—might they adopt a somewhat nonchalant attitude and take a calculated risk; and it is just into these that the few bigger ones are stated to have gone. Then, the UFO buffs have for years been suggesting that the OINTs employ all manner of robotic and distantly controlled probing devices of sizes ranging down to that of a baseball (ball lightning?). Such would obviously be much more useful over land surfaces and especially in areas of human occupation and residence. Our robotic space probes have often gone balmy due to extraneous influences that we did not expect and have seldom detected—*vide* Mariner 7 when making its first pass over a Mars pole. They also develop internal and intrinsic mechanical or other faults from time to time. Why not also such devices constructed by even the most superior OINTs? They may well have monitored all our little gadgets and computed their potentials, but they just might have missed some of the potentials of other, nontechnical animals. And many animals have the most unnerving projection systems as well as reception ones.

All in all, it would seem that the majority of freshwater UAOs are small; second, they would seem to be remote-controlled; and third, those that are observed to go into waters are in trouble. We will come back to this also at a later date.

6 · A SIXTH MYSTERY

Subaquaplanes

Put pointedly, the implications of all this are twofold; first, that there is something going on under water on this planet; and, second, that this engages intelligently controlled devices that can come out of and go into water and also proceed on out of our atmosphere into what we call space. Both concepts will naturally at first sound quite preposterous, but unless all the reports of such are some form of mass hallucination or a gigantic "plot" that has been going on for some three thousand years, we have either to accept these two premises or come up with a better alternative—better, that is, from the point of view of traditional thinking and acceptance. Despite all the wringing and twisting of hands by all and sundry orthodoxies, I have yet to hear of any such suggestion out of them that makes a ha'pennyworth of sense. Moreover, there are other items seemingly connected with this matter that also cry out for lucid explanation. I shall now tackle one of these.

In 1954 the government of Colombia, South America, sent a representative collection of their priceless state gold treasure on a tour of the United States. This consisted of a hundred specimens of ancient gold-work selected from the fabulous collection that that country has housed in the Banco de la República in Bogotá. This selection was placed on exhibit in twelve of our leading museums, including the Metropolitan in New York. The collection was in the charge of a Sr. Sanchez, representing his government. Along with it, there was presented for sale to the public a magnificent catalog of those objects displayed, four hundred pages in length and with no less than ninety-nine plates not just in full color but artistically indicating the metallic surfaces of these exquisite gold pieces.[152] I now turn to what should probably be called the purely human interest aspects of this business. At first this might well appear to have nothing whatsoever to do with the matter at hand, but I would ask you to bear with me, for this is the strange way in which real discoveries come to light.

Just about the time I started writing this book a very old and respected friend of mine, Emanuel ("Mannie") Staub of Philadelphia sold his business and was clearing out his workshop. Mannie is one of this country's leading jewelers, designers, and technicians in that field and has for twenty years been one of a very few experts who have been entrusted with making copies of the priceless collections of our leading museums. The beautiful gold displays that you see in many museums are his work— gold-plated; an insurance against theft of the originals, which are kept locked up in vaults. Mannie has never thrown away a mold, and in clearing out his shop, he was somewhat jolted to find a certain item. He cast a copy and sent it to me, with a note on its origin. (This little object is shown in the frontispiece of this book.) How all this came about was as follows:

When this collection was on exhibit in New York a most remarkable man, by the name of Al Jahle, obtained permission from the Sr. Sanchez who was in charge of the exhibit to make casts of six of the items, using a new plastic developed for dental surgery that could not possibly harm the specimens. Mr.

Jahle, I should add, was the senior technician of the Cardiology Department of Hahnemann Hospital in Philadelphia and the inventor of the electric heart-stimulator. He sent his molds to Mannie Staub and asked for casts. This little thing turned up among them. So much for the background, which is rather essential, before one attempts to go into an analysis of this thing, because such is going to lead us into the wildest realms of speculation.

First question is, of course, what is it? Having been trained as a biologist primarily, I perhaps rather naturally at first jumped to the conclusion that it was some kind of animal, such as a skate or ray or other batfish. But then I put it under a high-power lens and began to have the gravest doubts—and more especially when I looked at it in profile and spotted what is for all the world the Aramaic or early Hebrew letter "beth" or "B" on the tail fin. The whole thing became even more disturbing when I tossed a copy of the little model at an old friend who happens to have been a longtime aviation editor. He fiddled with it for a couple of moments and then said: "Who's trying to make a pendant out of one of these newfangled vertical-take-off planes?" Real trouble is that, whoever did so try and made this little thing, lived at least one thousand years ago—and, so help me, in South America!

There are several types of animals that fly in the air—birds, bats, insects; and several gliders like flying opossums and squirrels, and some little lizards in Indonesia, plus a snake! There are others that come out of the water and literally fly in the air—the true flying fishes and the flying gurnards and several shellfish called squids. Then there are others that sort of "fly" in water. These are the skates and rays and other selachians, a group of animals which are not really fish but are closely related to them, and which includes the sharks. These skates and rays or batfish literally "fly along" under water, in a horizontal position, and by undulatory movements of the edges of their delta-type "wings." These fish have upright fins on their tails but invariably have long tapering "tails" behind these. Many do have fleshy things behind these "wings" which are called claspers and which they use during mating. What is more, several have prominent eye-like markings on the "wings" which are probably to distract attackers from their real eyes which look out sidewise and are under ridges on the tops of their heads.

Rather naturally, as I said above, I first thought that this was an ancient artist's conception of such an animal, but then we photographed the little model and blew it up many times and traced its outline, and all kinds of things immediately came to light. Seen from above, the gold model proved to have practically no fishlike attributes at all but, rather, to show some most explicitly mechanical ones. Protracting the curvatures of the hind edges of the wings, and what appear to be structures which are now called "elerons" (being a combination of ailerons and elevators), one finds that the latter have a slight forward curve. Allowing for some artistic license, these being attached to the fuselage rather than to the wings, would indeed seem to be elevators (not ailerons) on such a device as an airplane, rather than the backwardly directed claspers of a fish. Then, if the centers of the two squirls on the wings, or planes, are meant to indicate the eye-spots on a ray, what is one to make of the two very prominent little globules to right and left of the straight bar across the back of the "head"? And this more especially if the two little twirls out near the front end of the head are meant to be the real eyes of such a fish?

This is all odd enough, but when we come to view this object in profile or sidewise, we get some much more profound shocks. First off, why should anybody, skilled artisan or uneducated idiot, want to make a model, in pure gold, of a fish (or moth or anything else) with its head three-quarters cut off? Second, why make the nose, bonnet, or front end precisely rectangular like an old-fashioned Rolls-Royce, and then put louvers on the top of it on both sides? Then, why tilt the "windshield" (or the bit of flesh at the back of the head after chopping it almost through) forward, and put a couple of eyes (headlights?) out at either side, when a fish's eyes are far forward and near the center line? Then, what about the "seat" in the cockpit? What's this supposed to be—fishwise? And then there's the "scoop" under and a bit forward of the cockpit; and it *is* a scoop, not just a median ridge to punch a hole through in order to string the thing on a necklace.

So we move back to the fins or "wings." They are absolutely horizontal, but when viewed head-on from in front, their tips curve slightly downward. Come then the little "elevators." They stick straight out on the same horizontal level as the wings but are attached to the body, and are square-ended and of a definite geometric shape—*not* curved fins. Next, the four "somethings" above them on the top of the rear end of the fuselage. What are these? But—worst of all is the tail.

Here we come to something that really does need explanation. Fishes have tails of all sorts of form, and all are upright (except for the flatfish, that are really lying on their sides). However, none of them has only an upward-going flange of this form. Planes do! What is more, this tail fin has the exact shape of that on many modern planes; and this one also has this strange marking on it. (We will see what the noted plane designer, of the Bell Helicopter among others, Mr. Arthur Young, has to say on this score in a moment.) In fact, taken all in all, this bloody thing does not look like any kind of known animal but it does look astonishingly like some kind of small airplane. We've searched the world of fishes for anything that looks like it—even with its head half cut off—and we've tried the entire insect world too but, as any entomologist can tell you, it has nothing to offer either.

We submitted these pictures and a cast in brass of the first object to a couple of aerodynamics people, one of them no less than Arthur Young, as mentioned above. His reply read as follows:

> Have received the small "flying" object, and your request for an opinion. This small solid gold object certainly suggests an airplane, especially in the vertical tail surface which is not

present in birds and insects. But, the wings are in the wrong place—[they] should be further forward so that its ¼-chord coincided with the center of gravity—for anything other than a tail-engine jet. Also, the nose is very unairplane-ish. So, I have to confess while it *suggests* an airplane, it does not resemble one. Perhaps it is an artist's "impression." Anyhow it is quite fascinating. Whatever it is, the front end is inexplicable and, of course, in this area no one is an expert.

We most certainly are not "expert" in this field either, but what we still want to know is why some artisan a thousand years ago went to the trouble of making this thing in the first place, and why he made it just the way he did. The "nose" is definitely a sort of rectangular box with (as seen from the side) another slightly raised box on it, with three louvers on either side. Then again, if all this front end was but a sort of glove compartment and the heavy machinery was abaft of what appears to be the cockpit, the thing *would* have been perfectly balanced—fore-and-aft, that is, if held between its two wing tips. The thing *is* manifestly an "artist's conception," but what did that artist know of the machinery of anything so bizarre? What kind of power plant, if any, did it have? Or was it a glider? And here comes another engineer with another suggestion.

I presented this thing to him simply as a model of what the catalog of this collection calls a "Figura Zoomorfa," or animal-like figurine. His first reaction too was that it was no such thing, but some kind of airplane. But then he started to analyze it, and came up with just the same objections as did Arthur Young. However, he then suggested that it looked more like a freight-carrying glider to be launched from a flume of water at altitude and able to brake on water with its scoop. This may be, but now we have three completely independent opinions by qualified engineers, all stating initially that it "looks like an airplane" rather than an animal, but then suggesting, severally, that it is a vertical-lift plane, a glider, and that it must have had a back-end power unit.

Actually, none of this really got us very far, apart from the obvious multiple conclusion that this lovely little artifact seemed most likely to represent some form of airplane rather than a formalized artist's conception of any animal. The stickler was, and of course is, that it is confidently dated as having been manufactured between 500 and 800 A.D., or at least over one thousand years ago; and in northern Colombia at that. What were airplanes doing buzzing about South American skies about the time of the final breakup of the Roman Empire in Europe? But then we proceeded to the next stage of inquiry.

We assumed that this thing *was* a representation of an airplane. What then? So, I next tossed a copy of the thing to still another engineer, who was one of the first pilots trained to fly a rocket plane in Germany. I did not even hint what the trinket was or where it came from or anything else about its background. In fact, I suggested that he have the protuberance underneath drilled, so that his eldest daughter could put it on her pendant necklace. My friend, Jack A. Ullrich, naturally asked me immediately what it was. I told him to figure it out for himself; and like the other aerodynamics boys, he retired into a shell—in this case another room—with a tape recorder, and came up with the following:

> I was asked to give my thoughts and opinions on this little gold "pendant" which Ivan gave me. He did not tell me where it came from or what it was. He simply asked me: "What do you think this is?"
>
> The first impression I got from this thing, not knowing its origin or anything else about it, was that it represented some form of aircraft; and a high-performance one at that. With its delta-wings it looked like an F-102 Fighter.
>
> Since first impressions are often the best, let me start off by assuming that it *is* an aircraft, and then let me try to analyze its external features, and then make some tentative suggestions as to what might be hidden in its interior as a propulsion unit.
>
> Starting at the nose, we find, first, two decorative "whirls" on the top and then two things that look like eyeballs arranged

laterally at the back end of said "nose." Such items are not normally found on aircraft as we know them. They could be due to what is called "artistic license," but the funny thing is that, if such things were put on modern airplanes, said planes would still fly. Many modern aircraft have more junk than that hanging on their outsides, and they still manage to "stagger" into the air. Take a look at some of the fighter-bombers flying today in Viet Nam. They are literally "hung up" with stuff hanging on their outsides.

Reverting to the model, the cockpit is broad and, depending on the over-all size of the craft, which of course we cannot estimate, could accommodate one, two, or more persons. Again, I refer you to the F-102, which is about the size of a C-47, and you may then see what I am talking about. The body could have been streamlined with a bubble over the cockpit. In fact, since the delta-wing configuration implies high performance—by which I mean speed—it would be a necessity. Otherwise, the occupants would not do so well with the resultant air turbulence.

The body of this "plane" is nicely tapered and has enough volume to allow installation of a power plant, which should be, in this type of thing, a turbojet engine. It would not make sense to put a reciprocating engine, or anything like that, into a fuselage such as this. (Propellers do not give the performance required to match a delta-wing construction, though they can be made to perform with such a structure up to several hundred miles per hour. But we are talking here of much greater speeds.) But this object spells out but one thing to me—namely, *jet*. But I wish to analyze this further. If it be a jet, where the exhaust should be—i.e., near or under the tail —detail is lacking in this little image. But what if there was *no* exhaust? Maybe it could have had a propulsion system other than that which we call a jet; but I will not speculate on that.

The only difference I see between this and today's delta-wing jets is that ours all have a different type of fuselage, which was developed more or less by accident and which is called the "coke-bottle fuselage." This specific shape has been created in order to make it possible for the plane to pass through the atmosphere at very high velocities and, at the same time, to decrease buffeting.

Considering next the underside of the object, an air-intake for an engine may be indicated on the belly-side, under the cockpit. Then again, this may be nothing more than a protrusion to allow it to be drilled and a chain put through it so that it could be worn as a pendant.

As I mentioned at the start, this thing appears to represent a high-performance type aircraft, and for those of you not acquainted with these matters and specifically not with the F-102, I would ask you to look at the widely circulated designs of the proposed SS-T of Boeing.

Aircraft with this type of wing need great power for take-off and they rise at a remarkably steep angle in order to get lift. They then fly very fast and land at high speeds. What I mean is, no slow cruising or gliding for these. This is why cargo transporters cannot be constructed on this type of configuration, and the only way the SS-T can make it is with brute power.

This is why we have no delta-wing gliders, since the glide-angle ratio would be prohibitive—somewhere on the order of 5:1, which means that for every five yards forward motion, the plane sinks one yard. The most efficient glider configurations are seen among birds, which have very high aspect-ratio wings; by this I mean wing-span versus width of wing. Powered aircraft do not have high-aspect ratios—with the notable exception of the U-2 of Gary Powers fame.

Unpowered gliders—i.e., sail planes—do have a very high ratio, and the best performance was exhibited by a flying wing design of the brothers Horten in Germany during the 1940s. Their glide ratio was 1:45, greater than an albatross, and which I do not think has been exceeded till now. This is diametrically opposed to the performance of delta wings. There isn't a rubber band made that could launch this thing in flight.

Looking at this model from in front, I note something particularly. Most planes have their wings slightly dihedral—in other words, when you look at it from the front, the wing-tips point slightly upwards. This helps to control the plane so it will be flying properly in relation to the horizon; with the exception of the high-performance aircraft, whose wings point downward; in other words, the wing-tips droop a little bit. (I'm not referring to the B-52 type of wing, which is extremely flexible, but to fighter wings, such as you see on the F-84, and the F-105 fighter bomber made by Republic Aviation.)

Now to get to the rudder. The rudder is conventional, but where body and rudder meet there are a few strange humps, which are mystifying, and I shall allow myself no opinion on them. We have also *elevator* surfaces at the tail, which modern delta fighters do not have at the rear end of the fuselage, as the model has; but, if and when they do have these surfaces, they are on the tip of the rudder. It is shaped like a "T" when you look at it from the front. Let me explain that modern Deltas can do without these surfaces entirely, since they now have what are called "elerons," a contraction of the words aileron and elevators. And these elerons are located at the wing's trailing edge and perform the function of both aileron and elevator. Then again, these two things sticking out at the hind end of this little model here may not be elevators, but possibly extended speed brakes, though their surfaces are parallel to the wing surfaces, which they should not be, for this way they will not grab the air and act as brakes. Perhaps it would have been difficult to do it some other way. I have no way of judging this. If they were eleron surfaces I think they should have been swept, as is the wing, since it would have made no sense to sweep the one and not the other.

Next came still another engineer, Adolph Heuer, onetime of the U.S. Air Force Quartermaster Corps, and designer and builder of probably the most astonishing automobile ever constructed, which performs in a manner that scares the pants off the licensing authorities! Similarly presented with a copy of this model, and similarly without comment, he too went into temporary limbo, and came up with an analysis; but this time with a new wrinkle.

Adolph knows his engineering and mechanics, and he also had long experience in the very factor of most significance in the analysis of this object—to wit, its "loading"—having spent years doing just that to all types of military aircraft. Put the freight in the wrong place in a plane and you court disaster; and the quartermaster had better know the specs of each individual plane before he starts giving instructions for loading. Adolph Heuer alone had the advantage of viewing not only the little model itself but also blowups of it made from photographs; and for this reason perhaps, he noted certain points that others had missed. Most significant of these was the fact that the wings, when viewed from dead ahead, were indeed perfectly horizontal but their tips distinctly—and apparently deliberately—curved *down* a little from the vertical plane. This confirms J. A. Ullrich's observation as being exactly the same as the construction needed and essential for super-powered, abrupt-rise aircraft, on which the tips have to "droop" slightly.

The significance of this clear difference is that, while such a craft with tremendous boost could indeed climb into the air and maintain itself there, it could also plunge into water and maintain equilibrium therein. As a result, Adolph Heuer, also before knowing even the origin of this little trinket, stated that he considered it to be an artist's conception of a delta-wing, super-powered plane but one that could plunge into water and proceed thereunder. This suggestion was then put to still other aeronautical engineers, and one and all concurred, pointing to the fact that we already have a plane that can do just this—not merely on the drawing board, but in fact, as reported in *Popular Mechanics*.[153] It is also alleged that a prototype of such a plane, named the "Flying Fish," was built by the Douglas complex for, and on the specs of, the O.N.R., but that the first one, flown in 1966 off the coast of southern California out of San Diego, disintegrated and the pilot was killed. We have been unable to confirm this. However, our informant—who is not given to making things up—states that some essential adjustments were made, and we understand exactly in accord with the suggestions made above, as to the dip of the wing-tips, and the next model performed as required.

The going-into and popping-out-of water by machines is actually not just logical but obvious. And well might this experimental machine be named the "Flying Fish." These splendid animals have been doing just this for countless millennia; and I would advise any who are interested in aerodynamics to take a look at these animals. What we call their "streamlining" is pluperfect; they have true wings which they *do* flap—whatever any marine biologist may say to the contrary—and they have "elerons" attached to the after-end of their bodies. They also have upright tails with the upper tine most suggestively like that of the "fin" on the little gold trinket. These creatures, of which there are literally billions all over the world, have for millennia been darting out of the surface of the sea, gliding and then propelling themselves over it in the air, and then plunging back into it. If these relatives of the admirable herring can do this, why not us?

But then comes another thing. I mentioned in an earlier chapter that I had the honor of being granted considerable time by the top notch scientists and technologists in our underwater research and development. The one who initially granted me ten minutes of his most valuable time, ended up by giving me an hour-and-a-half exposition of just what is going on. During this briefing he told me that there is a private citizen, a resident of Hawaii, who has the money to build and put into working effect an item that is really quite extraordinary. As I understand this, the gentleman concerned has completed his theoretical procedures and has already built a prototype at his own expense. Apparently he has offered to build a working unit, again at his own expense, and to demonstrate its abilities, with no holds barred or obligations, provided the Navy would supervise the entire procedure. What this gentleman offered to do—and it will probably have been done by the time this book appears—was simply to travel from the Hawaiian Islands to San Diego, a matter of 2,400 miles, with his device, in four "skips" under water.

His machine is "powered" only with liquid freon gas under pressure and in liquid form. This is dense, or "heavy" if you want, and with the weight of the rest of the device causes it to plunge down into the depths at very considerable speed. Then, some of the freon is released from its pressure and of course vaporizes or turns to a gas, and becomes enormously buoyant. When released it therefore boosts the device upward at really terrific speed, because even an air-filled object at great depth rises to the surface almost like a rocket.[154] Back at the surface, gravity takes over and the machine arcs over and starts to descend just as any other solid object does in water. The process is then repeated. Result: what used to be called hops, skips, and jumps, but with no energy expended except the natural forces of gravity and counter-gravity (i.e., buoyancy). I know nothing of the mechanism itself, but it would appear that those manning this device will have to be enclosed in a steel pressurized sphere in the body of the device in order to avoid the resulting compression-decompression dangers, of such kinds as are called by divers "the bends," which are due to the bubbling of the nitrogen in the blood. Further, said machine would, it would seem, have to have distance-measuring devices to detect the ocean floor on the one hand, and the water's surface on the other, in order to obviate banging into the solid bottom or roaring out into the atmosphere above. And this latter is the very point I wish to make here. Any such machine that does operate efficiently on such principles *could* dart out of the water and, if properly constructed, dive back into it. This "experiment" stems from underwater research; but, as I have explained above, the Office of Naval Research has already developed just such a unit, but working downward, as it were, from aerial principles.

Thus we have underwater devices that can skip and jump *under water;* others that can skip into and out of water; an ancient model of a device that displays all the little oddities and necessities for doing both (i.e., this little delta-wing pendant from the Colombian gold collection); and finally we have animals that in point of fact "fly" underwater—the rays and skates. This raises a number of most interesting questions.

First, going into and coming out of water by sealed devices is not only logical but demonstrably possible and in fact has been demonstrated. Second, living under water has now also been shown to be perfectly feasible even for gas (air) breathing entities, let alone liquid (water) breathers. Third, there is mounting evidence that there are now and have for a very long time been just such underwater dwellers. Fourth, if properly sealed and insulated devices can penetrate to depths of 35,000 feet in water on this planet (as our bathyscaphe *Trieste* did [155]), they could most certainly operate throughout the whole range of densities of our atmosphere, and also, just like our space capsules, proceed on into what we call "space" and continue to function efficiently therein too. This is all perfectly logical and definitive, but the aspect of it upon which not only the average person but even the specialist gags is the historical factor, meaning the chronology of all this. Just because we have only very recently wakened up to the fact that all this is possible, we seem to have developed the notion that "nobody" else could have come up with it previously. This is typical of our inborn egocentricity and what I can only call egomania. Our whole tradition—which ruled our thinking until only a few decades ago—asserted that we were God's ultimate effort; that we were unique; and that we alone were endowed with cogent abilities. The very idea of sharing the universe with other intelligent types, and especially with *more* intelligent ones was, and still is, almost universally abhorrent to us. That we might have been sharing our own planet with any such types constitutes such a complete horror that it just has to be dubbed phoney.

Before leaving this subject, for the time at least, I would again draw your attention to that group of animals which is closely related to the fishes, and which includes the skates, rays, sharks, and others that display the delta-wing outline of the little gold artifact. These creatures actually do "fly" under water, though their method of propulsion is not that of a jet or any other form of internal combustion engine, nor even a gas-release device. As birds do in air, they progress by complicated undulatory motions of their "wings." However, there are other marine animals that *do* propel themselves by the jet method; and some of these dart out of the water and then dart back down into it. I speak of certain squids, which are related to octopuses and are, loosely speaking, shellfish. A very large number of squids customarily come rushing out of the ocean and, opening their delta fins—they travel backward—sail for incredible distances above the waves and then javelin back into the water. They do this, like all of their ilk, which are known as cephalopods or the "head-footed ones," by filling their body sacs with water, then closing a sort of collar and violently ejecting a stream of this water out of a nozzle under their heads. So powerful are the muscles that compress the body cavity and so perfectly designed is this nozzle that these animals become the fastest things that move in water.

So here we have mechanical devices obviously modeled on the very efficient working principles of certain animals, and said animals having developed such principles, presumably by trial and error, over the millennia. And, considering the efficiency of the animals, both biologically speaking and from an engineering point of view, no wonder intelligent entities should copy their proven designs. That it has taken two million years for us landlubbers to get around to so copying is just a matter of time, or rather *relative* time. Apparently some such thinking entities got around to it at least a thousand years ago—*vide* the little gold delta-wing. But were these some of us humans, or were they OINTs? This we will discuss in greater detail later.

7 · A SEVENTH MYSTERY

Submarine "Lightwheels"

The time has now come for us to turn from the world of gadgetry to that which I suppose is best called Nature. Here too we are dealing simply with recorded facts; but here again said facts form a rather wide spectrum. They range from a "weirdie" that may, as I shall now endeavor to show, be subject to a fairly simple explanation, to much more incredible findings on the part of the oceanologists and geomorphologists during the past two decades. Then there comes another grotesquerie which, while being a discovery of a strictly orthodox scientific nature, has just about everybody baffled. Whoever said that fact is stranger than fiction said a mouthful indeed. One has great respect for the science-fictioneers because of their imagination, the one quality or factor that really keeps the intellectual world going, but I, frankly, do not think that even the best of them has ever come up with anything quite as fantastic as the items that we are now going to plunge into. What is now known of suboceanic terragraphy (as per three maps published by the National

Geographic Society), which we shall discuss in a later chapter, is so astonishing, even to a lot of oceanologists, that its significance has not yet really penetrated our thinking.

In the meantime, there is a most troublesome matter that has had some people in a mild uproar for quite a long time now and that has been adopted by the UFO buffs. Like so many other oddities and enigmas, it has, unfortunately, often been very badly reported, and then misquoted, and thus grossly garbled. As I will explain, I had thought this enigma solved, but now, once again, I am not so sure, and more especially in view of the matters discussed in the previous chapters and some further information that has come to hand since Dr. Wallace Minto and I tackled this issue back in 1964. Said issue then went as follows:

For just a hundred years now mariners—commanders, captains, masters of ships or their senior officers—have been reporting immense displays of what they rather naturally call "lights" under the surface of certain seas.

I have about a hundred cases in my files; I know of other sources of reports I do not yet have, and I am quite sure there are dozens if not hundreds more tucked away in nautical journals, both naval and mercantile, and in the records of every seagoing nation. I have been told they are mentioned in ancient Indian literature. And well these people might have recorded this strange business, for it is apparently centered on the Indian Ocean.

Of all the cases I have so far unearthed only one (originally given by the indefatigable Charles Fort (*might* be from outside this general area. This is from a statement made by a Mr. E. L. Moss in the British scientific periodical *Nature*, in April 1875, as follows: "When upon H.M.S. *Bulldog* a few miles north of Vera Cruz [he] had seen a series of swift lines of light" on the sea.[156] I have been unable to trace the cruises of said H.M.S. *Bulldog* during that year, but I will keep trying, because this might be a rather vital item. There was a Punta de la Vera Cruz on the west coast of Luzon in the Philippines, but it seems to have been dropped from the maps before 1875, and one supposes Mr. Moss meant the well-known port on the Gulf of Mexico.

All other cases, however, come from the periphery of the Indian Ocean, from the Persian Gulf to the South China Sea, with one somewhat doubtful record from the upper reaches of the Gulf of Aden and one ambiguous report from "the China Sea" [157] without specifying *which* China sea—the one north of Taiwan or the one south of that island. If we assume that it refers to the South China Sea, then all the reports fall between the equator and approximately 25° N. latitude. (Note that Vera Cruz, Mexico, is at 20° N., between 50° and 120° W. longitude.)

The greatest number of these "wheels of light" have been observed (1) in the Persian Gulf and notably the narrows of the Strait of Hormuz; (2) off the coast of Malabar in the channel between that coast and the Laccadive Islands; (3) in the Palk Strait, north of Ceylon; (4) in the Strait of Malacca between the Malay Peninsula and Sumatra; (5) in the Gulf of Siam; and (6) in the South China Sea. The reports from the latter are mostly without precise fixes, but one from the Gulf of Siam, dated May 30, 1962, in *Notice to Mariners* of the U.S. Hydrographic Office is most precise. Perhaps it is significant to note that although it is in a sea, rather than an ocean, it is not in a strait of any kind. One of the most remarkable aspects of all these reports is that there are none that I know of from the open *ocean* and almost all are from landside straits.

These observations have been made during every month of the year, but no less than 70 percent have occurred during March, April, May, and June, and 60 percent during the last of these three months. This, at first, looks like a natural seasonal phenomenon, but the seasons in the tropics are not defined (by our calendar) latitudinally, but rather longitudinally. Mostly, it is a matter of wet as opposed to dry periods. If, on the other hand, the phenomenon is life-induced or animated, it might be possible to correlate this April-to-June emphasis with some seasonal occurrence in tropical marine animal or plant life.

Just for the record, let us examine two typical sightings; the first, the *Notice to Mariners* mentioned above:

Luminescence, Gulf of Siam

Second Officer C. J. Boyes and Midshipman M. Hibbert of the British S.S. *Telemachus,* Capt. J. K. Edmonds, Master, reported the following:

At 1906 G.M.T. May 30, 1962, in lat. 7° 22′ N., long. 103° 18′ E., course 166°, speed 16.5 knots, dim rays of light were observed. These rays appeared to be traveling across or under the water and came from a 210° direction and extended in a 120°–300° direction. They passed the ship at a rate of 3 per second. At 1910 G.M.T. these rays changed from parallel lines to curved lines which rotated around a center, which apparently was on the horizon, in a clockwise direction. The center was bearing 210°. At 1913 G.M.T., the rays became confused and at 1916 G.M.T. another group of rays, this time on the port bow, appeared. These rays were curved but rotated in a counter-clockwise direction about a center which appeared to be bearing 120°. At 1921 G.M.T. the lines became less well defined and slower in movement and passed the ship at a rate of 2 per second. At 1926 G.M.T. the rays disappeared altogether. The depth finder was turned on but showed the charted depth with no variations.

Wind N by W force 1, no swell, rippled sea, barometer 29.76 inches, temperatures: dry 84° F., wet 79° F., sea 87° F.[158]

By way of contrast, and to bring out what is probably the most important fact of all, I wish to reproduce parts of an article that appeared in the *United States Naval Institute Proceedings* from the pen of Comdr. J. R. Bodler (USNR).

My vessel had passed through the Strait of Hormuz, bound for India. The night was bright and clear. The Third Mate called me to the bridge, saying that he had observed something I ought to see.

About four points on the port bow, toward the coast of Iran, there was a luminous band which seemed to pulsate. Its appearance suggested the aurora borealis, but much lower; in fact on or below the horizon. Examination with binoculars showed that the luminous area was definitely below the horizon, in the water, and drawing nearer to the vessel. With the approach of this phenomenon it became apparent that the pulsations seemed to start in the center of the band and flow outwards towards its extremities.

At a distance of about a mile from the ship, it was apparent that the disturbance was roughly circular in shape, about 1000 to 1500 feet in diameter. The pulsations could now be seen to be caused by a revolving motion of the entire pattern about a rather ill-defined center; with streaks of light like the beams of searchlights, radiating outward from the center and revolving (in a counterclockwise direction) like the spokes of a gigantic wheel.

For several minutes the vessel occupied the approximate center of the phenomenon. Slightly curved bands of light crossed the bow, passed rapidly down the port side from bow to stern, and up the starboard side from aft, forward. The luminosity was sufficient to make portions of the vessel's upper works quite visible. The bands of luminance seemed to pass a given point at about half-second intervals. As may well be imagined, the effect was weird and impressive in the extreme; with the vessel seeming to occupy the center of a huge pinwheel whose "spokes" consisted of phosphorescent luminance revolving rapidly about the vessel as a hub.

The central "hub" of the phenomenon drew gradually to starboard, and passed aft; becoming more and more distant on the starboard quarter. While it was still in sight, several miles astern, and appearing, by this time, as a pulsating bank of light, a repetition of the same manifestation appeared fine on the starboard bow. This was slightly smaller in area than the first, and a trifle less brilliant. Its center passed slowly aft on the starboard side, with the pattern of revolving, luminous "spokes" clearly defined.

It was my impression that the actual illumination was caused by the natural phosphorescence in the water, periodically stimulated by regular waves of energy. The shape of the "pinwheel," the well-defined "spokes," the revolutions about the center, and the speed with which each band of light traversed the water, all preclude the possibility of this phenomenon being caused by schools of fish, porpoises, or similar cause.

Approximately half an hour later, a third repetition of this manifestation was observed. The general characteristics, direction of rotation, etc., were the same as the others, but this one was much smaller and less brilliant. Its diameter was not over 800 to 1000 feet, and compared to the other two was unimpressive. It was first observed much closer to the vessel than had been the case with the others. Whether this was due to its lesser brilliance or the fact that it came into being at comparatively close range could not be determined.[159]

The first thing that strikes one is that these so-called "wheels of light" are not wheels at all but might better be called "sunbursts," like the old Japanese flag. However, some reports state that the beams, instead of broadening out as they leave the hub as do all other types of lights except laser beams, appear to continue as parallel bands. Second, these underwater "lights" appear to have a definite point of origin. Third, this point of origin invariably seems to be moving. As in Commander Bodler's report, sometimes this center or "eye" appears to have moved in under a ship and, if his statement does not delude me, to have stayed there, in the case he reports, for some time, presumably traveling *with* the ship.

The first major point to understand is that these displays are not "wheels" of light; for whoever heard of a wheel without a rim? Rather, they are a series of "spokes" that rotate or whirl horizontally around a diffuse center. (Several of the reports state that the center was not brighter than the rays, but that it was "mushy" or almost indefinite. This is significant.) Nobody seems to have noticed the outer ends of these beams— as to whether they dimmed off, petered out, appeared to plunge down, or came to an abrupt stop. Let me go back and try to give a composite picture of just *what* these seasoned mariners have reported for, lo, these hundred years.

Mostly, something like a pulsating light appears on the horizon or between the horizon and the vessel. In due course, this resolves itself into, not a pulsation, but a series of *beams* of intense light sweeping around, apparently just under the surface of the sea. In a few cases the witnesses report approaching a large luminous blob or mass. When they came close to, rays shot out from it and started revolving. In several cases more than one display has appeared at the same time, or in succession. In the latter instance they always seem to diminish in size.

In this matter of size there is apparently enormous variation. Many ships' officers have reported that, observed through binoculars from the bridges of their ships, the hubs were beyond the horizon yet the beams swept their vessels' hulls and in most cases seem to have continued under them and far toward the opposite horizon.

One report, made by Officer Douglas Carnegie, of a display in the Gulf of Oman, in 1906, states, "I noticed that an intervening ship had no effect on the light beams; they started away from the lee side of the ship, just as if they had travelled right through it." [160] Other reports appear to describe quite small displays only a few hundred feet in total diameter. But these reports are, one and all, frustrating because they fail to mention the exact form of the whole or how the rays ended. In one case, observed by the second officer of a Pacific and Orient liner in the Strait of Malacca, the shafts "appeared to be about 300 yards long," which would indicate they terminated abruptly. [161]

There is no agreement on the width of the shafts or beams, or on the distance between them. When given, the width of the shafts seems to be between 20 and 30 feet, and the distance between them about 100 feet. However, the matter is further muddled by instances in which the beam and intermediate unlit areas are said to have been equal and both about 100 feet in width. But if these beams emanate from a fairly small hub, it stands to reason that the distance the beams are from that hub would automatically alter their width if they expand like the beams of a car headlight, while the distance between them also must increase outward. The speed at which the beams are reported to travel along their circular course appears to range all the way from "motionless" to an estimated 200 mph, but most are estimated as traveling about 60 mph. This again would, of course, depend on the distance from the hub.

Some observers—and I am quoting only from ships' officers—seem to have felt that the beams were above the surface of the water, as from a light source protruding from the water. But this does not jibe with the fact that the hub always is described as being rather diffuse, or that beams coming from beyond the horizon do not sweep the *upperworks* of the vessel but always remain at the waterline. Further, they always seem to pass *under* the vessel.

Another curious fact is that the whole manifestation may turn either clockwise or counterclockwise; two may be going in opposite directions at the same time; or one may slow down and become dim and then come back, revolving in the opposite direction. This is immensely puzzling. But most aggravating of all, the beams, per se, cannot be "light" at all! For who ever heard of a *curved* beam of light, especially one making a flattened S? A high percentage of the reports describe the beams as being curved like a catherine-wheel firecracker or turning from straight lines to curves. One might think this to be some sort of optical illusion were it not that in more than one case where the hub moved directly under the ship, or the ship steamed over the hub, this curvature was very pronounced.

The sum total of recorded facts about this weird phenomenon is pitifully little to go upon, and I cannot understand how mariners, dependent for their lives as well as their livelihoods, can so persistently fail to include such further details as the color of the light, whether it appeared to follow the curvature of the earth, etc. So, now let us consider what is popularly called "phosphorescence."

Contrary to popular opinion, there is no such thing per se—at least in the sea. Certain substances actually may glow in total darkness owing to the release of photons caused by the breakdown of materials that has become "charged" through the absorption of sunlight. What we see in the sea is better called luminescence and is produced chemically by living things, including bacteria and all manner of higher animals, but most notably by a tiny single-celled animal known as *Noctiluca miliaris* (i.e., Night lights by the milliards). *Noctiluca milaris* is found all over the world, but mostly in warm water and most abundantly in tropical waters. These tiny creatures light up when stimulated in various ways—as mechanically by a ship's bow waves and wake. Sometimes diffuse patches of luminescence may be seen stationary near the surface of the sea. This is usually due to a school of fish feeding and so stirring up the tiny, normally dark creatures.

But that *Noctiluca* or any other luminescent animals or plants could be the *initial* cause of the whole business of the "wheels" of light is so improbable as to be well-nigh impossible. However, it is possible they may be the cause of the light itself. It is known that fireflies may synchronize their flashings, precisely, over a wide area, and *Noctiluca* can do the same in the face of sundry stimuli. Hence Commander Bodler's observation is very acute.

Let us suppose that some source of energy starts broadcasting some invisible "waves" on the electromagnetic (or other) spectrum which stimulate or activate the light-producing mechanisms of the *Noctiluca*, and let us also suppose that said energy is broadcast in the form of a series of radiating bands whose source of origin is revolving; we would then have a progressive and, to our eyes, instantaneous turning on and off of the *Noctiluca* as the beams swept by them. I cannot overstress the speed of the "make-and-break" mechanism of these and other intermittent light producers. The flash can be of as short duration as a millionth of a second! This suggestion leaves us with two appalling questions. First, how can the beams or shafts curve? Second, what is the initial source of stimulation?

Let's try the first one. Consider a single straight—be it parallel-sided or expanding like a car headlight—shaft of this energy that stimulates the luminescence of the little animals. As any skater who has played "crack-the-whip" knows, the skaters at the end of the circling line, going around the outside, travel much farther and faster than those near the center. If one forms two strings starting at right angles, like four spokes of a wheel, you will end up with four strings curved very much as Commander Bodler describes the "wheel" of light.

Now neither light nor any other electromagnetic wave can bend like this (as Einstein showed, light can be bent only by gravity), so that the beams or shafts actually are straight. The curvature might be due to the minute time lag on the part of the *Noctiluca's* lighting mechanism, which, although incredibly rapid, is not instantaneous nor even anywhere near the speed of light. Moreover, there is a known curve of this order than can be mathematically correlated with such time lags. The triggering energy could be of an order that proceeds to infinity but that loses its potency progressively with distance, or its wavelength could be such that it would activate the luminescence up to a specific distance only. Of course, this "explanation" of the phenomenon is not the only one, nor can it claim an iota of confirmatory evidence. Nonetheless, it is the most logical of the dozens that have come to my attention. Let us, therefore, investigate the possible *source* of such a triggering energy.

First, the energy acts like a radio or radar beacon in that it "sweeps" the horizon. There are three possibilities: it is either inanimate, animate, or mechanical. It has always been suggested that these displays are "electrical" phenomena. This, in a manner of speaking, is reasonable, because electrical flux belongs in the same scheme of things as radio beams; but it begs the question. What *sort* of electrical displays, and how come their unique form? What this suggestion is really driving at is that they are natural manifestations of electromagnetic disturbances, like lightning or northern lights. However, we do not know anything remotely like this elsewhere, in any other medium.

The second idea, that the source is animate, assumes that it is some manifestation of marine biology such as the *Noctiluca*. There is more to this story. Certain kinds of deep-sea worms, of the group to which our lugworm belongs, come to the surface near reefs in the Indonesian and West Pacific area, but on one night only in the year. This they do as part of their breeding cycle, and at this time the back part of their bodies is nothing but a thin-skinned, elongated sac, containing eggs. These eggs are brilliantly luminous. Arrived at the surface, these egg sacs break off the wriggling multitudes, which then sink back into the depths. These eggs are delicious to eat raw. I once sampled them off the Aru Islands in company with the locals. By the end of the orgy all of us and the canoes were completely luminous too. A most eerie sight! My initial notion was that a mass of these worms could form into a vast ball and by the creation of a mass rhythmical motion somehow "broadcast" and then cut off their light, while revolving as a whole. But I am afraid the idea did not and does not wash. These worms do not move rapidly. Besides, they are not known from the Persian Gulf.

There are luminous squids, and they could move through the water fast enough to match some of the reported speeds. But how account for the beams, all equally spaced, emanating horizontally from a diffused mast that is never the brightest part of the display? And why turning?

We are left then with the third, last, and most "unpleasant" notion—i.e., that the source of the triggering energy is mechanical. A mechanical source could account for the regular beams, of regular width, regularly spaced, and revolving at a regular speed; hub not the brightest spot; hubs moving on their own; beams changing from straight to curved (with increased speed), slowing down; beams appearing apparently on the surface, just under it, or deep down and even sinking!

Charles Fort first suggested that these sources of energy were what he called "constructions." [162] He also called OSFs ("Objects Seen Floating" in the sky, now better known to us as "Flying Saucers" or UFOs) constructions. By a nimble juxtaposition of reports and cases Fort tried to point out the significance of all manner of "fiery" objects allegedly seen plunging into and rushing out of the sea. He never quite says that extra-terrestrial devices, mechanisms, craft (either robotic or manned by intelligent entities) constantly come and go, to and from this planet, and use the bottom of the seas (as opposed to the oceans) as their landing fields and "outposts." But he does hint that the "masses of oily substances" reported floating near these light displays could be oil or other waste from such machines. There he stops. But let us continue this speculation—as a mere intellectual exercise, of course!

If the energy that triggers our luminous sea creatures comes from such "constructions," how and why does it occur? Why are they seen only around the periphery of the Indian Ocean (and possibly the Caribbean)?

Any craft that can travel through space should be able to continue on and down into a liquid medium, since said craft must be completely sealed. What better place to land than the bottoms of the seas (not the oceans, where the pressure is great, the silt deep, and the atmosphere far away). But why pick on the fringe of the Indian Ocean only? Possibly they don't. But it is only here, and maybe in the Caribbean, that our local conditions (*Noctiluca* in abundance; clear water of a certain constitution, etc.) cause some of their beamcasts to become visible to us.

Perhaps they are all over; perhaps they prefer water of a certain temperature; perhaps they need the enhanced "spin" of the equatorial belt to help in their braking for landings and thrust for take-off; perhaps they just stumbled on a base in the Indian Ocean, as the Europeans did in Singapore, as a highly suitable center for activity with ready-to-hand raw materials in greater abundance than elsewhere. We could speculate on and on with this wild idea.

I admit to having been shaken by the submarine photograph taken by the Russians of what was described as "the track of some enormous bottom-living creature" in the Indian Ocean a few years ago.[163] Admittedly, this looked somewhat like the tracks left by a sea turtle when it comes out of the surf to lay its eggs far up on some sand beach, but its very size gave me pause. Where had I seen anything like this before? Answer, in the Canadian Northwest Territories at the end of a new road being pushed through the spruce forest and muskeg! It was the track of an enormous "crawler" that toted tens of tons of gravel up to the roadhead!

Having considered this wild, way-out theory as to the origin of these lights, we now must ask: Why their form? For this, all I can suggest is that hypothetical circular "ships" could have constantly running radar-type scanners; that the "rays" these use become apparent to us only when they happen to trigger the luminosity of a mass of little, one-celled creatures indigenous to our warm seas and present there in countless multitudes. Maybe these "constructions" are all over all the continental shelves, but there just aren't enough little *Noctiluca* elsewhere to show up their presence. Now you think up a better one.

I tossed this at Wally Minto and asked him, as a leading investigator of underwater radiation, to rip into it. Rather than paraphrase Dr. Minto's expressions I have sought his permission, and that of the magazine in which the article containing them was published, to reproduce it in full because it contains so much that needs most precise interpretation. It goes as follows:

As a scientist interested in the various types of radiation given off by living creatures, I wish to advance an explanation for these remarkable wheels of light observed in oceanic waters. I fully realize that advancing one possible explanation for these phenomena does not thereby eliminate other, more esoteric possibilities, because we know so little about the world in which we live. But trying to fit observed fact into the framework of our present knowledge often serves to call attention to unnoticed gaps in that framework. So let us see whether scientific deduction can shed some light on this luminous mystery.

First, since the observations of this phenomenon seem confined to tropical seas—or at least to warm water—this is a compelling indication that the source of the *light* is in some form of luminescent organism which requires such warmth for growth and activity. Because of the uniformity of illumination within the beams and at the hub, it is evident that the light sources must be dispersed through the water, in contrast to the appearance that would result if the light emanated from a single central source. Therefore, the evidence clearly indicates that luminescent plankton must be the immediate source of the light, as suggested by Ivan Sanderson. However, this leaves unanswered the mystery of the extraordinary pattern. Why would the plankton give off light in the shape of a rimless wheel?

We know that the luminescent plankton found in tropical seas emits light when subjected to a mechanical stimulus, as shown by the luminous wake of a boat plowing through an area suffused with these tiny organisms. But what sort of stimulating force do we know of that could induce this pattern of radiating beams? A source of stimuli that fills the requirements very nicely is underwater *sound*. If there are two closely adjacent sources of sound at the hub, an interference pattern will be set up. In the radial zones where the sonic waves from both sources are in phase, they will reinforce each other, stimulating the plankton to emit light. In the alternate zones, where the sonic waves are out of phase and cancel each other, there will be no luminescence-stimulating vibrations. Thus, we can see how a radial pattern could be generated, but, let us test this hypothesis against the other observations to see whether it stands up.

First, it is fully in accord with the notation that the beams pass through the ships, since their hulls would transmit the vibrations, exciting the plankton on the far side.

Second, if the two central sound sources rotate slowly about each other, the radial interference pattern will also rotate. Further, because of the limited speed of sound in water, such rotation would produce a pattern of spiral spokes, rather than lineal beams, again in accord with the reports.

Third, the intensity of light will be essentially uniform, both at the hub and throughout the length of the radial arms, because the intensity of light is dependent upon the concentration of plankton in the water, not on the intensity of the sound waves. As with most biological phenomena involving excitation, the sonic stimulation of plankton is an "all-or-none" effect. Below a certain threshold level, the individual organism remains quiescent; when the stimulus is above threshold, it gives off light. But increasing the intensity of the stimulation does not increase the brightness of emitted light after the threshold level is surpassed.

Again, this fits well into the observation that, in some cases, the beams had a fairly sharp termination. Naturally, the intensity of sound decreases with distance from the central hub, so, at some radial distance, the intensity will fall below threshold. As a result, though the sound waves continue outward with slowly diminishing intensity, they will be unable to stimulate the plankton, resulting in a fairly sharp cut-off point.

In every respect, the observations are entirely compatible with the results we should expect from sonic excitation of luminescent plankton. But what is the primary cause of this spectacle? What can we deduce about the source of the sonic waves? A wide variety of marine animals produce underwater sounds. Let us examine the clues and try to narrow down the list.

Since the wheel of light is so large, the sound must be intense to disturb so large a volume of sea. Yet, if the sound were so intense, why did the observers fail to mention its presence? Logically, because its frequency fell outside the spectrum of human hearing, which extends from about 20 cycles to 15,000 cycles per second. To generate sub-sonic frequencies at less than 20 cycles under water requires the expenditure of tremendous amounts of power. No living animal could generate a sub-sonic output capable of agitating the plankton at the reported distances. So, the only possibility at this end of the spectrum is some incredibly powerful machine. Because of the historical dates of sightings, we can be sure that this hypothetical machine could not have been made by man.

On the other hand, at the upper end of the sonic spectrum beyond human hearing, it takes much less energy to generate ultrasonic vibrations. Sounds of the required intensity could be generated by a large marine animal; indeed, dolphins and other whales generate just such sounds for communication and sonar detection of objects in their vicinity. It would be virtually impossible for a host of small creatures to vibrate so exactly in phase as to produce an interference pattern, but the powerful whale is a good probability. This highly intelligent mammal could well be the focus of this display.

But we are left with one tantalizing problem: the generation of a radial interference pattern requires the presence of two adjacent sonic sources. Could it be that a solitary cetacean is "talking" out of both sides of his head at once? If so, why? Nature rarely does anything without a purpose, though it may be difficult for us to discern it at first. Possibly this is a deliberate search pattern in a very empty ocean? If so, our sonar experts could profitably learn from it.

Another possibility is pleasantly beguiling. The same beautifully coruscating whorl of light could be engendered by two porpoises "singing" in close harmony! Let us hope that the rigors of scientific analysis do not lead us to reject this enchanting possibility.[164]

Before we go any further, I wish to present a list of the precise cases on which this theorizing is based—both those available to Dr. Minto and us when we first wrote on this, and some that have come in since that date. Once again, this is but a gleaning of a considerably longer list and is confined to those items for which there are at least specific references which we have been able to confirm.

1875.   E. L. Moss, on H.M.S. *Bulldog.* (See p. 97.)[165]

May 15, 1879.   Comdr. J. E. Pringle of H.M.S. *Vulture* in the Persian Gulf, saw revolving wheel of light well under water, centered east; but another wheel to the west revolving in contrary direction Shafts 25 feet broad; space between 100 feet. Traveling about 85 mph; lasted 35 minutes.[166]

1880.   R. E. Harris, Commander of A.H.N. Co.'s Steamship *Shahjehan*, at Malabar saw unidentified stuff floating on surface. "Waves of brilliant light with space between." Floating substance did not give light, but it and all the sea illuminated by shafts of light.[167]

1891. China Sea, "Shafts or lances of light that had the appearance of rays of searchlight." [168]

1901. Captain Hoseason on the Steamship *Kilwa* in the Persian Gulf saw vast "ripples" of light for 15 minutes; then they died out. No phosphorescence on the sea.[169]

1906. Mr. Douglas Carnegie on ship in the Gulf of Oman saw a bank of quiescent phosphorus; when within 20 yards, shafts of brilliant light across ship's bows at 60 to 200 mph. Bars about 20 feet across. Intervening ship had no effect on light beams; seemed to travel right through it.[170]

1907. Mr. S. C. Patterson, second officer on the P. & O. S.S. *Delta* in the Malacca Strait, saw "shafts which seemed to move round a center—like spokes of a wheel—and appeared to be about 300 yards long." Went on for half an hour.[171]

1909. Captain Gave on the Danish ship *Bintang* in the Strait of Malacca saw "a vast, revolving wheel of light, flat upon the water; long arms issued from the center around which the whole system appeared to rotate." So large only half could be seen at a time; center on horizon. Lasted 15 minutes. Disappeared when dead ahead of vessel.[172]

August 13, 1910. Captain Breyer on the Dutch ship *Valentijn* in the South China Sea saw "a rotation of flashes like a horizontal wheel turning rapidly just above the water." [173]

1949. U.S. Navy Captain Bodler in the Strait of Hormuz. (See p. 99.)[174]

1962. Mr. C. J. Boyes, of the S.S. *Telemachus*. (See p. 99.)[175]

Jan. 23, 1964. At the northeast Point of Groote Eylandt, W. Australia, large lights were seen in the sea. Compass went "haywire." Shadow in center of lights rotated clockwise, causing lights to pulsate.[176]

There are not enough items in this list to permit any real statistical analyses except the very crude ones alluded to above.

The Indian Ocean continues to be the center, and almost the sole center, for these appearances; but it is just this that gives me pause to wonder. The luminous or light-emitting protozoan named *Noctiluca miliaris* is not confined to the Indian Ocean or even to the tropics. Nor are mating whales and other cetaceans! I have plowed through oceans of luminous sea surface in the far north off the coast of Norway. The same sight may be encountered just about all over every ocean in the world, apart from the polar and subpolar areas. It is particularly prevalent in the Caribbean, and that sea abounds in cetaceans, and in several cases of the same species found in the Indian Ocean. This being so, why have these "rimless light wheels" not been reported from all over?

Then again, whales and other cetaceans are not the only marine animals that emit sound. Just listen to the cacophonies that were recorded by such institutions as the Oceanographic Center at Wood's Hole, Massachusetts. Under water is a positive uproar. So why don't these sounds made by fish and crustaceans and so forth, and often rhythmically, be it noted, also activate the little *Noctiluca*? There is something dashed rum going on here.

Personally, I am also not fully satisfied with the explanation of those rays which form sinusoidal curves while revolving about their apparent hub. Despite elapsed (or relapsed) time in the propagation of these light beams from their center, I have failed to obtain a clear explanation of the actual method by which such precise curves can be created by switching microorganisms on and off. Also, I'm not quite satisfied with the parallel-sided, laser-like beams. Just how do you so confine a beam of light and then keep it confined while revolving it like a spoke of a wheel?

Thus, I am afraid that I have had to resort back—though most reluctantly—to the notion that these appearances may be caused by some kind of machines. Prior to unearthing the material that I have put on record in Chapters 1 to 6, I considered this quite balmy; but if there *is* a submarine civilization, or the bottoms of our seas and oceans are being used by intelligent entities with advanced machines, one can but be forced to accept the notion that their scanning or other devices might activate the *Noctiluca* in these remarkable manners. We just have to accept the fact that there are sound waves in both air and water (and solid matter, as well); electromagnetic waves; and some other spectrum that we have not yet pinned down. The last may, as of now and for convenience' sake, be called bionic, in that its waves certainly produce effects and at distance but cannot be interfered with by the methods used to disrupt electromagnetic waves—such as Faraday screens and so forth.

So once again we are just about back where we started; namely, in the biological field of investigation. I have said repeatedly, and not only in this book, that *some* UAOs could, *themselves*, be living entities; that others could be constructions devised upon and running on biological rather than mechanical principals; and that some could have been "manufactured" by some living entities who may or may not travel in them. In any one of these three cases, any that prefer to land, operate, or reside under water might well produce effects on our physical and biological omnia of the nature described in this chapter. As I have said: *"I don't like it"*—but there it is! Is it another ringbolt in this watery coffin?

8 · AN EIGHTH MYSTERY
The "Bermuda Triangle"

We come now to a hairier one. I would have preferred to title it—with due apologies to the memory of The Bard— "The Much Vexed Bermoothes," but that would have put us right back in a bag which I wish to avoid at almost all costs. This bit first came to the attention of the general public only about six years ago, when that very splendid writer on matters fortean, Vincent Gaddis, coined the catchy moniker "The Bermuda Triangle" as the title for an article.[177] For some reason this phrase caught on like other such misnomers as "flying saucers," "abominable snowmen," "the great sea serpent," and so on.

Actually, affairs of this nature had been reported upon in that general area for centuries, as Gaddis pointed out. In 1947, however, matters became particularly acute thereabouts with the disappearance, first, of five Navy planes, and then of a large search plane which went off to look for the former. Still, the business was not put together until this article by Gaddis and his use, if not the original coining, of this catchy title. And we have to be extremely careful of catch phrases like "Sighted sub; sank same," which was alleged to have come from the American W.W. II effort, but which was coined by a Greek newsman in a bar and grill in Cairo! History is cluttered with these little epigrams, but there is not an iota of proof that any of them were ever uttered by those to whom they are attributed. Even items like *"Et tu, Brute"* and *"Semper aliquid de novis ex Africa"* can be most misleading, though probably both are perfectly valid platitudes. In the case of the "Bermuda Triangle" we have to face the fact that it is neither a triangle nor in any particular way connected with the islands of Bermuda, much "vexed" as they may be.

As we shall see, this turns out to be a worldwide problem and, although apparently concentrated in a comparatively few rather limited areas in widely separated parts of the seas or oceans, it also slops over onto adjacent land areas in many places. There is also now a growing suspicion that it may be just as atmospheric as it is alleged to be aquatic, and that at least part of the phenomenon can occur over land in the middle of continents (as in planes vanishing over Germany and Tunisia).[178] It could, of course, also have much to do with related matters such as the disappearances of grounded solid objects like barns[179] and people (see Appendix A, p. 217). However, we will endeavor to confine ourselves to matters maritime in this department.

We got engulfed in this matter when the nuclear-powered submarine, the *Scorpion,* failed to make her home port en route from the Mediterranean across the Atlantic in July 1968. This was a terrible tragedy from the human point of view but, horrible as it may sound, there's nothing really unique about it. Ships have been going down since the dawn of maritime history. So, more recently, have planes, and now space vehicles and submarines. So what was so exceptional about the disappearance of the *Scorpion?* First, it was a nuclear-powered sub; but second, it *could* have gone down in a sea country that is alleged to be of a very special and peculiar nature.

Many subs have just plain vanished, and not only in wartime. Two of them disappeared at the same time in the Mediterranean only a few weeks before the *Scorpion*—one Israeli, the other French. Also, we have lost other nuclear-powered subs, such as the *Thresher*. Whenever a sub fails to surface, there is an emotional outburst. And why not, since almost all of us are basically claustrophobics. But sometimes there enters another ingredient in these sorry events—namely, mystery.

Just how to define this has not as yet been determined or even attempted. Why is it that the public singles out one horror from all the countless others that occur every day and concentrates on it to the exclusion of all else? As I say, submarines have been staying down since they were invented and there have been some very dramatic rescue stories, but when two go down in the same sea, as in the Mediterranean recently, the story just sort of dies away. The individual event, in fact, seems to be of less importance than the *place* where it occurs. Ships have been going down in the Mediterranean since long before Greek times; so, more recently, have subs and planes. By the same token, all three classes of craft have been ditching in the North Atlantic one way or another for years. In fact, they have been going down all over the world, but only the maritime historians pay much attention. Yet, if so much as one dirty old freighter disappears in certain areas, thousands of people start speculating. In the case of our *Scorpion*, half the reading public of the world seems to have gone balmy. Why? Because there is a sort of folklore building up about this so-called "Bermuda Triangle."

Perhaps the greatest problem within this problem is that no differentiation is made in any official records that I have seen between *disappearances* and mere sinkings, founderings, and wreckings, and, if we are to get any further on this score, someone is going to have to undertake a monumental bit of research entailing the prying loose of all records of all maritime insurance agencies, commercial airline and shipping firms, and those of the navies and airforces of all maritime nations. Frankly, this can't be accomplished except by some official international body such as the UN, and even then I can hardly envision our friends, the Russians, disclosing their losses, and more especially the unexplained ones. All navies—as sort of corporate bodies, which they are—are excessively discreet as to what they say about anything. Being an ex-Navy man myself, I do not blame them, and more especially when I note the appalling trouble that the poor U.S. Air Force has been pushed into by being instructed to handle the matter of UFOs.

Commercial shipping companies are not much better when it comes to what is called frank disclosure. This, too, is perfectly understandable, because obviously nothing could do more damage not only to the image but the profit-and-loss statements of such enterprises than their vessels just vanishing. What of the freight, not to mention the crews and any passengers there might be aboard? And then comes insurance, along with a lot of other awkward questions from all manner of people and organizations, from widows to federal government agencies. It's a hard world indeed, and made even sterner in this case because nobody, including the navies, has the foggiest notion what is going on, let alone what the causes might be. I have been poking into this business for over thirty years, having initially become interested owing to my work as a counterespionage agent for a navy. My jurisdiction covered a considerable area of tropical seas infested with hurricanes, outright pirates, rotting coastal vessels, Nazi subs, Japanese so-called "fishing boats," coral reefs that were on no charts, sandbars that built up in a matter of months, smugglers, crooks, nuts, other intelligence and counterintelligence agents, people like the Black Caribs who don't like anybody anyway, and you name it. I was responsible for numbering thousands of craft in the area, ranging from oil tankers to large sailing canoes, and almost as fast as we discovered them and assigned them a number, dozens of them vanished.

Since there was then a fine war going on, it was virtually impossible to ascertain the cause of these disappearances; but despite the happy little practice of switching assigned numbers, or remodeling and repainting boats in out-of-the-way creeks that were often not even on the maps, we did get an astonishing number of answers which seemed to check out. Yet the residue left over was just too much, even for a critical boating area in the midst of a knockdown global war. And it was the owners of the missing vessels, were they pirates or large oil companies, who gave us the most help. You see, even if a sub plugs a ship at dead of night there is usually something left floating and radio usually had at least a chance to report the point of being hit. Still, the owners, after doing all they could to get at the facts, quite often found themselves completely baffled by the absence of *any* evidence of said plugging. Then came the airplanes.

At one point I had one submarine and five PBYs to operate with; at least, I had five for about twelve hours—for, on awakening at dawn in my own home port the next morning, three were on the bottom of the harbor (sabotaged by somebody drifting down on them in a canoe and drilling a hole into their floats), one was euphemistically called "crippled," and one was just plain gone—and this pun is fully intended. This got us involved with the then Navy Air Force and, in endeavoring to explain events within my bailiwick, I was subjected to a positive cascade of reports of "missing aircraft." Yet there was *no* aerial warfare within three thousand miles of the area. Nobody could understand this, but the brass seemed to think that, since I boated about the area and had reported missing ships, I ought to know the answer to the missing planes. As I said above, it's a hard world.

There were literally thousands of square miles of uninhabited and forest-covered land surfaces around this area in which whole squadrons could have "ditched" and nobody ever have seen them or found them; but of major concern to the aerial boys was the problem of planes vanishing over the sea. Here the riddle was even more baffling than with surface shipping. Did subs shoot them down? Were they sabotaged before take off? Did they run into a hurricane or a twister (and these were not pre-reported in those days)? Did they just conk out, or go home, or what? There was just no answer, and this was compounded by the fact that very, very few ever gave their location when something went wrong because radio contact with base was in those days also primitive, to say the least, while many planes were flying on official "blackout." At the end of W.W. II everybody was so happy, and we had so many planes left over—and all over the world—that nobody could be bothered with this business any longer, and anyhow, it was still under tight wraps. But then the now famous incident of the Avengers popped up.

This occurred on the 5th of December, 1945, out of Fort Lauderdale Naval Air Station in Florida. The incident has been written up many times, but there are some discrepancies among the many versions, all of which were first published in the most reliable newspapers. I take my facts here from Vincent Gaddis' version as published in his book *Invisible Horizons* [180] as being the nearest both to the official version and to the better public reports. However, the very well-known radio commentator, and more or less the original D.J., Art Ford, has now spent many years investigating all aspects of this case, even to tracking down and interviewing the families of the lost men, and he has run into some really very extraordinary and disturbing facts concerning the affair. His book on the case is to be published shortly, as of the time of writing this, so I will not go into further details. What is more, these would seem to concern more the dilemma of officialdom than the incidence of whatever natural phenomenon caused the disappearance of these planes and their crews.

Five TBM "Avenger" torpedo bombers left the Naval Air Station on a routine patrol flight. Each plane was operated by a pilot, a gunner, and a radio operator; however, on this occasion one man failed to report in for duty, so that the group left one short. A further complication arose later because one of those aboard turned out to have volunteered for the Navy while under age and under a false name, but this point was later cleared up. It was a brilliantly sunny day with clear skies. The planes had been carefully checked, and each plane carried an inflatable life raft, and each man wore a life jacket. All airmen were experienced. They were airborne at 2 P.M. and were scheduled to fly for two hours some 160 miles due east out over the Atlantic, then turn north for 40 miles, and subsequently return directly to their base.

The first radioed communication from the lead plane did not come in to the base until 3:35 P.M.—and, curiously, this did not request landing instructions but instead reported: "Calling tower this is an emergency. . . . We seem to be off course. . . . We cannot see land. . . . (Repeat) . . . We cannot see land." Asked by the tower for their position, the astonishing reply came back: "We're not sure of our position. We can't be sure just where we are. We seem to be lost." Advised by the tower to head due west, the even more astonishing reply came back: "We don't know which way is west. Everything is wrong . . . strange. We can't be sure of any direction. Even the ocean doesn't look as it should."

The land base then listened in to the interchanges between the flight commander and the other pilots for some half-hour. Unfortunately, either this was not taped or the conversations have not been released, but it was brought out at the subsequent investigation that the planes were still within sight of each other but their crews were becoming increasingly bewildered and distressed. According to Gaddis, quoting from reports of the enquiry: "Shortly after 4:00 P.M., the flight leader, for no apparent reason other than panic suddenly turned over flight command to another pilot." At 4:25 this new flight leader reported to land base: "We don't know where we are. We think we must be about 225 miles northeast of base . . . it looks like we are . . ." And that was the last heard from this flight.

Within minutes a Martin Mariner Flying Boat, specially prepared for rescue missions, was airborne and headed for the last assumed position of the Avenger flight. It kept in contact with the tower for some fifteen minutes, but then, when called back in a routine manner, it did not reply. And that was the last heard of it and its crew of thirteen experienced men! Next, the

Coast Guard was alerted and they sent a fast plane off into the descending dusk to scout the whole route assumed to have been followed by the Avengers, but when they got to the last assumed point of contact they found nothing but a clean sweep of ocean surface and clear horizons. This plane returned safely. The Navy then joined the search with Coast Guard surface craft, and this continued all night. Nothing was found, and so an aircraft carrier was dispatched and launched her thirty planes to square off a vast area of sea and ocean, while land parties started a search of all coastal land areas. In the end there were over twenty surface craft and over three hundred planes combing the area and considerable peripheral areas. Even the British RAF launched and searched from the Bahamas. This went on for days, but not one iota of hardware or any other evidence that might account for the disappearances was found.

The incident, if one can call it that, naturally hit the newspapers and created a considerable commotion despite the fact that the world was at that time almost immune to huge lists of missing planes, owing to the war. This was a little too close to home, and the turnout of military and civilian forces for the search led a number of reporters to speculate. As a matter of fact, it was an unnamed British reporter who happened to be on official assignment to naval bases in the South who really started up the hare. His modest heading to an article in, as far as I have been able to ascertain (by its print and paper, since it bore no date), the *Manchester Guardian* of England, read: "Sargasso Graveyard now claims planes as well as ships." This is just the kind of reporting that is best calculated to stir up a storm; and it hit a bull's eye. This was the interjection of the famed and infamous Sargasso so-called "Sea."

This is a large lozenge-shaped area in the western Atlantic stretching from about 25° N. to 35° N., and from the eastern edge of the Gulf Stream about 150 miles east of Fort Lauderdale to 40° W. in the mid-Atlantic. It is notable for the fact that the whole of its surface is strewn with floating seaweed, sometimes in enormous mats. From the time of the earliest trans-Atlantic voyages, which happened to use a route through this area, a legend has been growing up about it, to the effect that it caught ships and held them fast until they rotted and sank. It is just possible that small sailing vessels, over-built and carrying inadequate canvas, during periods of light winds in the very early days, may have been truly impeded by these masses of floating seaweed, but a properly rigged ship, let alone a powered one, just plows merrily through the mess. In other words, the menace of this Sargasso Sea lies somewhere between myth and legend, though, as a reality, it does exist.

When, therefore, our agile reporter casually attributed the loss of these planes to this sort of maritime Moloch, it hit the front pages. Quite how one equates a mass of seaweed with the disappearance of six airplanes I fail to be able even to suggest, but the logic of the press is quite unfathomable at times. In any case the almost immediate result of this bit of reporting was that all manner of other agile persons started digging into the past history of this Sargasso Sea and inevitably came up with all kinds of horrors. And, since they were committed to this "Graveyard of Ships," they clung to it and ignored all else. People hate having their myths destroyed, while they are almost equally averse to the creation of new ones. Of the Sargasso Sea they had heard; but it had been taken away from them when scientific exploration investigated and explained it. Now here it was back again with all its air of mystery.

The really aggravating aspect of all this is, however, that this Sargasso Sea just about coincides with our No. 1 Vile Vortex, and the disappearances of the planes and of most of the ships of old that the eager beavers dug out of old newspaper morgues and maritime records, had indeed occurred in this mysterious, lozenge-shaped marine area. A word of warning, nonetheless: since this investigation was intially kicked off by a glaring incident in it, the resultant research naturally concentrated upon it. Thus the stress on this northwestern Atlantic area probably gives a quite erroneous impression. Nonetheless, we herewith present said findings in order to demonstrate the massive nature of the phenomenon.

DISAPPEARANCES IN NORTHWESTERN ATLANTIC

1840	French ship *Rosalie* en route to Havana, found deserted except for a half-starved canary[181]
1854	Schooner *Bella*, vanished in so-called Triangle [182]
March 1854	*City of Glasgow*, en route Liverpool to Philadelphia, vanished, 450 on board [183]
March 1866	*Lotta*, vanished north of Haiti [184]
1868	*Viego*, vanished in so-called Triangle [185]
1870	*City of Boston*, en route New York to Liverpool, vanished, 177 on board [186]
1872	*Mary Celeste*, found deserted [187]
Jan. 1880	*Atlanta*, en route Bermuda to England, vanished, 290 on board [188]
1881	Deserted schooner picked up by *Ellen Austin* west of Azores; salvage crew disappeared in fog en route to St. John's, Newfoundland [189]
1884	*Miramonde*, vanished en route to New Orleans [190]
4 Nov. 1918	*Cyclops*, vanished en route from Barbados to Norfolk [191]
1921	*Carol Deering*, grounded at Diamond Shoals, N.C., deserted [192]
1923	*Swift Star*, vanished en route from Panama Canal to Atlantic [193]
1925	*Cotopaxi*, vanished en route Charleston, N.C., to Havana [194]
1926	*Suduffco*, vanished south of Port Newark [195]
Oct. 1931	*Stavenger*, vanished south of Cat Island, Bahamas, 43 on board [196]
Apr. 1932	*John and Mary*, found deserted 50 miles south of Bermuda [197]
March 1938	*Anglo-Australian*, vanished off Azores, 39 on board [198]

Feb. 1940	*Gloria Colite,* found deserted 200 miles south of Mobile, Ala.[199]
1944	*Rubicon,* found off Florida coast, only a dog on board [200]
1944	Five (of a flight of seven) USAF planes vanish 300 miles from Bermuda [201]
16 Oct. 1944	Two USN planes vanished off Hyannis, Mass.[202]
5 Dec. 1945	Five USN TBM Avengers and a Martin Mariner vanished off Florida [203]
24-30 July 1946	Three ships en route from Panama to New Orleans vanished, total of 115 on board [204]
1947	American Superfort vanished 100 miles off Bermuda [205]
29 Jan. 1948	BOAC *Star Tiger* vanished 400 miles northeast of Bermuda, 29 on board [206]
28 Dec. 1948	DC-3 vanished en route from San Juan to Miami, 35 aboard [207]
17 Jan. 1949	BOAC *Ariel* vanished between Bermuda and Jamaica [208]
March 1950	Globemaster vanished en route to Ireland [209]
June 1950	*Sandra* vanished en route from Georgia to Venezuela [210]
2 Feb. 1953	York transport plane vanished en route from England to Jamaica, 39 on board [211]
Oct. 1954	Super-Constellation vanished north of "Triangle," 42 aboard [212]
Sept. 1955	*Connemara IV* found abandoned southwest of Bermuda [213]
9 Nov. 1956	USN patrol bomber vanished in so-called Triangle area [214]
16 Apr. 1960	*Ethel C.* vanished off Virginia coast [215]
8 Jan. 1962	KB-50 vanished en route from Virginia to the Azores [216]
Apr. 1962	Private twin-engine plane vanished en route to Nassau [217]

2 Feb. 1963	*Marine Sulphur Queen* vanished near Dry Tortugas [218]
1 July 1963	*Sno' Boy* vanished en route to Jamaica, 40 on board [219]
28 Aug. 1963	Two KC-135s vanished 800 miles northeast of Miami [220]
17 Jan. 1967	Chartered plane vanished in the Caribbean [221]
May 1967	Sixteen-foot boat found abandoned, Gulf of Mexico [222]
24 Dec. 1967	*Witchcraft* vanished off Miami (sent distress signal, but had disappeared completely when the Coast Guard arrived 20 minutes later) [223]
July 1968	Plane vanished between Grand Bahama and Florida; within a few days of this a boat also vanished [224]
21 Oct. 1968	*Ithaca Island,* vanished en route from Norfolk to Liverpool [225]
July 1969	Discovery of five unmanned ships west of the Azores (the same area in which the *Mary Celeste* was found abandoned); two had turned turtle, others were totally undamaged [226]

This list, however, presents us with still another problem, which obviously falls into two parts: first, the disappearance or vanishing of planes, ships, and subs, and/or man-made constructions, and the coincident disappearance of people; and second, many instances of the equally coincident *non*-disappearance of animals on said ships. Seamen are very fond of their pets, and the ship's cat is normally considered by everybody aboard, however hardboiled he may be, with some veneration. This is doubtless a residue of ingrained tradition from throughout the ages, and pets and mascots usually get preferential treatment, even with women and children aboard. A captain goes down with his ship, also by tradition, but he usually heaves the ship's cat into the last lifeboat. But what to say when the cat and all lifeboats are present and accounted for, but all humans have vanished.

This is a very odd one, and it behooves us to present the details of some cases that demonstrate this profound enigma. It is all very well to assert that hundreds of people have disappeared at sea and that in quite a number of cases they alone did so—as apart from the ships they were on—but this means nothing unless some facts are presented which can be checked. I am well aware that the average person is much more interested in details than in theories and that the buffs are interested only in specific cases or, in the case of UFOs, what they call "sightings." I am afraid that I do not subscribe to this attitude and, while I keep massive files of details and from time to time initiate analyses of them, I simply cannot read seed catalogs for fun or even enlightenment. It is not the "what" that interests me but the "how" and even more, the "why"; because without such speculation and dependent investigation, the "whats," however numerous, massive, and variable they may be, don't really amount to more than a mass of statistics, and they prove nothing. I will therefore cite a few specific cases and then see if we can pick holes in them.

As in the analysis of any mystery or set of mysteries, it is best to start off with examples that have been explained (at least, to the satisfaction of marine insurance companies); then, proceed to those that have not been but which might logically be so; next, to any for which there would appear to be no logical explanation; and finally, come to those which seem to be totally inexplicable. The last two categories are not the same in that there are cases which *could* have logical answers but for the explanation of which just too many "ifs" have to be conjured up, while there are others for which nobody can supply either logical or any other suggestions at all by way of explanation. Of course, there must be a "logical" explanation for *all* events, so that even the inexplicables must be susceptible of explanation; however, the explanation may call for the exercise of a logic other than that to which we currently subscribe or—*and this is much more pertinent*—it may call for knowledge of processes that are entirely within our logic but of which we do not yet have knowledge or even an inkling.

I will start with a case that has been very widely publicized; namely, that of the converted yacht, the *Joyita*, in the Pacific in 1955.[227] I start here because, although the 25 persons aboard were no longer aboard the vessel when it was finally found half keeled over and with one deck awash, there was considerable evidence that violence had taken place aboard, as shown by some bloodstained bandages. The vessel, a twin-engine motor yacht built in California, had been converted to passenger and cargo for interisland trade in the southwest Pacific, and was owned by a Welshman who had fallen upon hard times. She was chartered by two New Zealanders, in Western Samoa, to make a trip to the port of Fakaofo in the Tokelau Islands, and carried also the newly appointed district governor of these islands. The mate was an Amerindian, and there were two crew members from the Gilbert Islands who were bosun and engineer and who had been with the captain for many years. The vessel was not authorized to carry any other passengers on that trip.

The *Joyita* left on the 3d of October for the 280-mile passage, under clear skies and upon a calm sea. She failed to arrive on schedule at her assigned port, and after some time a massive air and sea search was initiated, but it was not until the 10th of November that a British ship found her. She was awash but, having a cork sealing, was virtually unsinkable. There was nobody aboard. Evidence of some storm damage was found when the hulk was towed to the Fiji Islands and examined. There was damage to the upper structure and evidence that one of the engines had malfunctioned or been interfered with. Then the bloodstained bandages were found. A great number of other curious details were brought to light, but all remained unexplained. The inquiry and examination of the vessel were, of course, conducted upon normal lines, which seek only for normal and rational explanations, yet the findings were so strange and in some cases so contradictory that the theories evolved to explain them became ever more complex. In sum, they called for at least three separate disasters aboard, including boarding by some piratical group, suicide, and final abandonment of ship by personnel who then foundered and were lost. All of this may have taken place, but it puts an enormous strain on our credulity. This episode did not occur in one of our vortices, and personally I feel that it has all the hallmarks of a perfectly natural disaster, though perhaps aided by piracy. We don't know what happened aboard the luckless ship and we will never know.

The most famous case of all in the annals of disappearances at sea—though for just what reasons I have never really been able to make out—is that of the *Mary Celeste*.[228] Everybody who has ever had any interest in maritime matters, and just about everybody interested in mysteries of any kind, has heard of this case, but it has to be briefly reviewed here because it forms such a prominent feature of our main theme in the estimation of the average person who has heard of it. Actually, I am not sure that it has anything whatsoever to do with our subject any more than has the case of the *Joyita*. It has always appeared to me to be a clear-cut, albeit subsequently complicated, case of either piracy or barratry, but I have to admit that the attempt to explain what happened to produce the results found and recorded, once again begins to stretch our credulity almost to the limit. Straight piracy would at first seem to be the obvious answer; but why all the trouble of pirating a crew and a few papers and leaving a very valuable cargo afloat?

The *Mary Celeste,* a brigantine of approximately 280 tons and just over 100 feet on the waterline, was built in Nova Scotia in 1861 and originally christened the *Amazon.* In the fall of 1872 she took on a load of commercial alcohol in New York, consigned to Italy. Tied up alongside her was a British brigantine named the *Dei Gratia,* whose captain, David Morehouse, was an old friend of the captain and part owner of the *Mary Celeste,* a young but experienced mariner from Massachusetts named Benjamin S. Briggs. The *Dei Gratia* was loading petroleum. The

Mary Celeste sailed on the 5th of November, the *Dei Gratia* on the 15th of November. After being held back by strong head winds for two days, the *Mary Celeste* proceeded straight across the Atlantic for, according to her log, eighteen days. However, on the 5th of December, the *Dei Gratia* came up with her halfway between the Azores and Portugal and, noting that her canvas was in disorder and partly shredded and that she was yawing erratically, Captain Morehouse came about and bespoke her. There being no response and nobody visible on deck, he launched a boarding party.

Not a living soul or a dead body was found aboard. The logbook was in the mate's cabin open on a desk, and a chart indicated that the vessel had passed the last of the Azores on the morning of the 25th of November. Apparently she had been adrift for eleven days. All small boats were gone, the wheel was not lashed, all deck ports were tightly sealed with canvas and timber, but the main skylight and both fore and aft hatch covers were open. There was no evidence of violence, but there was of the crew having left in a great hurry. Rain and flurry had soaked the cabins, and there was water to the coaming in the forepart. Yet there was ample food and water aboard and the standing rig was in good order. Captain Morehouse put aboard a prize crew, who sailed her to Gibraltar.

There was a court of inquiry which dragged on and on and during which all manner of accusations, rumors and innuendos were aired, and a lot of quite wild assertions made. Just about the only additional fact of any significance that came out of all of this was that the ship's chronometer, sextant, and registration papers were missing. The inquiry was finally wound up, Captain Morehouse received modest compensation, and the *Mary Celeste* proceeded to her port of destination. Only later did other people start making allegations to the effect that Captain Morehouse had engineered a piratical seizure with all manner of dire adjuncts such as having murdered the crew, and so forth. This is all imagination and sensationalism, and the only facts are that the brigantine *Mary Celeste* was found adrift, sans crew. The circumstances, moreover, are not by any means unique, as literally dozens of sailing vessels have been reliably reported as having been found in just such a condition over the centuries.

The odd thing about this case is that it became a classic. It would seem to have been the publicity given to the case by the inquiry in Gibraltar to which the Queen's Proctor, one Frederick Flood—an appropriate name—was sent as investigator for the Crown. He appears from all accounts to have been an appalling little publicity hound with a penchant for criminal investigation; and, as the *Mary Celeste* was an American bottom, everybody had a field day. The only really mysterious thing about the business is that the crew *did* disappear. Once again, it is Vincent Gaddis who draws our attention to the number of abandonments that are known to have been caused by pure panic on the part of the crew, and so often when the captain had died or suffered an accident and inexperienced officers were left in command. He gives case after case of vessels abandoned for this cause which were duly established since the crews were rescued; and time and time again he mentions the same reasons given—namely, that there was an explosion, sign of fire, a shifted cargo, failure of pumps, unidentifiable leaks, and so forth, which prompted the crew to take to the boats in the belief that the mother ship was in imminent danger of foundering.[229]

Certain facts should here be noted. First, even an inexperienced or leaderless crew seldom if ever abandon ship because of storm. To do so is obviously asinine, because if the ship won't hold up, no yawl, gig, or other small lifeboat can do so. Only today are true lifeboats so constructed and equipped that they have a chance of survival when a large vessel founders. Second, I would like to point out that after years of research into this matter—and it is rather close to home for me as I was virtually brought up on the sea and lived for many years on my own schooner—I have yet to come across a clear-cut case of piracy without evidence of violence, the transfer of cargo and valuables, or deliberate wrecking. It is this that makes these cases of disappearances of people from sound ships so mysterious and puzzling.

At the same time, there are many cases of ships found drifting with all hands still aboard but dead. These are mostly, if not invariably, sailing vessels, though I will give a classic case of a modern power vessel in a minute. The cause is probably disease or food poisoning, and it is to be noted that almost all the cases have been recorded from the tropics, and of vessels that comparatively recently sailed from tropical ports where virulent strains of such diseases as typhoid might be acquired just before sailing by a crew not immune, having come from elsewhere. And the incredible virulence of some diseases in the form of local strains is sometimes hard to believe. An English officer acquired syphilis in central Nigeria, boarded a powered river vessel to go to the coast in 1930 without showing any symptoms, but threw himself overboard five days later. Infection by even comparatively mild afflictions of the so-called temperate zones can be violent in the tropics.

The other cases of abandoned vessels with only corpses aboard are almost without exception recorded from the Arctic or Antarctic, and in several cases the cause of death is recorded in logbooks found aboard. This is invariably being caught in the ice, starvation, and inability to rekindle the fire. There is nothing mysterious about these cases. Between the outer polar belts and the deep tropical there are nonetheless a small number of records of abandoned ships found with only dead bodies aboard, but they are one and all, as far as I have been able to ascertain, small fishing vessels with a crew of two or three and usually dismasted and without food or water.

We are then left with the cases of ships in perfect order, and particularly of larger size, and even modern, steel, powered vessels, that are found intact, with no signs of violence, but just lacking all signs of life—or at least with all *humans* missing. At this point, we have progressed from the obvious through the possibly obvious, to the potentially explicable. We now come to the unexplaineds and the inexplicables: and this, I contend, is where we enter another "world." I offer four cases in ascending or descending order of "impossibility" as it were, and can only ask you to make up your own minds while trying to pick holes in the illogicality of the cases. To reiterate first, let us get it quite straight that ships—and we are not dealing with planes or subs here—can disappear for all manner of perfectly simple reasons. Their crews can likewise disappear for several good reasons such as mutiny, abandonment due to panic or other cause, or piracy. Yet, when they disappear virtually within sight of others afloat and on shore in broad daylight off well-populated coasts, one begins to question.

Let me start with the case of a vessel named the *Holchu,* a modern motor vessel found adrift between the Andaman and Nicobar Islands in the eastern Bay of Bengal by a British freighter in February of 1953. "The crew of the freighter hailed the motorship. There was no reply and a boarding party was sent to investigate. No one was aboard. Her crew had disappeared. The vessel was in excellent condition. A meal had been prepared in her galley and was ready to be served. She was well supplied with food, fuel, and water. Her radio was in working order. There were no signs of trouble or violence. The only damage was a broken mast, but this would not have affected her operation since she was a motorship and her engines were in good condition. The freighter towed the derelict to Colombo, Ceylon, where harbor officials carefully examined the ship. They could find no clues as to why the *Holchu* was abandoned and the fate of her crew is unknown." [230]

In this case there is a distinct possibility that the crew or certain members of it had cause to "take a powder." They were not too far from land on three quarters and they had two powered lifeboats on deck, though the *normal* compliment of these was still aboard. They could have had a rendezvous with accomplices at sea and just vanished ashore, and more probably on the mainland of the Malay Peninsula than on the islands, as their appearance there would undoubtedly have been noted and bruited about. There is some difficulty in accepting this explanation because the crew was multinational and multiracial. The white men aboard would have found it very hard to avoid detection before getting to a major port and shipping out. Those of Asiatic nationalities could, if carrying the necessary papers, have merely filtered back into the general maritime community. After all, who ashore, even officials, knows precisely where any one seaman is at any specific time? I know, because it took me two years to trace the two men who had chartered a schooner I once bought; and nearly a year to trace the owner. (It turned out that he was running a gas station in Florida under an assumed name, as he was a Honduran and had been in the United States illegally for ten years!) There is no evidence that I knew of that either this ship or her owners had ever been involved in smuggling of any kind, but in that part of the world in that decade, owing to the disturbed political conditions, almost everybody had to be. willy-nilly; and so who was to say what the crew was up to, who they were, or what organizations they had behind them?

If you will look at a map, you will see that this incident occurred not too far from the Straits of Malacca, and it was from there that perhaps the most extraordinary of all modern reports emanated. Rather than paraphrase this case I have asked Vincent Gaddis' permission to quote his summation in full, since, having examined what reports there are extant on it, I have nothing to add factually and this account is extremely succinct. It goes as follows:

On a morning in early February, 1948, the S.S. *Ourang Medan,* a Dutch freighter, was steaming through the Straits of Malacca between Sumatra and the Malay Peninsula, bound for Jakarta, Indonesia. The sun was warm above a calm sea.

Suddenly Dutch and British marine radio listening posts picked up SOS calls from the vessel, followed by the ship's location. Other vessels in the general area were notified and rescue ships set out from shore.

The distress calls were repeated. Then after a short silence, came a final message: "All officers including captain dead, lying in chartroom and on bridge . . . probably whole crew dead." Now came a series of indecipherable dots and dashes, then, quite clearly, the words, "I die."

Radio directional equipment established the ship's position as slightly different from that given by the radio operator. With this advantage, rescue ships located the *Ourang Medan* within a few hours. The steamer seemed to be in good condition, but drifting with the current and leaving behind her a thin ribbon of smoke from her funnel. Repeated hails brought no response.

Boarding parties found a ship of the dead. The captain lay dead on the bridge. In the wheelhouse, chartroom, and along the deck were the silent bodies of the other officers and the crew. In the radio shack the body of the operator was slumped in a chair, his lifeless hand still resting on the transmitting key.

"Their frozen faces were upturned to the sun," stated a report in the *Proceedings of the Merchant Marine Council*, "the mouths were gaping open and the eyes staring." The doom that had struck the vessel had been complete. On the deck was the ship's dog, lifeless, its lips drawn back and teeth bared.

The rescuers held a conference on deck and decided to tow the freighter with its eerie cargo to the nearest port. Suddenly smoke and flames belched out of the hold and spread rapidly. The boarding parties, unable to fight the fire, hastily left the ship and returned to their own vessels.

Minutes later the boilers of the *Ourang Medan* exploded, and trailing flame she rolled over on her side, then sank beneath the waves.

In view of the ship's destruction, we may consider carbon monoxide or other toxic fumes from a smoldering fire or a leak in the boiler system as the cause of the deaths. This can easily occur in closed spaces, but it would be most unusual for a poisonous gas to asphyxiate men on an open deck even in the absence of a breeze.[231]

We have here the only known case of both an appeal for help and verification of some form of disaster to *all* personnel aboard, *including*, be it noted, a dog. It could hardly be a case of disease, as no illness is known that could lay so many people low unto death in that space of time. Poison, on the other hand, might do so, provided all members of the crew, *and* the dog, partook of the same lethal substance at the same time; yet there is no mention of stomachic or other pains or other symptoms by the radio operator. The most likely cause is indeed escaping gases of a lethal nature but, as Gaddis observes, it is indeed unusual that any such should kill people on an upper deck in the open air as well as those in confined quarters below deck. Then again, deaths from carbon monoxide and such lethal gases do not cause dogs to die with their mouth and eyes open. Finally, the sudden fire so many hours after the alert and just when the would-be rescuers were aboard, followed by the explosion of the boilers—at least as presumed—is also extremely odd. They could have just as well blown any time before or after the boarding. The timing is suspicious, to say the least. Unfortunately, there is no record of the exact number of persons aboard nor of how many were counted dead by the boarding party; thus, we cannot say how many were unaccounted for, and how many might still have been below—dead or alive.

This would seem to be a clear case of a "strike" against both humans and other animals—the dog—by some "outside influence," for, if it had been illness, surely the dedicated radio operator would have at least mentioned the fact. Gaddis makes a point of the observation by the boarding party that all those above deck were staring at the sky and that the dog was sort of frozen in death with its lips withdrawn and its teeth bared. Neither of these appearances are normal for death by asphyxiation from lethal fumes or gases. People who have committed suicide by fixing an extension from the exhaust pipe of their car to its interior appear simply to be peacefully asleep, and animals deliberately asphyxiated for humane purposes pass away in quietude just as if they had gone to sleep—which indeed they have—and appear altogether without signs of fear, panic, or any other kind of distress.

Should the rescue party not have arrived on time in this case, it is to be presumed that the vessel would have blown up and sunk in any case. Then, it might have been declared "vanished," or if perchance flotsam had subsequently been found in the locality, it would probably have been classed as a mere sinking due to explosion or other cause unknown. If, on the other hand, some "outside influence" had meticulously removed the bodies but left the ship intact, it would have gone down in the annals as a mystery. Have there ever been any incidents of this nature?

Reverting for a moment to cases of pure abandonment, I must give some details of an extraordinary case of what I can only call double vanishment. This is that of an abandoned schooner in the North Atlantic that was found by a British ship named the *Ellen Austin*, in 1881.[232] The schooner was never identified. There was no one aboard; everything was in perfect order; she was well found, had ample food and water, and there was no sign of violence or accident. Her rudder was lashed, but she had gotten below the wind and was pursuing an erratic course with loosened shrouds although the wind was light. The captain of the *Ellen Austin*, bespeaking her and getting no response, came up with her and sent a boarding party over. There being nobody aboard, he decided to attempt salvage and placed a prize crew aboard. The two vessels then headed for Newfoundland, but a dense fog descended and it was nearly two full days before it cleared. The prize was spotted not too far distant but again appeared to be performing in a most erratic manner. Once again the *Ellen Austin* came about and made close contact; and once again a party went aboard. For the second time the ship was utterly deserted, but everything was in perfect order—even to the repaired rig and the set of the sails. The remaining members of the crew of the *Ellen Austin* refused flatly to stay aboard, and this mysterious vessel was left abaft and never seen again.

What have we here? One can hardly accept any explanation of piracy or even barratry in this case. There is absolutely no evidence that the *Ellen Austin* had ever heard of this mysterious schooner; there was no implication of her master or any of her considerable crew having any knowledge of her existence; the *Ellen Austin's* course had been changed several times en voyage owing to the exigencies of weather; and no attempt was made to certify the incident. There is the rather strange fact that the ship's papers were not found in the first instance and the temporary log instituted by the prize crew in the second instance was either also lost or not picked up, and was not further mentioned. The only alternative to the acceptance of this as a complete mystery, and a double one at that, is that the whole encounter was a myth or delusion and that the prize crew either never existed, or were murdered. However, their names are on record, and it is very improbable that all those remaining would continue party to such a dastardly crime under cross-examination.

So far we have been dealing with disappearances at sea of ships or their crews and with deaths of the latter either attributable to possible known causes or to inexplicables. Perhaps there could be explanations for all of these, however abstruse and complex such might be, but when a large vessel comes ashore in broad daylight having been hailed and spoken by others afloat only a short way offshore who even received acknowledgements from her and clearly observed a working crew aboard, and is then found to be totally without human personnel, we begin to wonder. Once again I reproduce Vincent Gaddis' account because, despite perusal of the other statements on the case that he refers to, there appears nothing to be added. It goes as follows:

The sea was rough and the sky was sullen on a day in 1850 when fishermen and residents at Easton's Beach, near Newport, Rhode Island, observed a large sailing vessel heading for the channel reefs and disaster. The men close to the shore ran to the water's edge, shouting and waving their arms, waiting for the splintering crash.

And then, under strange guidance, the vessel swung around, maneuvered past the reefs and through the narrow channel and headed straight for shore, the wind filling her sails. As the ship hit the beach, a large wave lifted her bow and grounded her gently in the sand, undamaged.

The fishermen swarmed aboard to congratulate the captain for his seamanship. But there was no one *except a mongrel dog sitting quietly on deck* to greet them.

Coffee was boiling away on the stove in the ship's galley. Breakfast had been laid out on the table for the crew. The odor of tobacco smoke was still strong in the crew's quarters.

The ship was the *Seabird,* under command of Captain John Durham (some accounts give the last name as Huxham), and due to arrive that same day in her home port of Newport. She was returning from a voyage to Honduras with a cargo of hardwoods, pitch-pine, coffee, and dye-woods.

Captain Durham, a rugged New Englander, was known to many of the fishermen. The last entry in the log noted the sighting of Brenton Reef several miles offshore. The crew of a fishing boat reported that they had exchanged signals with the Seabird at sea about two hours before she was beached.

It is possible that the crew, frightened by the breakers on the reefs, had abandoned the ship and drowned. It is not clear in any of the accounts that the lifeboat was missing. But no bodies were ever washed up along the coast in the weeks following the abandonment.

The cargo was unloaded and transported to Newport by wagons. Attempts were made to refloat the vessel, but it had fallen deeper into the sand.

Several months later a storm struck the coast at night, hurling mountainous waves over the beach. In the morning the beach residents expected to find the ship pounded into pieces, her remains littering the shore. But the ship was gone and the beach was bare. The *Seabird* had returned to the sea and vanished.[233]

This is an entirely different matter from all the cases previously given,[234] but it is by no means unique. Anything that happened before W.W. II is highly suspect to the current generation, and anything that happened more than a hundred years ago is doubly suspect. However, our ancestors were not all wild-eyed mystics or gullible bumpkins. On the contrary, they appear often to have been a lot more sensible and pragmatic than we are, and they had what was perhaps a great advantage in that there were no kooky ideas current then about reality, while, at the same time, they had a much greater respect for honesty and the law. What is more, this was a case of a known object, with a known group of operators, seen by everybody in broad daylight and having been in physical contact with others only two hours before. If the crew of this vessel vanished within sight of land and no bodies were ever found, while no boat could have put off her without being seen, where, may we ask, *did* they go?

But it is the matter of the mongrel dog sitting quietly aboard that gets me. "Sitting quietly," indeed! I was trained as a biologist, and I have "owned"—or at least have had living with me —hundreds of both originally wild and born domestic animals, and quite a number of them aboard my schooner. In case of disaster they don't just sit quietly; on the contrary, they normally become hysterical, and often some time *before* the disaster— though this is another matter that I will not go into at this time.[235] Then again, as I said way back, ship's pets constitute a rather special category of pets and probably because of some age-old and even atavistic custom or belief. How many brave men have lost their lives trying to save a pet when their mates were drowning? You landlubbers may think me mad, but I've sunk more than once and only later did I realize that I had behaved in a quite irrational manner in my (in all cases successful, I am happy to record) efforts to save a pet at no disadvantage to my mates. I repeat, it may sound quite mad, but one just does not abandon ship and leave the ship's mascot aboard—ask any sailor. And this mongrel dog is not by any means the only pet left alone after a complete human vanishment. Cats and canaries predominate, but parrots seem to vanish with the humans!

It is cases like this that give us pause to consider rather deeply. Try as we may to explain away these mysteries, from time to time cases crowd in upon us that stretch first our powers of credulity and then our very imaginations to the limit. But we're not through yet!

AUTHOR'S NOTE

After we published our article in *Argosy* magazine on this subject of vortices, we began to receive an ever-increasing flood of letters from terrified tourists and other travelers and potential travelers asking whether it was safe to take a trip to Bermuda. This imposed a somewhat embarrassing question in that not only I but several others, including the Navy by a kind of tacit agreement, had publicized all these disappearances. One began to feel sorry for the air and shipping lines, let alone the Bermudan trade and tourist bureaus. As a result, we went to considerable trouble to track down some rumors to the effect that military planes and surface vessels, and commercial airlines, had received instructions not to fly or boat over the area originally designated the "Bermuda Triangle."

We found that all such allegations were pure fabrications and gross examples of sensationalism. No such orders were ever given by either official or commercial authority. Moreover, we obtained some statistics that showed at a glance the really enormous volume of airborne and sea-surface traffic through and all over this area, and learned that submarines operated regularly and normally throughout it. If only a couple of thousand souls are listed as having disappeared in this vast area in a century while literally millions have crossed it safely in a quarter of a century, it would seem that any hazard or risk therein is greatly less than that of traffic accidents on our highroads and not really much more than that of lightning strikes. What is more, this nasty business cannot possibly be a permanent feature even of the vortices; and even if they exist, *per se*. Many types of mysteries, and accidents, appear to crop up in sort of waves, though whether this is simply due to some kind of contagious psychology on the part of the reporters cannot be said. I know of no evidence that the disappearances in vortices is cyclical or periodic in any way. Thus nobody need worry about taking a trip to Bermuda—or the Mediterranean, Japan, Argentina, Capetown, or the southeastern coast of Australia. The risk from this mystery is so much lower than the usual accident hazards as to be insignificant. Were this not so, Lloyd's of London would long ago have been offering odds on it.

Supramarine
Time Anomalies

Could it be that excessive disappearances in these areas are only apparent compared to the rest of the surface of the hydrosphere, simply because there is more transit there? As I said before, we will have to do a complete survey of all recorded sinkings, wreckings, and disappearances before we can start to analyze the matter statisically, and even then we would have to conduct an equally wide survey of the possible factors involved.

But what do we have on record that might throw light on the physical constitution of these alleged vortices, which might lead us to conclude that conditions therein are truly anomalous? Do we have any direct observational data?

The most interesting account I have ever read was passed to me by Vincent Gaddis some years ago, and I have obtained its writer's permission to reproduce it here in full. It goes as follows:

Dear Mr. Gaddis,
After just finishing your book *Invisible*

Horizons, and especially the chapter on the Bermuda Triangle, I thought you might be interested in an experience I and a friend had in early April 1952.

I had just completed a 14 month tour of duty in Korea, and my friend, a surgeon, was expected to be called back into the navy. At that time doctors were being called back in. We decided to spend a couple of weeks in Bermuda for relaxation and fun. We left the then Idlewild International Airport in Queens around 7:00 P.M. on a Saturday night, on a BOAC 4-motor prop aircraft. At that time I think the plane carried around 57 passengers but there were only about 10 on this flight. Once we were airborne the captain gave us permission to wander about as we pleased as our weight was so negligible it would not upset the balance of the plane. The flight was routine and although there were storm clouds around, we were flying above them and our trip was very smooth.

We were finally served dinner and had just settled back with a scotch and soda when the huge aircraft suddenly dropped straight down a couple of hundred feet. The nose did not go down; it was as if we had suddenly stopped all forward movement and just dropped straight down. Needless to say, whisky and soda, glasses, magazines, people, and everything loose on the plane went straight up in the air. We were just beginning to comprehend what had happened and were trying to get back in our seats when the plane shot straight up, forcing us down hard in our seats. It was as if a giant hand was holding the plane and jerking it up and down. We finally managed to strap ourselves in and sat with eyes glued, watching the giant wings as they vibrated up and down. The wing tips were fluctuating as much as 20 feet and the whole plane was groaning under the strain of what seemed to be two forces, one pulling up and the other pulling down. My companion and I were terrified as we had both travelled a lot before, but neither one of us had ever experienced turbulence such as this. The up and down movement continued for about half an hour, gradually decreasing.

Meanwhile the captain had come back to reassure his ten frightened passengers that the aircraft would not shake itself to pieces, and also to give us a new worry and a decision! With charts, he explained that we could not find Bermuda, and were unable to make radio contact with either the U.S. or Bermuda.

It was as if the U.S. and Bermuda did not exist. We could turn back now and land in Florida or we could fly past Bermuda, and try to establish contact with a radio ship stationed in the Atlantic out past Bermuda. Assured that we still had enough fuel to make it back to the U.S. and as the turbulence was subsiding, we all decided on the radio ship and to try to approach Bermuda from the Atlantic side. During the next hour the pilot's door was open and we were able to hear the radio operator's efforts to raise Bermuda, the U.S., or the radio ship, with occasional reassurance from the captain that we would make it O.K. Finally, after what seemed hours, a voice loud and clear came over the air. It was the radio ship. We got our bearings, turned back the way we had been coming, and in a very short time had Bermuda on the radio.

Needless to say, the lights of the island were a welcome sight and we all breathed a sigh of relief as the big craft touched ground and rolled to a halt. What surprised us more was the fact that the sky was clear and starry with just a little ground fog around the airport. No storms or reasonable explanation for the radio blackout.

Although this happened over 10 years ago I am still wondering if we were a few of the lucky ones who were caught in the Bermuda Triangle, *where time and space seem to disappear,* but successfully made it through. I have often thought we could have been just another missing flight, down somewhere between N.Y. and Bermuda, on the books as another mysterious disappearance.

My companion on the trip was Dr. S. M. M., now a surgeon in New York City.

> Very truly yours,
> *Gerald C. Hawkes*

All very puzzling but, you may well say, what has all this got to do with suboceanic civilization and vile vortices? Just this. Whatever goes wrong with space and things in it, in these vortices, something definitely goes haywire with time as we see it. Mr. Hawkes' letter only hints at this as a sort of aside, and unfortunately no check was made of the possibility of a contraction or extension of time during that hair-raising flight. This is not the case with the next two reports. Herein, *time* was the basic anomaly, and it was on a chronometric basis that the anomalies were spotted, though the reporters, both being experienced aviators, rather naturally plunked for winds. This business is so exceedingly interesting, at least with respect to the disappearance of planes, if not to the disposition of vortices, that I give the reports in full together with an analysis of them by a high-ranking airline pilot.

Dear Sir,

Re: your "Bermuda Triangle" article in *Argosy,* I have an item of information which might be interesting.

In the fall or winter of 1955, I was a navigator on B-26's in Korea. We were returning from a training mission, heading close to due south, and I found that we had a ground speed of about 550 knots. This would have meant a wind of 265 knots. We were at 7,000 feet. Both the pilot and I laughed at this, but I rechecked it at the next two check points, and the results were close to the same. We made our home base and forgot about it.

I afterward became quadruple rated (pilot, navigator, bombardier, radar observer), and got a little more experience. I admit the possibility of some error in this wind computation, but not too much. And in several years of flying thereafter I have never heard of, nor experienced, anything like it. As a rule, the jet stream does not dip so low. And if it did, the velocity of 265 Kn. would be unusual. I have no explanation for this phenomenon. Korea *does parallel* the NW-SE line linking your two mystery areas.

The action of wind shear has become known to pilots in the last 15 years. This applies mostly to vertical wind movements. I leave it to your imagination then: what would happen to an aircraft moving at an airspeed of 250 *into* a wind of 265. (I can see not only a negative ground speed, but a sudden stall if the wind quit with no notice.)

Sincerely,
J. F. O'D.

COMMENT BY CAPT. DURANT

If the reported incident had occurred recently it would be valuable to obtain the aircraft's navigation log and the fixing data used by the navigator. It is doubtful that these records are available, or that Mr. O'D.'s memory is that good at this late date, so we must take his word for the extraordinary ground speed achieved by his plane. Unfortunately, this is not a detail but the central question, for if he did in fact encounter a 265 knot wind at 7,000 feet the meteorology texts must be rewritten and we might have a new insight on many cases of lost aircraft.

On rare occasions the "jet stream" dips as low as 20,000 feet, and on equally rare occasions it reaches a speed of 300 knots. A speed of 175 knots at 35,000 is typical. The direction of flow is easterly with some north-south wave motion. The stream normally flows over latitudes including Korea. In other words, a 265 knot wind at 7,000 feet in a southerly direction is not only unheard of, so far as I can determine, but nearly impossible according to meteorologists. [That's all I need to know that Mr. O'D. must be telling the truth!] The aircraft must have been in a body of air moving at 265 knots *rather than* reacting to a selective force one might imagine pushing or pulling the aircraft. That is, the B-26 was operating naturally; the air mass enveloping the B-26 was unusual. This is an important distinction. If the aircraft had been pushed by a "force field" the airspeed indicator would immediately show an increasing speed. Apparently the B-26 was indicating 285 knots which is close to the maximum for that model. Even a slight increase would have alarmed the pilot. Mr. O'D. makes no mention of such an increase. Let me repeat that a 265 knot wind at 7,000 feet would raise hell at ground level, even assuming the maximum recorded diminution of wind speeds from jet stream cores and the effect of surface friction.

Let's find out the following from Mr. O'D.:
1. A map showing the entire flight path of the B-26, noting checkpoints and the segment where the unusual groundspeed was observed.
2. Total elapsed time of the high groundspeed leg.
3. Fixing data used (ADF, Loran, celestial?).

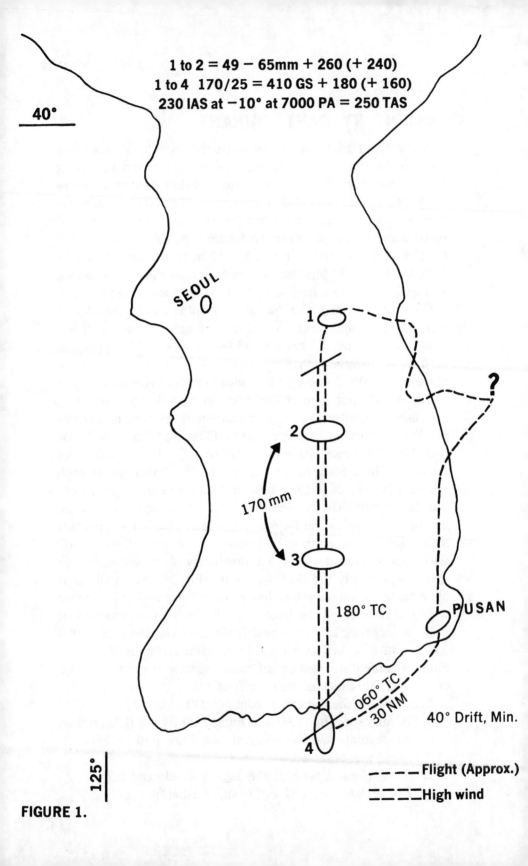

FIGURE 1.

4. Did he at any time record an unusual drift, turbulence, variation in indicated airspeed, variation in air temperature, or unusual altimetry readings?

5. General weather conditions during the entire flight, and ground weather reports.

6. *Any* additional "odd" things that may have occurred on the flight.

Hope this is some help.

Sincerely,
R. J. Durant

REPLY FROM MR. O'D.

I'll answer your questions in order, as best I can. I might mention, though, that from the questions, I know you have an advisor who knows what he is talking about.

1. Rough map enclosed. [See Fig. 1.] I can't do any better unless I go over to MacDill A.F.B. and get a flight map. And that may be not much of an improvement.

2. The southbound leg *should* have taken about 40 minutes with an IAS of about 230 K, 7000 ft., temp. about $-10°$ C, distance approx. 170 naut. miles (I don't have an E6B, so I'm approximating). There was a predicted tail wind of about 20-30 K. I got a fix at point 1 on the map, and also point 2. The ground speed showed up as about 490 K, but as it was only 6 or 8 minutes, I assumed an error. I got a G.S. between 1 & 3 and it was about the same. I got a G.S. between 1 & 4 and 2 & 4 and they all pointed to a wind of about 225-240 K. We made the leg about 15 minutes fast.

3. Fixes were visual on my part. ADF was available to the pilot, but not used, except for the final turn.

4. No unusual drift. Wind was from astern. No unusual turbulence. (Did have IAS meter, plus temp. & alt.) Don't remember anything unusual. (Must mention that another pilot had flown the B-26 at take-off power and indicated about 425 K)—Don't believe that could be the case here.

5. Weather—was during the winter months. High pressure,

cold and clear. Only ground wx. reports were from our base, K-9—clear.

6. No other odd things, to my knowledge.

I was the group navigator at the time, and daily briefed 3 squadrons on navigational routes. I knew the area extremely well, and allowed for errors. However, it does seem as if a freak wind did come down to low altitudes at this time. Our eastbound leg was too short to show it, and also we were descending for landing.

Sincerely,
J. F. O'D.

COMMENT BY CAPT. DURANT

The additional information in Mr. O'D.'s letter of December 16, 1968 leads me to believe that his report is credible and deserves SITU's continued attention. Only a ground radar plot confirming the visual navigation would finally establish the veracity of this report. However, O'D.'s background and the type of fixes taken [visual] are both reassuring.

I conclude that the aircraft was caught for 25 minutes in a truly anomalous body of air. The B-26 turned to a southerly heading, accelerated to a very high groundspeed, then turned 120° away from the high-speed flight path. Except for the groundspeed all other flight conditions and parameters remained normal. It is this lack of side effects (which we must believe if we are to believe any of the report) that makes the case so unusual and bizarre. The wind was forecast to be 20-30 knots but the aircraft reacted to an equivalent of *a wind ten times as great*. As per my last analysis, not only the weather stations but the whole world would have quickly known of such a wind. Nevertheless, let's assume such a wind existed and that it had an extremely small diameter, on the order of several miles laterally. This is a valid assumption because no unusual wind velocities were reported on the ground 1.3 miles below the B-26, and there was no drift to speak of when the plane was flying at right angles to the wind. I have drawn the diagram below to illustrate this hypothetical situation.

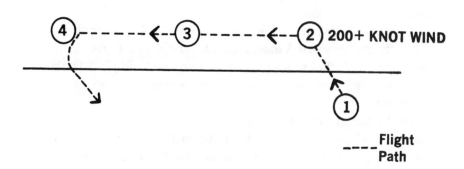

FIGURE 2.

(1) Indicated airspeed 230 knots, pressure altitude 7000 feet, outside air temperature $-10°$ C, true airspeed 250 knots, no turbulence. Navigator in visual contact with ground.

(2) Aircraft enters "wind." Extreme turbulence, extreme indicated airspeed fluctuations, possible control loss in turn.

(3) IAS stabilized to 230 knots, if power setting remained same. Mild turbulence, possibly smooth, no drift, GS 450 plus.

(4) Same as (2). Both (2) and (4) would give an initial drift angle of close to 45°.

In sum: a wind *flow* extending along the 170-mile southerly flight path is completely ruled out. A very strange picture emerges from all this. It seems the B-26 was enveloped by a small mass of air as it turned south. The envelope accelerated smoothly to about 240 knots within six minutes, then slowed to about 160 knots for the last leg of the speed run (points 3 to 4 on O'D.'s map). In the last few minutes it slowed to well below 100 knots, allowing the plane to turn away into the normal surrounding atmosphere. I know how absurd this sounds, but it is the best "explanation"—the only explanation which fits the reported facts.

Sincerely,
R. J. Durant

The second report was as follows:

Dear Mr. Sanderson,

I read your article in the August issue of *Argosy* with great interest, and recalled Vincent Gaddis' 1964 piece. As far as I am concerned, this subject which you are exploring has far better scientific credentials than flying saucers or abominable snowmen.

In the Spring of 1966 I was a basic navigator aboard an Air Guard C-97 aircraft flying from Kwajalein Island to Guam. My duty position at the time was that of Air Force Advisor to 106th Air Transport Group, N.Y. Air Guard, based at NASNY (Floyd Bennett). Air Guard had difficulty at the time manning a Pacific mission because of time limitations, and advisors filled in crew slots. Regular AF navigators aren't necessarily better than Guard navigators, but they do tend to know when they goof because they get more practice goofing. Anyway:

Kwajalein weather gave me a pleasant forecast, no significant weather, winds at our level approximately 040/10-12 knots. Terminal weather at Anderson on Guam was standard, and we all looked forward to a pleasant night flight of approximately 6 to 6+30 hours. When the tropics are nice, they're nice. Period. We climbed out to about 12,000', leveled off, and settled down for the flight. There are several atolls 45 minutes to an hour west of Kwajalein that can usually be picked up nicely on radar, Eniwetok is about 50 miles off course to the north, and these provide nice position fixing, visual or radar, about an hour out. I logged such a fix, saw that the weather briefing was about right, pointed the aircraft toward Anderson for another hour, and relaxed. Second hour out, since the weather was so good, I decided to use a Celestial Fix for a position. Loran is good for the last three hours into Guam, dubious for the first three out of Kwajalein because of distance from the station. So, for my second hourly position, I shot what developed on the chart as a perfect three-star fix. It was a true pinpoint. It left no doubt as to where the aircraft had been at that point in time. I logged it all and blessed our forecasters.

Third hour out, with a tremendous feeling of security in my own ability, and confidence in our meteorologists, I shot a second celestial fix. Weather was excellent: high, broken overcast, no turbulence, wonderful results. Another pinpoint fix. Only problem was (and I almost fell out of the airplane when I put this on the chart), this last fix was about 340 nautical miles down intended course. A C-97 at that altitude works at a true air speed of about 220 knots. With the pertinent information stuck on a computer I came up with a wind of approximately 110 knots from 070. I rechecked and re-rechecked. There was no error. It is, as you know, a very serious thing in the business when ground speed changes for inexplicable reasons by a full third. Such an unknown could shatter overocean airline flying, for instance.

Fourth hour out, you can imagine that a really interested navigator was taking positions. I was using good Loran and shooting celestial. Groundspeed was down to about 230 from the previous fix. Some slight left drift. No problems. Except for the fact that, in ostensibly good weather, a plugging old '97 had, in fact, covered 340 nautical miles in one hour of time for no apparent reason.

I debriefed weather on Guam with a young 2nd Lt. and was kind of ashamed to press this. I asked him if anybody had reported any really big winds that night, and he said no; and looked at me as if to say "You old duffer, what are you doing flying anyway?" There had been no aircraft over that track at any level for quite a few hours. But off behind the swinging doors in the section was a very fine Major type who was then CO of the Anderson weather outfit. He knew the Pacific Ocean. I mentioned my problem to him and got certain straight, if not definitive, answers. He was aware of such inexplicable phenomena. It always occurred at night. The incidence was not even monthly, but perhaps 8–10 times yearly. The phenomenon lasted not more than two hours.

After putting together what this weather officer told me, my own experience on this particular flight, Gaddis's article, and your own, may I wish you the best of luck in pursuit of uncovering a mystery of major importance in many fields.

Very truly yours,
Frank P. Hopkins
Lt/Col, USAF (Ret.)

COMMENT BY CAPT. DURANT

Once again we have a report of unforecast, inexplicable, etc. winds, made by a very experienced navigator. The type of fixing used in both the O'D. report and this one is very accurate and reliable. Jet stream is ruled out by low altitude and wrong direction.

Am including for your files a portion of a navigation chart showing the Hopkins flight. [See Fig. 3.] The chart shows the

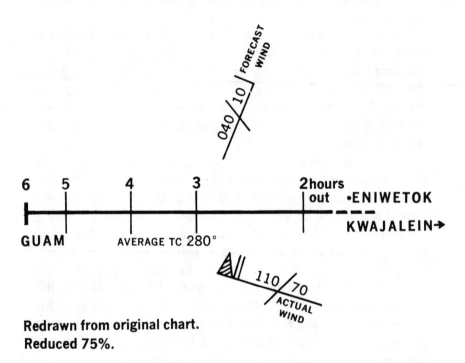

Redrawn from original chart.
Reduced 75%.

FIGURE 3.

flight path from a point 50 miles south of Eniwetok to Guam. I have marked the approximate positions of the aircraft at intervals of 2, 3, 4, 5, and 6 hours out of Kwajalein. . . . When a navigator computes a wind he divides the distance between 2 fixes by the elapsed time. Consequently, the computed wind value represents an *average* between the fixes. Hopkins found himself moving in accordance with forecast winds at both the 2-hour and the 4-hour checkpoints, so it is probable that the wind was normal for at least a small distance at the beginning and end of the high-speed zone. If this was the case, the actual wind in the middle of zone 2-3 would be much greater than 110 knots. For instance, let's suppose the winds were normal 50 miles beyond the 2-hour point and 50 miles before the 3-hour point. [See Fig. 4.] In the illustration—which in no way con-

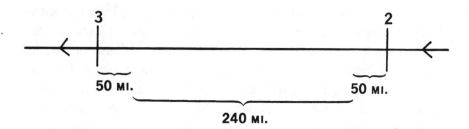

3   **2**

50 MI.   **50 MI.**

240 MI.

FIGURE 4.

flicts with the reported data or common sense—the average wind in the central 240 mile portion would be 190 knots. This line of reasoning could, of course, be extended to an absurd point, but my specific example probably shows most accurately what happened to Col. Hopkins. A 200 knot "wind" out of no-where, *gently* moving a four-engined aircraft, diminishing to the normal forecast wind. Where is the turbulence and drift?? Something very weird going on here.

Sincerely,

R. J. Durant

The feature of these reports that is not at first apparent to us ordinary mortals was pointed out to us by a physicist who hap-pened to have spent his young life in the Air Force; and it is just this hang-up on the part of the fliers with the wind factor. This scientist stated that he, frankly, did not believe this any more than Capt. Durant appeared to do. If such extraordinary winds of such velocities suddenly appeared at those low levels within such limited areas, and one of them over a populated land mass, there would have been an outcry below and, as Durant points out in the Korean case, the whole world would have heard about it. Moreover, no such winds in such confined areas are on record anyway, while both were running quite contrary to the jet stream in that they must have been blowing from north to south instead of west to east.

Both cases record an anomaly of space—and I do not mean just air space—and, moreover, a complex one as between the lower atmosphere and the land surface below. These anomalies appear to have occurred, yet observations on them both from the air and the ground seemed to imply that these were impossible. You can't have it both ways. Either the observations were valid or they were not; either something went amiss in the comparatively confined space traversed by the planes, or it did not. The alternative is that the planes ran into a local *time* anomaly, rather than into incredible, undetected and seemingly impossible winds. To put it simply, the planes "appeared" to get to their destination much faster than they should have done according to their maximum speed abilities, and by their actual speeds as clocked by their instrumentation and with reference to ground points, yet the only *known* possible cause would be excessively high-velocity winds. No such winds were recorded; and if they had occurred they would most certainly have been detected, as they would have had a devastating effect on the ground.

If, on the other hand, the planes slipped into areas wherein time ran slower the planes would have comparatively longer to get farther and thus come in early. If they ran into a faster time slot they would be late on arrival. In the latter case, however, the delay would naturally and undoubtedly be attributed to head winds. Tail winds can account for extra speed of travel, but when that excess speed is of the order reported in these cases, ground meteorological stations just cannot miss them.

PART II

The Disposition
of Anomalies

We have spent a perhaps inordinate amount of time discussing the things that called attention to these "Vile Vortices" in order to demonstrate the extent and character of the phenomenon. I think the time has now come for some detailed analysis of and comment upon this business as a whole; and from this we may proceed to some speculation.

The popular idea has been that there is one roughly triangular area with sides running from Bermuda to central Florida and thence to Puerto Rico in which a large number of planes have simply vanished without a trace.

This is a glamorous notion, but on proper analysis, it does not stand up. It is *not* a triangle, and its periphery is much greater than the one outlined above. In fact, the area in which such disappearances, or alleged disappearances, have been recorded forms a large, sort of lozenge-shaped area which is neither centered on the oceanic island of Bermuda nor can in any way be depended from it. We have plotted all the "disappearances"—and please remember that this is something quite different from mere sinkings of ships and submarines, or ditchings of planes—reported from this area and have found that it slops way over the original so-called "triangle." After this discovery, the question naturally arose as to the uniqueness of this funny blob, which extends from about 30° to 40° north latitude, and from about 55° to 85° west. Was it unique?

We knew already that there was at least one other such area *alleged* to exist. This lies some 250 miles south of the Japanese island of Honshu about longitude 140° east. We therefore started to work, gathering records of ships lost and planes vanishing around this point which, as a matter of fact, had up till then been only mentioned—and rather casually, at that. The outcome was not just amazing; it was positively startling. Plane after plane on its way south to Guam appears to have vanished, and this with disturbing frequency. So we started plotting again, and despite the usually very vague locations given —and no wonder, considering that these ships and planes disappeared without radio signals or any trace—another lozenge-shaped blob came to light.

This startled us a bit, but then one of my colleagues had the brilliant idea of getting out a map of the world! Once we had a map before us, we saw that both lozenges lay precisely between 30° and 40° north and also spread about 30 degrees east to west, latitudinally. This really did spark us, so we made a concerted grab for a globe.

Now the surface of our earth as seen on a globe is really very different from what we look at on a two-dimensional map, and especially one on what is called the Mercator projection. Just where did these two blobs lie relative to each other as one went around the globe? It turned out that they were centered 160 degrees apart (going around one way) and 200 degrees (going the other). In other words, there did not appear to be any noticeable pattern. If they had been at 180 degrees going both ways, they would have been exactly opposite each other on opposite sides of the earth. But then something else cropped up.

We had been inundated with letters asking for more information on the *disappearances* of the Israeli and French submarines at the east and west ends of the Mediterranean, respectively. We were naturally unable to add anything to the news reports and official statements. However, the Mediterranean Sea just happens to form a lozenge-shaped blob, also lying between 30° and 40° north, and just about 30 degrees from left to right, latitudinally.

Naturally, we measured the distance between these three blobs. Then something else rather startling came to light. They were arranged on an apparently strict numerical progression— from the Bermuda bit to the Mediterranean, four; the Mediterranean to the Japanese, five; and the Japanese to the Bermudan, six.

Now, I don't like such neat patterns emerging in anything in nature; it looks far too much as though somebody had got the idea first, and then tried to fit the facts into it. You can fit almost anything into almost anything else if you try hard enough; as any mathematician, statistician, or police officer can tell you. However, Nature is to a great extent fairly orderly and *does* display rather neat patterns.

So we had three "blobs" in a line—and the same line, please note—of something. But just what? At this point I started doing some hard thinking. If there are three such areas between 30° and 40° north latitude, could there be equivalents at 30° and 40° *south* latitude? A subsequent investigation into plane, ship, and sub losses in the southern hemisphere yielded some amazing results.

There turned out to be three exactly similar areas situated below the equator. These lie off the east coasts of South America, South Africa, and Australia. All proved to be precisely within 30° to 40° of latitude south, and also to be about 30 degrees of longitude in width. But *very* strangely, they were all tilted up to the right or east, as were also those in the northern hemisphere! Frankly, this does not seem to make sense, because our planet is a sphere and the southern hemisphere should *mirror* the northern. So we started looking for some physical reason for this clear pattern.

The first thing that emerged was that these vortices in the southern hemisphere were precisely shifted the same number of degrees to the east in all cases. Then one further fact came to light. Of all the possible known physical factors that could cause this pattern—temperature, barometric pressure, and, above all, geomagnetic anomalies—only one fitted, and this was surface ocean currents!

Five of these six areas—the Mediterranean alone being in a different category—lie on the right or east sides of the continents, and all *precisely* in curious areas where hot surface currents stream out of the tropical latitudes toward the colder waters of the temperate, subpolar and eventually polar areas. What is more, the two principal ones in the northern hemisphere, in accordance with the simple behavior of waters on a spinning globe, turn clockwise, while the three in the southern hemisphere turn counterclockwise. There is nothing odd about this; but there is about the fact that said twirls all make their tightest turns precisely in these five locations.

As there is a very good scientific reason for these twirls of hot ocean currents being just where they are, anything strange or mysterious that is common to them should probably be an outcome of their existence. And do not for a moment think that the disappearance of planes, ships, and subs is the *only* odd occurrence reported from these six areas (including the Mediterranean this time). Other oddities include wild reports of all sorts of UAOs therefrom.

That five of these six areas were where hot tropical surface waters jet in comparatively narrow streams into cold-water areas, though, *is* of enormous significance. These are the areas of extreme temperature variabilities which alone would predicate a very high incidence of violent marine and aerial disturbances. What more likely areas for storms and wrecks and founderings, and even magnetic anomalies? Moreover, since all these areas also happen to be near major areas of human population and maritime enterprise, is it small wonder that they would be those wherein the most losses of ships, planes, and subs would be recorded? However, there still remains one really mysterious factor.

Planes, ships, and subs have, as we have stressed, been disappearing all over the world. But it has to be admitted that many more are reported to have done so in these six areas than in any others; and, which is much more important, *the number of disappearances is out of all proportion to such recorded losses anywhere else.* This is the point upon which not only our Navy, but a lot of other navies, maritime commissions, and even Lloyd's of London have become baffled.

When a ship or plane sinks into the sea, *something* almost invariably comes back to the surface. A large liner goes down, and at least one wooden deck chair surfaces; a small plane ditches, and the whole area is immediately covered with an oil slick. But these are ditchings, founderings, sinkings, or just plain wrecks. Disappearances are something quite else. In our six mysterious areas, planes, ships, and subs often just *vanish*.

I would like to state that the disproportionately high number of losses in these six "vile vortices" is due only to the fact that they fall in very rough areas of contrary currents, winds, temperature inversions, and so forth, but I am afraid I cannot do so. Allowing for all of these, we still have to explain this business of disappearances *per se*.

Since we never get any fact as to just what *did* happen in these cases, how can we even start to try to explain them? The Services, and notably the air forces and navies, know perfectly well that there is something "not right" about this, but they haven't any more idea than we have as to what it could be. Thus, the picture is wide open to suggestions, and most unfortunately and particularly from those who have none of the known facts.

The most vociferous are the UFO buffs who have suggested that these "vortices" are sorts of holes where gravity, earth magnetism, and perhaps other natural features are weaker or otherwise different from those elsewhere around the surface of our planet. They have then proceeded from this assumption to the speculation that extraterrestrial intelligencies may know of these anomalies and have picked these vortices through which to descend upon us and collect specimens of us and our machines; or through which to take off from our planet. A lot of UFOs have been reported from the skies over this area by utterly reliable flyers, both military and commercial. Second, even the most pompous "ufologist" still has a sneaking idea that flying saucers are machines and must therefore be made by very clever chaps who live elsewhere in the universe and come here for one purpose or another. On this account, UFO buffs immediately claimed that this Bermuda Triangle was some kind of special place that the "space people" had picked out to use as a sort of collecting ground. Actually, I have a strong feeling that this is nothing more than an old wives' tale.

And so this matter of the vortices rested as of the middle of August, 1968—at least from our point of view. But I, personally, was far from satisfied; and on half a dozen different scores. As the old adage has it: there was definitely "a screw loose somewhere," and this bugged me. Then, as so often happens, the spark came from a completely unexpected and previously unknown source. In this case, it was in the form of a very simple and straightforward letter from a young lady in the Southwest who made it quite clear that she had no scientific training but had brothers in the Navy and Air Force who had recounted to her certain experiences that they had had, and certain "stories" they had been told.[236] Being close relatives, they had spoken frankly of these matters to her, and my correspondent had shown them an article I had written on the subject. Then she lobbed me the shell!

In substance, this was that her brothers seemed to feel that there were two more "lozenges," or vortices, in the North and South Pacific Ocean respectively and that they appeared also to be shifted to the right in the southern hemisphere. In reply I asked her if she could pinpoint these or even give me some indication of their general localities. Her reply, in turn, was almost as vague as my request, but one point gave us a great jolt. This was that the area in the North Pacific lay just about where one of the most extraordinary things I have ever heard of in my life was found.

This is a little difficult to explain because, as I have found to my ire, the use of the simplest terms, which I had always considered to be the best, gives a completely false impression of the facts. The phenomena herewith reported are, simply stated, "depressions in the ocean"; but the average person naturally assumes that one means extra-deep places below which the hard surface of the earth either bows down or reaches less far from the center of the earth than the surrounding ocean bottom. This is not the case at all. Nor does it mean that these areas are gravitic anomalies in which, to oversimplify, things weigh more and thus sink lower into the surface of the water. Such areas are known. This is quite different in that the *surface* of the water—which, according to all textbooks, should "find its own level"—bows down somewhat over a large bowl-shaped area. There is even a story, which I have been trying for four years to have confirmed or disproved, that some old freighters sold to Japanese scrapyards had failed to make the grade *up* the slope out of one of these patches and had had to be helped out by ocean-going tugs. (This may be apocryphal, but if there are such "depressions" some poor old vessel just about able to make five knots in a calm sea might well find even a few feet rise an insurmountable obstacle, even to its most obstinate efforts.)

As a result of this curious coincidence—and I can call it no less—I put out a call to all my friends who are practicing oceanologists and oceanographers, geophysicists or geomorphologists, and any spare mathematicians and geographers who could join us.* We were, shortly after, "nearly a score attending," as they used so delightfully to put it. And then things began to pop.

* The Society for the Investigation of the Unexplained, Columbia, N.J.

First of all we cleared the decks. Then we obtained a dozen globes—two showing national boundaries, and two, physical features of the earth. The rest were simply plain outlines of the borders between land and water surface of the earth. We then plotted the positions of the initial six lozenges, or vortices, that we had found; and then we put in (on one globe) the two alleged in the Pacific. Next, the mathematicians took over with their slide rules and tridimensional trigonometry. This was fun to watch, and it lasted for four days; but, at the end, they had all agreed with both the geographers and the geomorphologists upon one thing; and we of the straight geological and biological contingent were quite satisfied with what they had to offer. (But, I am sorry to say the geophysicists were *not*!) And what did they come up with? Simply this.

They averred that there would appear to be *ten* lozenges, or vortices, ringing our earth in two belts, one in the northern, and the other in the southern hemisphere. These are approximately, if not precisely, centered 72 degrees apart, and those in the southern hemisphere are all shifted to the east (or right) by exactly the same distance—to wit, about 40 degrees. All but two lie over water, but there is no evidence for one in the southern Indian Ocean; probably because no ships or planes ever pass through or over it. The two that are not wholly over water are the Mediterranean and the upper (northern) reaches of the Arabian Sea and the Persian Gulf. But as a clincher, it was demonstrated to us that the nine (plus the hypothetical tenth in the southern Indian Ocean) all lay on the western (or to the left) bulges in the northern hemisphere, and to the eastern (or to the right) bulges in the southern hemisphere of a set of five perfect sinusoidal or S curves.

The significance of this may be lost on most of us ordinary and non-mathematically orientated folk, so I asked our chief geometer, who is also a specialist electronics engineer, to tell me how to put it. His reply was very clear and, to me at least, simple; namely, that there would appear to be ten funny places on the surface of our planet which lie opposite each other in a particular manner. Seeking further clarification, he sought permission to demolish one of our plain globes, and forthwith did so by inserting five long skewers through said globe, entering as near the center of one lozenge as could be determined and coming out very near the middle of another one on the other side of the earth and in the other hemisphere. Then he carefully sliced the globe in half and, without materially disturbing the skewers, demonstrated that all five of them were battling to pass through *the exact center* of the earth.

This may mean nothing in that the disposition of these points was initially defined trigonometrically, so that the five axes should be just as they were found to be on opening the globe. However, the position of the lozenges was initially suggested quite empirically from mere lists of disappearances. These records, moreover, were statistically insufficient, often lacking complete data, and were actually almost entirely random. So is it not rather odd that, working with such paltry and almost hypothetical data, a result so geometrically precise as this should be obtained?

There are various known anomalies of our earth's surface, such as the gravitic, magnetic, etc., but one of the most interesting studies of such items is that of Rouse and Bisque.[237] This theory was first released in 1968, just about the time we were endeavoring to grapple with our vortices, and we at first thought that this might give us a logical answer; and it just might do so, but for a few discrepancies.

The basis of this theory is simply that Rouse, working on the origin of deep seismic or earthquake impulses, noticed that they all appeared to hit the surface at a certain angle. Applying this worldwide, he suggested that they stemmed from a certain layer within the earth's near surface, and he went on to plot these epicentral areas. His works should be read in the original, but it may be said in simple terms that he presented evidence of the existence of a sort of continuous trough or low point in the surface of the core of the earth, and swinging up and about and around it. Between the loops of this low trough, the core must naturally form comparative domes or "high points." All of this was founded on a detailed statistical analysis of earthquakes, but, as the authors stated later, just about everything else of a geological, geomorphological, and other nature, when compared with their findings, seemed to fit in a most remarkable manner. This went for nodal points of seismic and volcanic activity, the distribution of heavy mineral deposits, and much else. In fact, this exposition has been hailed as a truly unifying theory for much of the earth sciences.

At first we were extremely taken with Rouse's map because it showed five lozenge-shaped areas circling the waist of the globe, and another large, more diffuse one in the southern hemisphere. What is more, these five all lay more or less on, or very near, five of our major areas of anomaly—i.e., that in the southeast Pacific, the Bermuda "Triangle," the Mediterranean, the Persian Gulf-Pakistan area, and that east of Australia. However, the second most significant vortex—that south of Japan—is not so covered, and the other most vital one, off the east coast of South America, is also in limbo. Therefore, if the vortices and their distribution have any validity they, once again, cannot be correlated with the distribution of other known anomalies. It is manifest that we are dealing here with a set of factors that are not, or have not as yet been, correlated with any other physical features of our earth. But . . .

11 · SOME MORE FACTS
Whirligigs and Vortices

As noted in the preceding chapter, we thought that we might be on the track of a possibly realistic and pragmatic explanation of the Vile Vortices and thus of supra- and sub-marine disappearances. This was at the end of our conference which I described above. Our hopes were further greatly bolstered by the outcome of another conference, held under official auspices, in New York and which was attended by some engineers, geophysicists, and two extremely prominent theoretical physicists, one a household name. This was to listen to an exposition of a rather revolutionary paper then recently published by a geophysicist who had done his research under the terms of a grant from the Office of Naval Research.[238] Being unaware of the modest endeavors of our Society, this scientist—Dr. John Carstoiu—had listed one of our publications in his bibliography, and thereby caused a near (official) "riot" that had taken quite an effort at very high levels to quiet! The trouble was that the item listed was a purely popular article by this writer in the magazine *Argosy*.[239]

The substance of the paper under discussion was a detailed mathematical exposition of a theory that there is a *second* gravitic force, which its author permitted us nonspecialists to refer to simply as Gravity II. This postulates certain effects on the surface of our earth and notably under, on, and over certain maritime areas, that are now readily detectable by our present techniques for the exploration of the phyiscal behavior of our planet. Our article happened to be brought to this scientist's attention, and he noticed the possibility of a correlation between our findings, stemming from a crude analysis of mere records, and his, which had been developed on a purely mathematical basis. As his paper states (and he wrote this before we met), "This could explain a number of anomalies and oddities that have been recorded, such as those in (11) below." [240]

I would not dare attempt to explain this theory, even if I could do so in terms that you and I could understand. Further, the author had not considered so applying his theory until this meeting was called, and he has not yet developed it for general dissemination. All I can say with safety is that, should his theory prove out and be applicable, as his formulae suggest, there would be very valid reasons for the disposition of the vortices and some possible explanations of some of the seemingly incomprehensible events that have been reported to have happened in them. What is more, such a conclusion was reached at this meeting.

No sooner had this encouraging possibility surfaced than two other papers were published that still further encouraged us. The first was by Dr. Joseph Weber of the University of Maryland offering evidence for the existence of a gravitational—in this case ordinary gravity, or Gravity I, of the Newtonian type —field acting in a manner equivalent to (but not, of course, on the same spectrum as) electromagnetism.[241] Just such as this had been suspected for some time and searched for diligently. One of its significances, to us at least, was that it greatly enhanced Dr. Carstoiu's theoretical exposition of Gravity II.

The reasons Dr. Carstoiu gave us for having made the statement in his footnote as stated on the previous page are almost impossible to put into our layman's language, and I will therefore not attempt to do so. Nonetheless, it boils down to a contention by that scientist that there could be good reasons for some form of gravitic anomaly being disposed around the earth in just such a pattern as we had postulated from a mere analysis of what records we had of these "disappearances." This will sound awfully abstruse, I know, and I apologize for it, but in matters of this nature it is better to be noncommittal rather than attempt an oversimplification. Let the statement therefore stand. The proof, for any who desire to peruse the matter further, is published in his paper referred to above.

The other paper was not quite so spectacular, but was just as signficant to us.[242] In this the authors described the simple mechanical effect upon a circular dish of mercury when a naked flame, or other concentrated heat source, was slowly revolved around underneath it. The mercury in time began, and then continued, to revolve in a *contrary* direction. At first, the average mechanically minded person or any with even a smattering of training in thermodynamics says something like "Well, of course" and goes into a near diatribe. However, the curious thing in this case, as pointed out by Messrs. Schubert and Whitehead, is that the mercury gathers speed until it is circulating way ahead of the flame, which is not, according to our current view of things mechanical, so bloody obvious. This seemingly simple observation has two quite different and very far-reaching implications.

The first is not related to the matter at hand but rather to a most odd and esoteric one. This is the extraordinary descriptions of the motive power employed or used by alleged flying machines in India thousands of years ago. Be these nothing but myths or legends, it would still seem to be odd that more than one of them states that the "engine" was composed of a container of mercury with a naked flame below. (See Appendix B, p. 221.) What a funny thing for an ancient Indian scribe to think up! Why mercury; and why the emphasis on a naked flame, or "ordinary fire," as they put it? But all this must be read in context; though it would not at first reading seem to have much, if anything, to do with UAOs, except that it might point to a general physical property that has not yet been investigated either from the point of view of manufacturing mechanics or been applied in a much larger sense to geomechanics.

The second thought that this demonstration brings to mind is a geophysical one. Might other materials react in a similar manner to the mercury if heated from below by a circulating body at a higher temperature? And what happens if the heat is applied from above? Might this have anything to do with the age-old question as to where hurricanes get their power (energy) from? For, be it noted, these monsters spin in a contrary manner to the ocean whirligigs, and in both hemispheres. What is more, they are also overcoming what is called the Coriolis effect—i.e., the tendency for everything to be pushed to the north and right (as seen on maps—i.e., east) in the northern hemisphere and to the south and right in the southern. Does it not strike you as rather odd, to say the least, that a body of air that starts revolving over an ocean should gather speed in a contrary direction to that of the aqueous spin?

What, then, of vast bodies of water at one temperature jetting into either still water at another temperature (colder or hotter), or already circulating? Does the top layer start going around the same way as the layer below, or does it behave like the mercury and start going the other way? It would seem that the cold waters from the polar regions that jet into our vortices go around the same ways as the layer below and in accord with the push of the Coriolis effect; but contrary currents have now been found at greater depths. What are the physical—mechanical, electromagnetic, and/or gravitational—results of, on the one hand, a combination of the lower atmosphere and the surface of the hydrosphere going around together and, on the other hand, of the former going one way and the latter in a contrary way? Then, there is the further matter of straight earth magnetism that has to be taken into account.

At this point, I am quite frankly going to turn you over to

the experts and refer you to their most recent publications.[243] The disposition of magnetic anomalies and of their movements are still being plotted, and in great detail, and what is emerging is unexpected to say the least. The same may be said for gravitic—i.e., Gravity I, or normal gravity—anomalies; but the distribution of these, as so far plotted, does not coincide with the disposition of the vortices. The purely mechanical whirligigs in the surface layers of the oceans, on the other hand, do seem to do so. What we would like to know is whether these vast "machines" generate still another kind of anomaly that might cause something to "go wrong" (from our point of view) in our space-time continuum. In other words, could they create just what we are talking about—i.e., "vortices"—into and out of which material objects can drop into or out of other space-time continua?

This has been the thought of the UFO buffs for some years now, and it is a perfectly splendid idea. Should there be proof of it from strictly pragmatic and scientific angles, one might even say that at last we are getting somewhere; but I am afraid that there are still other aspects of this concept that have to be taken into consideration. These again are twofold.

First, there is as of now totally insufficient evidence even for the existence of these vortices, per se. If they are arranged absolutely precisely and on a trigonometrical basis around the globe, not only longitudinally but also latitudinally, two of them fall almost wholly over land—namely, one over Morocco and Algeria in northwest Africa, and the other in northern Pakistan and Afghanistan! It has been suggested that the five in the northern hemisphere might lie on some kind of undulatory curve of their own, but this does not help much. Trying to fit anything to a preconceived theory is exceedingly dangerous. Then again, we have no actual proof that any such vortices occur in the southeast Pacific and in the southeast Indian Ocean—and for the very simple reason that hardly anybody ever goes there, and there are no records. The obverse of these observations is rather naturally to ask if—ignoring the south Pacific and south Indian Ocean ones—anomalies such as are reported from the remaining three in the northern and the southern hemispheres, occur in the other two which would appear to lie over land. This is a tricky question because we don't know the true extent of those vortices that have allegedly been defined, nor exactly what their conformation is, or where their exact centers are. What is more, maybe those centers drift. Thus the northwest African one could extend well out into the Atlantic on the one side and into the western Mediterranean on the other. Likewise the Pakistani one could slop over into the Persian Gulf and Arabian Sea. Should this be the case, and be due merely to a necessary enlargement of all these areas, we would end up with the whole earth being covered with "anomalies" contiguous and even maybe blending but more concentrated at ten points.

Let us contemplate further whether these may be time anomalies and whether this factor might not be variable or intermittent in any one area, or wander about spatially. Perhaps this factor might vary in intensity in accordance with any or many of a whole host of other variables like the sunspot cycle. Such cyclical variability calls for a statistical analysis of a lot more cases than are on record and of a large number of factors connected with each. In fact, the whole thing is so appallingly complex that we find ourselves more or less back where we started; which is to say, with nothing much more to go on than a couple of hundred reports, and a lot of speculation. Nevertheless, there are indications that our planet is constructed upon, and does function in, a considerably orderly way and in conformity with known physical principles for gross bodies. Perhaps there will, one day, be a general field theory correlating and integrating gravities, geomagnetism, oreogenesis (mountain building), continental drift, the distribution of heavy minerals, various meteorological and hydrological (oceanographic) phenomena, volcanicity, seismological events, and even our vile vortices.

If they are time anomalies, there is frankly nothing we can

do about this, as nobody really has any idea what is meant by this term apart from a mathematical factor. We constantly say that time passes, and we have always thought that this was so obvious as to be a platitude, but even this has now been questioned. Does it pass us, or do we pass it? Does it pass (whichever way you look at it) from what we call the past to the future—the so-called "present," of course, not being able to exist by this theory since the instant anything happens it is past? Then again there is currently considerable speculation as to whether there may not be a sort of counter-time that flows from our future to our past, and there has been speculation as to whether things ranging all the way from galaxies, suns, planets, and all that is on them might not therefore start off in old age and at its limit which is what we call death, and spend *their* allotted span getting younger until they vanish back into The Whole by a process of getting unborn! I would advise some study of Buddhist philosophy before deriding this unnerving notion. Then again, we have to contemplate there being an infinity of "times" running every which way at multidimensional angles. For this one, try the good Professor Einstein. Then, of course, time may not exist at all.

Nevertheless, these disappearances did occur, and those of us who have puzzled over the matter have had to admit that we are completely stymied. However, I have had a lingering suspicion for some time that we may have been looking at the whole thing back-end-befront, as it were. I don't like theories, but I indulge speculation freely, as I think it is quite legitimate and may lead to reappraisals of things, which in turn may lead to solid theories being put forward by specialists who know all the factors involved. Nonetheless, I make so bold as to put forward an idea, and will endeavor to give my reasons for so doing.

Let us imagine for a moment that these vortices are not themselves grim molochs that suck people, planes, ships, and subs into their space-time vacua, on their own time and at their own whim; but that they have a latent potential for so doing, given certain stimuli or a certain combination of factors. Might it not then be that something(s) on said planes, ships, and subs does/ do the triggering and that once "fired" said perfectly natural forces perform just as do any other natural phenomena like tornadoes, hurricanes, earthquakes, *et alia,* once they get going? Be it a time-warp or some electromagnetic or gravitic anomaly, it might perform upon perfectly natural principles that we do not yet know about or which, like this Gravity II, we are only just becoming cognizant of.

The first obvious question that any thinking person will ask is, What triggering, and by what, and how could it be a potential of subs, planes, and modern mechanical ships as well as old-time sailing vessels? More so, why the selectivity, in that sometimes only *people* go, while the ships remain and other animals aboard are also not whisked away? This is going to be rather sticky, so I would suggest that those of you who are not interested in further technical matters just skip ahead to the next chapter. For those who find the incredible new discoveries in the field of electromagnetics of particular interest, please read on and see if what I have to say makes any sense.

The basic fact is that our tiny bit of our universe—that is to say, this planet—runs on electromagnetism. We and all other life forms here are essentially electrical devices, and our planet with its magnetic envelopes is likewise. The whole thing hangs together by what are called in popular jargon "electrical forces," and it functions on a sort of vibratory system. The speed, size, or whatever you want to call it, of these vibrations or pulses or waves may be laid out as a band and calibrated. These "wavelengths" presumably go on beyond, both ways, to infinity, but for our immediate requirements as of today we have taken a spread from the over-all resonance of this planet to that of those protons that come to us from outside. This band we have chopped up into manageable pieces and then studied the products of each bit. These bits encompass those electromagnetic effects that we know about, and more are being found all the time within these.

Now, this is apparently the way this world evolved. This natural order was, one might almost say, created out of cosmic chaos, and then established a natural balance. But then *we* come along and start collecting and propagating electromagnetic energy. What is more, we learned how to divert this energy from one frequency to another, and then started spouting it out, either by "broad"-casting or unidirectionally by beam or line; and each frequency without any regard to all the others being shot out. Result: sundry frequencies sometimes combine or interact and get in what is called phase, so producing quite a different impulse from either of its components. And when this happens, as it is doing with ever-increasing frequency as our technology elaborates and our gross power output burgeons, and throughout the whole electromagnetic band or spectrum, all manner of nasty things happen. And it does not take any great output of power to set off these imbalances. Innocent little electronic devices drawing very little power can throw a vast and enormously power-consuming complex out of phase, and with the direst results.

What I am driving at is this: Let us suppose that the radio contacts of the five Avenger planes were using a "frequency *x*" which just happened to lock into phase with some natural frequency in the area over which they were flying—say a vortex caused by a cold whirlpool of lower air over a hot sea surface, as per the bowls of mercury, and hurricanes—to produce something quite else which happened to be the trigger that set off other natural procedures in that area: what might not happen? I will not speculate on this, because we do not know what if any connection there is between whatever purely mechanical, electromagnetic, and gravitic forces there may be, though as we have noted above, scientists are rapidly working toward a possible unified theory of what they call "fields"—as per Einstein and others who have come after him. All I am trying to say is that the oddities, enigmas, and horrors allegedly noted in the vortices may be entirely natural and indigenous to certain areas of our earth's surface and be perfectly stable therein until *we* come along and upset their balance. In other words, the best way to discover just what the potentialities of these areas is would be to analyze just what we and our devices really *do* do.

This tenative suggestion might be acceptable to the EMI—i.e., electromagnetic interference—experts, but I imagine (and I almost hope) that it will not find favor with any others. Its weakness would at first seem to be its apparent illogicality; namely, what triggered these forces *before* Faraday and the resultant introduction of electromagnetic studies and their practical development and application? More so, what about the animate forms such as human beings and canaries? Can these individually, or in groups, likewise trigger such forces? Let us consider the matter calmly and with the exercise of what logic we can muster.

There would appear to be two alternatives. Either said vanished persons "triggered" their vanishment in some manner similar to electromagnetic gear interfering with other frequencies, or the act was accomplished by so-called "Outside Influences." This is a sort of catch-phrase and is probably an unintentional divarication which is merely being made use of, rather than having been deliberately devised, to get around just such an awkward situation. Moreover, it has sprouted from a most unexpected quarter; namely, that of orthodox scientific research and the most advanced technological enterprise. Let me give you two instances.

When Mariner VII was orbiting Mars before buzzing off sunward, it was guided to make some passes over the poles. On the first pass, however, it suddenly deviated from prescribed course. As reported by those in charge of its flight, there was no detectable malfunction of any of its gadgetry, either before or after this deviation; and when asked what these technologists might consider the cause to have been, they made only this simple statement: "Some outside influence." Then again, a group of scientists headed by a Dr. Gohed have for a year been searching for sealed chambers in the Great Pyramid of Khefren in Egypt by recording cosmic-ray penetration of that great mass of stones to a deep, sublevel chamber. Hearing that all was not well with these experiments, the *Times* of London sent one of its top-notch science reporters to interview Dr. Gohed. His report makes the most astonishing reading, and goes in part:

> More than $1-million and thousands of man-hours have been spent on the project, which was expected to reach a climax a few months ago when the latest IBM 1130 computer was delivered at Ein Shams University computer centre, near Cairo. At Ein Shams, Dr. Amr Gohed, in charge of the installation at the pyramid, showed me the new IBM 1130 machine surrounded by hundreds of tins of recordings from the pyramid, stacked in date order. Though hesitant at first, he eventually told me of the impasse that had been reached. "It defies all the known laws of science and electronics," he said, picking up a tin of recordings. He put the tape through the computer, which traced the pattern of cosmic ray particles on paper. He then selected a recording made the next day and put it through the computer. But the recorded pattern was completely different. "This is scientifically impossible," he told me. Dr. Gohed said that earlier recordings that had raised the hopes of a great discovery were now found to be a jumbled mass of meaningless symbols. After long discussion, I asked Dr. Gohed: "Has all this scientific know-how been rendered useless by some force beyond man's comprehension?" He hesitated before replying, then said: "Either the geometry of the pyramid is in substantial error, which would affect our readings, or there is a mystery which is beyond explanation—call it what you will, occultism, the curse of the Pharoahs, sorcery, or magic—there is some influence that defies the laws of science at work in the pyramid."[244]

My basic question is, "What influence?"

These two alternatives—electromagnetic or other "triggering" and "outside influences"— are actually considerably interwoven, as we shall now see, since we humans may have learned, or may be in the process of learning, how to engineer vanishments. However, no human beings as far as we know had even conceived of such a procedure *prior* to about 1940 A.D., or *later* than about 500 A.D. For this reason, and in view of the large number of said disappearances at sea prior to 1940, we can but presume that those which were not due to normal procedures like piracy were engineered by these Outside Influences. Moreover, said influences almost *must* be intelligent, or at least intelligently controlled. The selectivity as between ships and other constructions and people on the one hand, and between people and other animals on the other, is just too much to be credited to chance, coincidence, or some physically simple happening.

After over forty years of investigating and pondering the unexplaineds in the world of what we call nature, and of reality as we materialists know it, I have seldom run into a truly *inexplicable*. By this I mean an event or series of events for the explanation of which nobody was able to think up at least *some possible*, logical answer; and I do not take into account any such theory or explanation that is based on the mystical, occult, or other as of now intangible aspect—or possible aspect—of existence. Even the seemingly most wildly abstruse and esoteric reports are, almost without exception, at least amenable to some logical and usually perfectly "materialist" explanation; though this does not mean that this is necessarily the right or correct one. At first sight, this business of the selective vanishing of human beings would seem to be inexplicable. But perhaps what we need is simply a complete reorientation of our thinking.

12 · STILL MORE FACTS
Our Hydrosphere

Our hydrosphere is the water envelope that encloses our earth and is represented by the oceans, seas, lakes, rivers, ponds, and—though this is seldom realized—everything between these under the air down to at least a few miles. For instance, we ourselves are four-fifths water and even such dry-looking things as desert sand and granitic rock contain water (H_2O) in combination with the other minerals that constitute their recognizable composition. Let us not forget that this hydrosphere lies between the atmosphere and the lithosphere (i.e., the solid surface) of our planet but that in the form of water vapor it is diffused up into the former as an included item in the air. This is why our earth is sometimes referred to as a "Water Planet," and this is apparently a great rarity, at least in our part of this universe. Water exists in a liquid form only between (within somewhat fine limits) the temperatures that we have designated 0° and 100° Centigrade. Compared to the known range of possible temperatures, from what is called "absolute zero" (minus 273° C.) at which all molecular motion stops so that it is impossible to have anything "colder" —heat being due to such molecular movement—to several million degrees as predicted for the centers of certain stars, this hundred-degree range is so absolutely minute that it is small wonder it is a rarity.

What is more, the fact that life as we know it is entirely water-based and cannot exist (for long anyway) below or above the limits of that tiny range, we may infer that the mean average temperature of our earth has not varied outside this range for *at least* 500 million years.

And here we should define the difference between seas and oceans. They are not the same.

It must be clearly understood that an ocean, such as the North Atlantic, is not just the water area between Europe and Africa on the one hand and North and South America on the other. True, this ocean is contained within that body of water, but an ocean is not just a body of water; it is a very definite geographical entity with most precise limits and a highly complex structure. Complete definition of an ocean would require a large volume, but the salient facts may be summed up as follows:

There are six true oceans—the North Atlantic, the South Atlantic, the Indian, the North and South Pacific (though the division between these two is arbitrary in that you may separate them in any of four different ways according to the over-all criteria you choose to employ), and the Arctic Ocean.

There is a theory that disturbs many geomorphologists. Briefly stated, this is to the effect that the earth is really a sort of vast crystal and is trying to adopt a tetrahedral form—namely, a three-sided pyramid with an apex at the Antarctic and a flat triangular base around the North Pole. This would give us apices at four points, as we actually have in the land masses of northeastern Asia, Europe, North America, and the Antarctic. We should thus get three triangular continents depending south— and we have these in Asia plus Australia, Europe plus Africa, and the Americas; and the three triangular oceans running up between them, which we have in the Indian, Atlantic, and Pacific complexes; and a flat triangular area at the top, filled with the Arctic Ocean or Basin.

The true oceans are great areas of apparently permanent depression that have never been dry land. Their rocky bottoms are said to be covered with the second layer of the earth's surface, known as the *sima* (silicon-magnesium predominating), as opposed to the continents, which are bits of the outermost layer, known as the *sial*, (silicon-aluminum predominating). The continents of sial are said to float on the sima. The continental rafts are at present partially flooded or sunken so that a shelf extends seaward from all of them to a varying degree in all directions toward the oceans. They are notably wide off the southeastern coast of South America and to the east of Australia. These shelves are comparatively shallow—vis-à-vis the true oceans— but they are also clearly defined. Upon them, and upon them alone, are to be found what are called terrigenous deposits, namely, sediments derived from land surfaces and washed into the sea. Beneath the true oceans are only five kinds of silts, formed from meteoric material that descends from the sky, or muds derived from the coverings of tiny single-celled animals that die in the water above or from those of little free-swimming shellfish. The division between terrigenous deposits and these others marks the boundaries of the true oceans. All the rest of the water constitutes seas, which are something quite different. Seas are of two kinds. There are those, like the Caspian Sea, that are entirely separated from the oceans and completely surrounded by land, but there are also others, like the Scotia Sea— that area of water which is surrounded by the tip of South America, the Palmer Peninsula, the South Orkneys, and the South Shetlands—which are almost entirely surrounded by water, but which nonetheless are clearly separated by shallows. These "sea-islands" or "sea-countries" often have very distinctive climates and other environmental features, and they are often populated by most characteristic assemblages of animals.

At this point we should take a look at just what is known about the bottom of the aqueous world. For this we refer you to three maps prepared for and published by the National Geographic Society.[245] Comparing these marvelous maps with the best produced up till a decade ago, one realizes with a considerable jolt just what incredible strides have been made in this field of exploration. Further, quite apart from the now somewhat precise and detailed depiction of the terragraphy—i.e., surface conformation of the bottom of the hydrosphere as well as that of the lithosphere under the atmosphere—this new mapping shows up just how the continental rafts may have drifted apart. The old bugbear connected with the idea of continental drift was that, if the continents were once all one (or two) and then split and started to drift apart, how come the bottoms of the oceans (not seas, please note) to be paved with immensely deep deposits of ooze and other sediments that must manifestly have taken hundreds of millions of years to accumulate? The answer to this conundrum is now apparent in that the initial cracks in the ancient supercontinent(s) were along lines of subcrustal volcanic activity and that it was an upwelling of material through these that was the cause of pushing the continents apart. Indeed, this took almost incomprehensible time to achieve, but as it did so, suboceanic sediments began and then continued to be deposited. Proof of this is that these sediments are deepest in the middle of the great troughs and thinnest or shallowest at their edges, just off the continental shelves *and also* on either side of those original rifts which now form vast mountain chains wandering all over the earth down the middles of the oceans. Just take a look at those maps. The average depth of the oceans and seas, which cover almost three-quarters of this planet's surface, is over two miles. The surface area of the earth is 196,940,400 square miles. If we add the area of rivers, lakes, and ponds to that of the seas and oceans we come so near to a full three-quarters of this* that we may adopt the figure 140,638,654 as

---

* The total area of the earth is 196,940,400 square miles.[246] Of this, it is usually said that 28 percent is "land" and 72 percent water. The only atlas we have found that gives figures lists the "total land area of

the total for the water surface, but we may likewise reduce the average depth to, let us say for convenience, a round two miles. This gives us roughly twice the area covered by water as the cubic volume of the hydrosphere, namely 281,277,308 (or say 280 million) *cubic miles.*

Turning then to the remaining quarter of our planet's surface, which is what is euphemistically called "dry land"—i.e., the surface of the lithosphere under air or the atmosphere—we find that it comprises about 60 million (actually 57,225,000) square miles. Things that live in air (which of course includes all of those which live in holes in the ground) do not go down even in exceptional circumstances more than an average of a hundred feet and, although some birds and insects can fly up to some 30,000 feet above sea level, no living things are known to exist perpetually in the air. Nevertheless, we may say that we aerial creatures have a layer of some 30,000 feet (or 5½ miles) thick in which to move about, *over land.* This gives us a volume of some 330 million cubic miles. This is slightly more space than the intraaquatic types have to operate in; and we must note first that we *can* "make use of" the air space over water surfaces also, which is to say the whole atmosphere or (at 5½ miles in depth) 1,083,172,200 cubic miles. Nevertheless, whereas subaquatic entities could use all of their environment

the earth, including inland water but excluding Antarctica" as 52,125,000 square miles.[247] Adding Antarctica (5,100,000), the total is 57,225,000. Then, subtracting the area of the 34 largest lakes and inland seas (783,755 square miles) and a rather arbitrary figure for the 95 "principal" rivers, ascertained by multiplying their combined length by 1 (mile in width) to get a figure (139,499 square miles), the "land" surface of the earth measures 56,301,746 square miles. This yields the percentages listed above, 28 percent land and 72 percent water. But this ignores all other rivers, creeks, lakes, ponds, swamps and marshes, canals, reservoirs, etc. that pepper the landscape. A very small map of Brazil, indicating only the largest natural features, shows 52 rivers; and a listing of natural features in another atlas reveals the following counts for rivers, lakes, creeks, canals, etc.: Alaska, 78; Arizona, 52; Colorado, 113; Florida, 108.[248] And these are only those that have definite names and are large enough to be included on maps that measure approximately 8 x 10 inches!

right up to its very precise and definite top, we aerial creatures are actually much more confined. Apart from some birds, we operate in the air only over land, and very few flying animals ever go more than a few hundred feet up. If we give airborne, terrestrially based animals an envelope of atmosphere even a mile thick to operate in over land, we find that our total work space is only this 50 million cubic miles, and this gives the water babies a five-to-one advantage over us in living space. With this in mind, let us indulge in some speculation.

PART III

13 · A SUGGESTION

Underwater Civilizations

So, once again, I ask the rhetorical question: Just what is all this about?

Basically, the dozen or so apparently unrelated matters that we have discussed would seem to have nothing much more in common than that they all have something to do with water. There is, nonetheless, an underlying unity, but this comes to light only when we review them together as possible aspects of and evidence for an over-all concept. This, moreover, is simply that there is an underwater "civilization" (or civilizations) on this planet that has been here for a very long time and which was evolved here, and/or that there are intelligent entities who have been coming here from elsewhere, probably for a very long time, and which prefer to use the bottom of the hydrosphere, and possibly also the surface layers of the lithosphere below that, on or in which to reside and from which to operate.

It is the consensus of all opinion, let alone the purely scientific, that life as we know it on this planet originated in water and only later came out of it onto land under the air. The atmosphere is therefore an "unnatural" environment for our life forms, and in order to function in it at all we have to expend most of our corporal energy creating an aqueous environment *within* our bodies—and one with almost exactly the constitution of sea water at that—in order to survive in this environment.

Now, we *presume* that we are the only form of what we call "intelligent" life on this planet, and since we live in the atmosphere, we *assume* that being the only form of intelligent life, no other such intelligence could evolve or exist in water. This notion has, however, been considerably shaken recently by the investigation of the mental abilities of the cetaceans (porpoises, dolphins, and whales), but panic has been held to a minimum by the observation that these fine creatures don't have hands and that "intelligence," as we think of it, is founded on technology, which in turn calls for the employment of what we call heat in order to invent and carry on metallurgical procedures. However, we can weld metal under water and we can mix concrete that sets under water, so it would seem that a technological civilization is not impossible in a liquid, and especially in such a delightfully inert one as water.

The problem we therefore have to face is: Could there have evolved a technological civilization, or a type of civilization such as we imply by that term, underwater? I am afraid I have to say that, first, there is no logical reason for stating that there could *not* be; and, on maturer consideration, and provided you are prepared to discard all your preconceptions, there would seem to be not a little evidence that there *is* such, and that it has been down there for a very long time indeed.

There is one alternative or corollary that we must not overlook. This may be either a little harder or easier to accept, according to which way you look at the problem. Once again, in the famous words of Gordon Creighton, "Bearing in mind that these things don't exist," and making every allowance for your natural conviction that they could not, may I ask you for a moment to consider just what the alternatives would be if they do exist? There are only two: namely, (1) they are indigenous to our planet, or (2) they originally came here from outside (off) this earth, and/or come and go from here to there and vice versa.

The latter runs us into the blurry field of ufology—i.e., that of so-called "Unidentified Flying Objects," which includes the even more damnable "flying saucers," "teapots," "corncobs," and what-have-you. This is a department that we would truly have liked to avoid; but, as you may have noticed in the previous chapters, we have been forced into it time and time again. After all, Dr. Villela's item that burst up out of the Antarctic ice was manifestly at least an incipient UFO, and all those things that we have seen went into oceans, seas, lakes, and rivers from the skies above must have been of a like ilk.

Accepting next, therefore, that at least some of the underwater babies can behave as UFOs, must we suppose that they all are? Also, must we accept that they initially came here from outside and took up residence here and that they prefer now (or always have preferred) to operate in water and from under water just because they demonstrate aerial and apparently space flight? Personally I think this is putting the cart before the horse —or should I say the blade on the back of the dozer. If a superior technological type of intelligent civilization(s) developed on this planet under water, they would very likely have gotten much farther ahead than we have, having had several millions, and possibly up to a billion years' headstart on us, life as we know it having started in the sea. Life by its very nature implies variation and thus evolution, so it must forever "progress" to ever greater complexity and sooner or later one or another form of such life would seem inevitably to reach a point where it desires to control its environment—just as we higher primates did when we moved from a sort of higher ape type to what we call a human one.

Control of or making changes in the environment by taking thought upon the matter need not at first mean more than developing simple tools. From this it should logically proceed to such interference with said environment as the clearing of vegetation for agriculture. Eventually the superiority of metals over stones for the fabrication of tools must almost inevitably be discovered, and when metallurgy gets started, come power sources —steam first, and then proliferation until the electrical basis of existence is stumbled upon. From there, as we now know, it is but a step to atomic analysis and the development of nuclear power. But was the late Willy Ley right when he postulated that none of this could be developed under (or in) a liquid medium?

Looked at from our point of view, and based solely on what *we* have achieved and until recently known, he is of course quite right. But if we ignore what we *have* so laboriously achieved and take into account what we now know *is* possible, and start to build from scratch in a liquid medium—and especially water—what do we find? Simply that everything we have done, including metallurgical expertise, *could* have been developed under water, and probably without a lot of problems that we have encountered, such as "explosions." Moreover, if you have a couple of hundred million years to develop the theory and do the job, God only knows where you may not end up.

If this *could*—and please watch these qualifying words— happen on a planet such as this, it could happen on other like planets, or other cosmic bodies having a liquisphere, be it water, ammonia, or whatever. And, as a matter of fact, it would be much more likely to do so on such than on gross bodies *without* any such liquid envelope. Also, development of such a nature in a gaseous medium, though not of course impossible, would appear to be much less likely and certainly more difficult to achieve—unless, of course, the end-product be diaphanous entities requiring (from our point of view) a minimum of material content. (This consideration runs us into another whole aspect of ufology; to wit, the UAPs or Unexplained Aerial Phenomena, many of which appear to be diaphanous to the point of total insubstantiality.[249]

Thus, there is just as much reason for supposing that any

things residing under the surface of our hydrosphere were initially developed elsewhere and either came here initially to reside, or have been coming here for a long time on a regular or an erratic basis, as there is for supposing that all those we encounter were developed here on our planet. If any of this conforms to actual facts, it is much more likely that *both* suggestions apply—hence the constant refrain by all kinds of people that there is and always has been a conflict between the "good boys" and the "bad boys" (for instance, angels "elevated" and "fallen"), the former defending their own, the latter trying to muscle in. So where do *we* come in?

In a case such as this we have to back off and start still again. At the risk of being appallingly corny, the best analogy I have to offer is the age-old one about us and the ants. The latter manifestly have some kind of intelligence, be it individual or corporate. At least they get things done; including, as the engineers say, "work." But, as many people have pointed out, we just tramp all over ants in the kitchen and in the woods without ever so much as a passing thought as to just what they may be up to. If we have a bunch of superintelligencies indigenous to the aqueous envelope of our planet who have been around for the Lord alone might know how much longer than we have, why on earth should they give a damn what we do or what happens to us? True, they might, when they have time to indulge in such a pastime as pure research, decide to collect a few aerial types of life, just as some of us become fascinated by the behavior of the ants and start collecting them as a hobby or to study. Be it noted that *we* seem to be going through just such a phase with regard to things that are indigenous to our atmosphere and beyond!

This, you may say, is all very well, but just where do these superbeings live, and why haven't we found them?

First, as stated in Chapter 12, three-quarters of the surface of this planet lies under the surface of water, when all the lakes and rivers have been taken into account; and this water, or hydrosphere, is on an average somewhat over two miles deep! This constitutes a volume of some 280 million *cubic miles,* a volume that is almost incomprehensible to the average run of us ordinary folk. This is not to say that any intelligent subaqueous beings were evolved in or reside *in* this space. Rather, they would more likely have originated on and go about their business upon the *bottom* of it. We live on the bottom of the atmosphere, and what have we done? First, it would seem, we lived out in the open along with other animals, then we started digging in, using what few caves there were for convenience and in their absence (which means about 95 percent of the earth's surface) began building domes and other structures on the surface to protect ourselves from the elements. Next, some bright lad invented the ladder and people started building upward to save space and digging. This phase lasted a long time, but eventually some even brighter boy invented a thing called a "lift." This made it possible to go farther up, somewhat faster, and considerably more easily than walking up stairs. These devices worked on the principle of counter-gravity (i.e., weights) or hydraulic principles. Finally some supergenius applied electrical power to an invention called an elevator and we really went up. From the point of view of what is euphemistically called "real" estate, this is a perfectly splendid idea, but it is absolutely asinine from every other.

We may well envisage some hardworking and industrious types evolved on the bottom of the hydrosphere going through all these primitive and then complicated maneuvers, but they would very probably eventually come to the conclusion—just as certain of our more enlightened engineers and architects are now coming to it—that they had got the whole procedure upside-down. Instead of going *up* into their living medium and encountering vile currents (winds), changes of temperature, mechanical dangers from earthquakes, chemical rot from aerial (aqueous) pollutants, they would—if they had a grain of real sense—drop the whole exercise and start digging down. There is already one fairsized corporation, New York Underground Facilities, Inc., that has burrowed into a mountain near Rosendale,

New York, and ensconced therein not only its executive offices but one of its officers and his family. Two other firms also have offices there, and housing is planned for hundreds or even thousands of people. There are parking lots, fresh clean air, and even green plants to enliven the scene.[250] This points the way that we are going to go, despite the inborn claustrophobia of most of us.

It is my contention that any subaqueous entities with intelligence would long ago have cottoned onto this simple and practical procedure. Further, they would not dig down into the deep accumulations of silt, mud, and other semiviscous deposits on the bottoms of the great deeps of the oceans but would drill into the comparatively firm surfaces of the continental shelves or into the sides of the great suboceanic mountain ranges. After all, if you have been evolved in a liquid medium and use it, as we do a gas (air), why not go below? This would not imply some "terror" of being discovered by miserable and primitive subaerial creatures like us, but would simply be for convenience and on practical grounds. That it might make it more difficult for the likes of us to discover them would never occur to such advanced entities. What the heck if ants do discover our houses? (Of course, if termites do, we have to do something about them!)

It has been said that in normal conditions our astronauts have not been able to detect anything, even lights, that might indicate the presence of sentient life on this planet from only a compartively short distance up. The only indications of what we might call "intelligent" activity that are large enough to be observed in the daylight zone were the long and somewhat wide logging trails cut straight through the Canadian taiga forest. This, moreover, is using the best photographic and visual aids that we have, which, be it noted, were invented and developed in air, and were specifically designed for long-distance inspection through our atmosphere—*not* through water or any other liquid. Just what and how much *do* we know about the bottom of the oceans or even the seas?

Then also, what in the name of all that is believed, does anybody know of what is at the bottom of any of the great tropical rivers, or even our own temperate and subpolar rivers that are deep and turbid? *Nothing.* I spent many years collecting animals in Africa, the Orient, and South America, and a good part of our time was devoted to fishing, netting, and dredging in such large rivers. Many of the things we brought up had previously been quite unknown, often even to the local people. For instance, a sting ray over six feet in width and of similar length with a five-foot tail turned up in a river that had been inhabited by intelligent African people born and bred to water for centuries and on the banks of which white settlements had been established for half a century, but nobody had ever seen anything like it before. And don't try to tell me that it was some sort of imagination. A dozen sturdy men toted it up to the house where we were residing and dumped it on our concrete verandah.[251] Fact is, we don't have the foggiest notion what is going on in, or what resides upon the bottoms of, even most shallow waters.

In the vastness of the oceans there is not just room for all manner of enormities but—at least according to the new maps of these vast areas—what might be called an open invitation for residence upon their bottoms for all manner of "things." So it is perfectly idiotic to say that there is no place for such things as we have mooted have evolved or now reside there. Aquatic creatures have a vastly greater living space than we aerial ones do—or, at least, had to start with. That any such creatures might, just like us, have discovered how to go up through the nonsolid envelopes that encase them and reach to the stars may be ignored for the moment, though we would point out that punching your way upward, against gravity, through successive layers of liquid of decreasing density is exactly equivalent to our boosting our rockets up through ever-decreasing layers of gaseous or atmospheric density.

Next, be it noted that "life" as we know it appears to have started at the bottom of the hydrosphere at least twice as long ago as that on land under the atmosphere. The oldest fossils known are now somewhat confidently dated at some 600 million years ago—if we allow a hundred million prior to what is called the beginning of the Cambrian for the date of some strange objects that appear to be the fossilized remains of organized bodies that have been found in Archaean or Pre-Cambrian rocks. However, the earliest fossils in the earliest Cambrian rocks are of really very advanced and complex animals that must have taken many more million years to have evolved. The earliest known subaerial animals are from what are called Devonian strata, now dated at some 300 million years ago. Thus, aquatic life forms had at least a 300-million-year head start on us of the air and, if we take into account our mutual aquatic ancestry, perhaps another billion. And we presume to think that we are the only lot who have really gotten anywhere!

We have now achieved "space travel," or have at least gotten out of our atmospheric envelope, and we are awfully proud of it. But we have only just now achieved this after some 300 million years. What might intelligent entities, having had more than twice as long to evolve, and, what is more, in a much more equable and favorable medium (i.e., water), have achieved? We are still currently banging and crashing and splashing around (with apologies to Dr. Wernher von Braun) in our efforts to achieve this enterprise; but unless we blow ourselves up, or decide to drop the effort, or just plain fail to be able to carry it forward due to the onset of the next Dark Ages, we should rapidly refine our procedure and make it a lot less noisy, in all senses of that word. Given an efficient propulsion system, like teleportation for instance, we would start slipping in and out of our atmosphere without all this rumpus and uproar. And we'll *have* to develop something like teleportation or we will run out of fuel because there will come a limit to our travels using chemical (molecular) fuel as we are now doing, and there will be a *time* limit on travel even with atomic energy and nuclear power.

Thus I contend that if we will only stick to being logical, and within the framework of our presently accepted logic to boot, there is no reason (a) why there could not be an extremely advanced "civilization" under water, (b) why it *might* not be up to twice as old as ours, (c) why it should not have developed what we call space flight, and (d) why it should not be so far in advance of us technically that we would never have even noticed it until *we* started to develop a few really sensitive gadgets.

You will please note that these four points are all couched in negative terms. Such expressions positively infuriate the average citizen, and particularly scientists and technologists. The reason is that most people, especially in our cultural zone, want a "yes-or-no" or "black-or-white" answer to everything, and they cannot stand the very thought of a yes/no or "gray" answer. In other words, they almost demand that anything and everything be either *possible* or *impossible*, and without any reference to the factors involved, while the *improbable* completely confuses them. This was splendidly laid out by Dr. Richard G. Van Gelder, Curator of Mammals of the American Museum of Natural History, in a filmed interview conducted by Ron Webster, then senior producer of the Second Program of the British Broadcasting Company. The subject was a film allegedly taken in the mountains of northern California by a Mr. Roger Paterson, showing what purported to be, and certainly looked like, one of the giant hairy hominids reputed to exist thereabouts and which are called Sasquatches or Oh-Mahs. Ron Webster had asked the perfectly straightforward question of Dr. Van Gelder: "Is this possible?" The answer, of course, should have been a simple "Yes" because there is no reason why such creatures, reported for centuries, can*not* exist, the past history of hominids and of the geography of the Bering Strait having been what it was in the immediate geological past. However, Dr. Van Gelder replied thuswise:

"Look; if this was radio and you told me that you were talking to me from the moon I could not say for sure that you were lying. However, although it would not be *impossible*, it would seem to me to be highly *improbable*." This was a truly scientific expression, and we would wish only that more scientists would follow this gallant doctor's lead. The weakness in his out-look, however, is that as of July 1969 such a conversation *could* have been conducted between the moon and the earth, and would therefore become *possible*. That it be *probable* would de-pend upon a number of factors, and all of those factors would have to be positive. Moreover, given sufficient such positive evidence, anyone assessing the probability would have to be most extremely cautious because both the quantity and the quality of said evidence would also have to be assessed.

When it comes to underwater babies we find that the quantity of positive evidence is almost overwhelming, provided we take enough factors or subjects into account. We have covered half a dozen of these subjects in previous chapters. The quality of these reports is, moreover, in our opinion, extremely high—much higher, in fact, than that in any other of the mysteries of natural phenomena. Unlike even UFOs, for instance, we have not only human observation but concrete records by machines and in the form of such solid items as ships, and, what is more, records and other proof that have been officially approved and published. Ghosts are entirely ephemeral; poltergeists are themselves likewise, but they produce measurable physical effects; abominable snow- and other persons leave foot-tracks and dung, and they are alleged to be photographable; lake monsters are completely solid, however elusive—*vide* the film of the Loch Ness effort; but these "babies" of the underwater are absolutely solid both in physical contact and in the effects they appear to produce and many other things that they do.

We have here, therefore, a rather curious situation. Here is a mystery that has been more or less overlooked and which at first appears to the average person quite balmy, yet it is sup-ported by far greater concrete evidence, both quantitative and qualitative, than any of the other popular mysteries. What is the reason for this anomaly?

After more than prolonged cogitation, I have come to the conclusion that the basic cause is that man as a species is a landlubber. Within land masses there are indeed river people, and there are those who for generation after generation have boated upon inland lakes. Around the coasts of the land masses there have always resided sea people who for at least ten millennia have been going out upon the salt waters, and to these must be added those of them who landed upon islands and have inhabited these ever since. These boating people constitute quite a body, but compared to the whole mass of humanity, their numbers are paltry indeed. What is more, the vast majority of them remained firmly anchored to the land, while the bottoms they sail in—and especially today—are but floating islands with all the appurtenances of life on land. The sea is to the inhabitants—and almost invariably only temporary ones to boot—of these artificial islands but a comparatively flat surface of an unfamiliar and in some cases hostile element. Fishermen and oceanologists are well aware of the life going on below this surface, but both have confined themselves to the investigation and collection of cetaceans, fish, and other animals. It is thus only the navies that, since the invention of our submarines, have had to take a harder and closer look at just what does go on underwater. And it is from navies that we get the most cogent reports—and the most startling, I might add—of things other than animals below the waves.

There comes here, however, a further complication in that of all the millions of humans manning the navies of the world either on a permanent or part-time basis, all were born landlubbers and very few have been permanently water-borne since childhood. What is more, attendance (i.e., duty) upon modern naval vessels becomes every year less "nautical." You *could* spend a year aboard an aircraft carrier without ever seeing the sea if you so wished; and without any dereliction of said duty. I was once in the sick bay—but not from seasickness—aboard a transatlantic liner which I boarded off a dock in Europe and from which I landed upon a dock in the Hudson River, and I never saw the sea nor even knew, to tell the truth, when we were even in forward motion. (That was the old *Aquitania,* surely the softest-riding ship that was ever floated.)

The naval personnel who really do come in contact with the underwater domain are the radar operators, both in subs and afloat above. They are virtually the only ones *penetrating* this medium in depth; and, be it noted, it is just from them that we get the most startling reports of what prompts us to suggest the existence of the underwater babies. Recently, commercial operators employing sonar devices like Simrad to spot and track fish have started, albeit rather tentatively and almost shame-facedly, to report "large things" down there. So startled have they been by the tracings that have turned up on their paper strips by entirely mechanical means, and the portraying of which could not have been tampered with by human agency, that they have tended so far to report only those that look like large animals, known or unknown. The items without fins or other protuberances they prefer not to talk about at all but, if persuaded to do so, assign them to malfunction of the apparatus or to something like a very large whale seen from an angle that did not show either any dorsal fin, flippers, or tail flukes.

Add to all these considerably valid reasons for not accepting this whole business, we still have to note the universal desire *not* to believe in *any* such thing. The whole concept runs contrary to the upbringing, beliefs, traditions, and even what we like to call the common sense even of mariners and underwater radar operators. How, the average person asks, can anything like this have been going on without our knowing about it? But I have already answered that question. It has always seemed strange to me that almost everybody not only believes in, but almost casually accepts, the existence of a Universal Power, God, the Almighty, or however they choose to designate a Supreme Being, without a single iota of the sort of concrete evidence for His existence that they so clamorously demand before they will even "believe in" anything as concrete as a lake or sea monster. (Please understand me: this is not to say there may not be perfectly valid and acceptable proof of a spiritual or non-concrete nature of the existence of a Supreme Being. Such is no part of this discussion.)

The basic trouble—and I reiterate, and shall continue to do so, even *ad nauseam*—is pure ignorance, both of facts and of possibility. There is every excuse for the former but absolutely none for the latter. Why, all religionists throughout the ages (and now even the communists) affirm that with God (or nature) nothing is impossible. Squaring the circle is *not* impossible, though that anybody at our stage of mental development and stuck with our present rules could achieve this trick is indeed highly improbable. What is more, as has been said rather often, you'll never find anything unless you know what you're looking for. This statement, of course, needs qualification and should better read: "If you don't know what you find, you'll not notice it." Thus, if you are convinced that no such thing as an underwater civilization could exist, you will tend positively to deny bumping into a supersub—and even by radar—and try every which way to explain it away as a whale, a partially deflated navy blimp, a vast log, or one of the other standbys of those dedicated to skepticism of the existence of as yet unidentified large aquatic animals.

If there has been for a very long time a "civilization" underwater, it would very likely have been observed throughout the ages. Until recently its operatives would not have cared much about being so observed, but now that we are probing the depths below and the skies above they might have become very cagey—if they desire that their presence not be known as yet, that is. Disclosing your presence to a bunch of Amerindian hunters or even to their sophisticated rulers a thousand years ago might be considered of no consequence to such superior intellects; but popping up in the middle of antisubmarine maneuvers being conducted by the most advanced navy in the world today might well present to them quite another situation. Modern radar operators are not going to log something that travels at 200 mph to a depth of 20,000 feet as a "sea god," and ships' captains with priceless cargoes and several hundred fellow humans aboard under their care are not going to report shallow-water or beached constructions as such gods in the process of coming ashore. In fact, we are slowly getting fairly smart, and any other intelligencies that may be around would have to start employing some protective strategies. And this leads me neatly to the last consideration of this whole business. This is the *"why"* of it all.

Frankly, we don't know *"why"* anything. We don't know why we are here, and we don't know why the universe exists, or seems to us to exist. There are those who say that it is God's will; there are others who contend that it just happened and that there is no "why" for anything. Yet, there are degrees of "why-ness," if I may coin another word. It would seem to be quite hopeless to ask "Why everything?"; but we may legitimately ask "Why something?" In the present case, we have suggested that any intelligencies there may be, who live in a liquid medium, may not want us to know about their presence and activities. Fair enough: but do we have any evidence of such a desire on their part? I think that we have, and that this is to be sought in the third set of facts that we presented above—namely the disappearing ship; ships disappearing and then reappearing; and planes arriving before time. Further, once such a procedure is developed it would undoubtedly be refined, so that the disappearances could be selective. Instead of just "grabbing" a whole ship and everything in and on it, one might be able to pluck off the men only; or the old men only; or the stupid ones, or all those named Ambrose, or just about anything else your computers desired. At the same time you (the superior intelligencies) would undoubtedly also know how to make *yourselves* invisible, and so "come aboard" as the saying goes nautically, to supervise. If not, you could presumably operate at long distance and from another medium. I begin to wonder just how much there might not be to the age-old stories of invisible entities that do things; people that flash on and off; and all the rest of those incredibles and unbelievables so beloved of the mystics and so abhorred by the skeptics and other pragmatists.

14 · A CONCEPT

Who and Where
Are the OINTs?

We have repeatedly alluded throughout this book to what we perhaps somewhat facetiously call OINTs. This was merely a time-saver for the expression "other intelligencies." It must be understood that this is far too vague a term in many respects, since, as we have found to our chagrin, the average person infers that by it we mean only some other sort of entity—corporeal or not—having about the same average, over-all "intelligence" as ours. This is not what we mean at all. There are endless "oints," in the general sense, living with us right here on the surface of our planet in the forms of other animals; and let nobody try to deny the fact that *all* animals—and now it seems even plants and the single-celled organisms—have some form of what we call intelligence.

But just how do we define any intelligence, including our own? And how do we assess its level or degree of competence, desirability, efficacy, or necessity? A human intelligence in an opossum's body would be in one hell of a fix, and an opossum's in a human body just would not be able to function at all. Starting with us, it is now plain that our activating forces may be rather clearly divided into three categories. First, we have a brain which is a corporeal entity and nothing more than an elaborate electrical computer. In other words, it is a machine, and machines can be wrongly constructed in the first place, can break down, can be damaged and fixed, and otherwise tampered with. Machines don't have to be made of metal and plastics put together with nuts and bolts or have precise geometric conformations, as the use of wire clearly demonstrates.

Second, we have what is perhaps best called a mind. This functions through the brain but is not itself corporeal; and it would not appear to be a machine—at least as we usually think of, and currently define, such an entity. Nonetheless, it would appear that we have made a beginning in the construction of, and in tampering with, human mentality. Furthermore, it can be most clearly demonstrated that by taking, as the old saying goes, "thought upon the matter" we can influence other mentalities both at our level of "intelligence" and below it. This, of course, raises the question as to whether entities at other levels can influence us. Further contemplation of this possibility will have to wait for a few moments.

In addition to a brain and, let us call it, a mind, all life forms, or living (by our definition) entities, have a third aspect or "machinery" that is at once much more ephemeral but much more potent. Throughout the ages, and presumably since he first started thinking at our level, man has groped for this force, having for some amazing reason always seemed instinctively to have felt that it exists. This is a "something" that is entirely non-material, but which, as the old philosophers put it, "vitalizes" living things. You may call it the soul, the spirit, the id, or a personality. It would seem to be individual to every living thing and thus be equivalent to our concept of individuality *per se*. So far, it seems that we can*not* tamper with this "bit," though we can apparently (at least) destroy it. Yet, for all its individual uniqueness, even this itself would appear to be but a "process" by which something even greater still operates. And here we come to the crux of the whole matter.

Until a few years ago it was universally accepted that all things could be clearly divided into two categories—the living or animate, and the inanimate. Doubts first arose when we dug downward in size to macromolecules and discovered that they individually appeared to have a high percentage of those proclivities and abilities of the smallest things that we had been calling "alive," some of which were composed of as few as four such molecules. Where to draw the line? Philosophical scientists began to devote a great deal of thought to this paradox, but it was not until 1966 that the matter was, in my opinion at least, logically summated. This appeared in the form of two articles by Andrew A. Cochran, in which he pointed out the place of what we call "volition" in the scheme of things.[256]

This, however, led to a further conundrum, because we humans in our boastful egocentricity considered that we alone possessed this quality, which we defined as the ability to make a free choice. However, when the science of ethology, or the study of animals in nature, got going, and even more so when behaviorism—which is the technique of observing living creatures in unnatural conditions—was developed, it was immediately perceived that all animals, right on down to the amoeba and even far beyond, possessed this marvelous quality. It was Cochran, moreover, who further pointed out that *everything*, right down to quanta, appears to have it too, in that, when presented with a dichotomy, they do not act merely upon the laws of chance. In fact, the whole universe seems to be nothing more than a vast computer running on the binomial system—namely the 1-or-0, or yes-or-no principle—but with the *choice* of the one of these as opposed to the other being apparently, at least to some extent, voluntary as opposed to purely haphazard. This becomes more than a little alarming if we go back and start again from our level and work "upward," as it were.

Could we be at a change-over point in cosmic development? If our universe is basically volitional, and started off with some such admonition as "Let there be light," a trend of events, or what we call evolution, would be set in motion. How many possible *different* trends might have been, it is not worthwhile to consider, let alone debate, because they were probably infinite. In other words, endless existences such as we call our universe almost *must* have been created and, time being of no consequence, doubtless still are being so. Let us, however, stick with our universe, and within it our cosmos (i.e., its material manifestation), and particularly with our infinitesimally small bit of that, namely our earth.

So our planet gets started, and in due course what *we* call life appears upon it, and this becomes ever more organized and more complex until our form of primate appears. Now, up till this time everything just seems to have bumbled along as if unaware that there might be a reason for all of it, or more so, a "plan"—though I do not mean by this a plan such as we draw up to establish an industry. In other words, nothing before the appearance of man was of itself—at least on this planet—sufficiently organized to be *aware* of its having this volition. (I must admit that, personally, and owing to my now somewhat long life of living with and working alongside other animals, I am not at all sure that some of them don't have a clue to this, and most notably the elephants.) There has been a great deal of talk about man being different because he is not only aware of his environment, but "has the brains (or intelligence, if you wish) to do something about it." This is true, but it is nothing more than another way of saying that somewhere along the line he became aware of the fact that he *could* make his own choice, and about *everything*, not just one thing, like a cat in a house or a rat in a cage.

So we've got Desmond Morris' "naked ape" all fired up with the idea of changing the world to the way he wants it, and what is more, he apparently did just that, though he made a lot of appalling false starts and subsequent mistakes, and may well have had the wrong idea in the first place. Yet, now here he (that's you and me) is, confronted with a frontier with which his (our) brain is not yet ready or able to cope. We have got very close to the limits of the understanding of our purely material environment. Now we are confronted by the non-material. Mystics, religionists, and other spiritualists of all kinds got there ages ago, but they had no true knowledge to work on and no tools to work with. They had but feelings, beliefs, and emotions to guide or misguide them. It remained for the development of what we so loosely call "science" to provide the real facts and the usable tools.

The real turning point in history was, of course, the incident at Hiroshima. From that day on the age of belief was dead and we were catapulted into the age of fact and reality (if not of reason!). Since we have now created our own environment, if you take thought upon the matter, either we are going to have to live with it or we are going to die in it. And if we prefer the former, we had better get to work exploring the (to our basic senses) invisible world.

We now have ample proof that there *is* an invisible world around us and even within us, and I am not talking about the spiritual business, but of entirely material matters. This unseen world appears to be vastly greater than the seen one; and that which is "in it" displays a much wider range of things than the little material world that we have been brought up in, both genetically and individually.

Please don't think that I am going mystical on you. I have neither the time nor the inclination to prove godheads, spirits, or any such. My personal interests are purely pragmatic, and I therefore prefer to confine myself to practical matters. And there are plenty of items calling for investigation in this field: for example, such simple things as electrical flux. Yet, while staying strictly within this field, we nonetheless run into an ever-expanding area of "unexplaineds."

Unfortunately, a lot of these have until recently been tagged "psychic"; and here we run into a most monumental semantic muddle. The following definitions of this word are found in Webster and the Oxford English Dictionary respectively.

1. Of or relating to the psyche. 2. *Lying outside the sphere of physical science or knowledge* [italics mine]; immaterial, moral, or spiritual in origin or force. 3. sensitive to nonphysical or supernatural forces and influences.

Non-physical force assumed to explain spiritualistic phenomena.

The trouble is that most of the things the average person calls and thinks of as being "psychic" are *not*. These are purely practical matters that range from hypnosis to sometimes even (so help us) UAOs.[253] These may be either wholly or partly intangible and they may be invisible, but they are just as real as a jolt of electricity or a hunk of moon rock. The truly psychic are, at least as of now, entirely mental or spiritual matters, though I personally believe—and I am not ashamed to admit this—that they will, in time, all be shown to be entirely real and subject to purely physical and materialistic principles.

Meantime, we are left with a seething mass of intangibles, "non-materials," and "invisibles" for which we have no popular collective name; at least, we did not until last year, when the Russians neatly coined the word "parapsychic," meaning *para* (like) the psychic. This is ironical indeed, in that when orthodox science finally admitted that there was/is a seemingly endless invisible world to investigate, they allowed such expressions as "parapsychology," "paraphysics," and "para-just-about-everything-else-in-the-material-or-visible-world," which they lumped together as the "paranormal." In other words, they had been looking at the whole thing, albeit reluctantly, from the wrong end. Instead of regarding these matters as being suspect aspects of known material realities, they should have—as the Russians have now done—looked upon them as very real manifestations of what they and their dictionaries had been tabbing "psychic."

Now, it doesn't matter if you are a scientist or a religionist, by which I mean an Einstein or a pope, it is quite useless any longer to attempt to deny that there is an invisible world around us. You can explain this any way you want to but, for the sake of the Almighty, would you please make up your minds how to divide up the field between you? To this end may I suggest just one simple guideline? This is between ghosts and poltergeists. The first apparently affect peoples' minds only; the latter throw things, make noises and stinks, and so forth. So let us for now at least define the first as a "psychic" phenomenon, and the latter as a "parapsychic" one. Since it can no longer be denied that there is a vast and seemingly endless invisible world around us, we might as well consider some of its possibilities. These, of course, are also endless, so I shall confine my observations to just a couple of items that are pertinent to the theme of this book.

Here we have to deal with two basic sets of facts. One is that UAOs, meaning both Unidentified *Aerial* Objects and Unidentified *Aquatic* Objects, are (a) objects and (b) unidentified. The other is that said objects are reported to behave in an "intelligent" manner, which is to say either as animals do or as machines controlled by animals do. The objects themselves have been adequately dealt with, at least to my way of thinking, and not just in this book but in literally hundreds of others. The intelligencies that motivate them (i.e., the OINTs) have, on the other hand, barely been touched upon. This discrepancy should, I feel, be rectified as far as possible and without further delay, since it is manifestly the crux of this whole matter. But here, once again, we come face to face with a whole series of clearcut dichotomies.

This is like asking the question: "If I hit that piece of glass with this hammer will it break or not?" Either it does, or it does not. It cannot "sort of" break. Thus, UAOs either exist or they don't. Then, again, another dichotomy: "If they do exist, are they what we call inanimate or are they animated?" Next, if some of them are the latter: "Are they themselves "alive," or are they machines built and activated (even though not necessarily piloted) by living or animate entities?" And finally: "If the latter, are these entities intelligent or not?" And it is here that we run head-on into the real stickler because we find ourselves right back where we started in that we have not yet defined "intelligence," either *per se* or relative to that form of it which we think we possess!

Apparently, a really very large percentage of all people believe in the reality of UAOs in that they finally admit either that they have seen one, or have some relatives or close friends who say that they have. Of these millions—and in this country alone —there is now quite a high percentage who feel that these things "come from another world." Within this group, however, there is still another minority that interprets the word "world" as meaning another universe (or space-time continuum, or estate), and an increasing number of these people are beginning to suggest that this other universe is normally invisible to us through our normal senses, but that it is detectable at least in part through some of our more advanced devices in the electromagnetic field. The corollary to this is, of course, that other intelligencies even a little ahead of us are able to do this from *their side*, as it were; and if they are only a little bit more advanced, they might be able to both "come through and then go away (i.e., vanish)" at will. But here, once more, we face a dichotomy: namely, do they come through (a) *per se,* or via machines, or (b) do they merely *project* themselves into our environment?

A number of very profound thinkers, all with much actual and practical experience in all aspects of this field, and particularly those with true scientific training and education, have been nibbling away at this suggestion for some years. There are people like Desmond Leslie and Brinsley Le Poer Trench on the one hand and Gordon Creighton, Charles Bowen, and John Keel on the other. But recently still a third group has surfaced. These are the working scientists, by which I mean men of keen intellect who earn their living in the established setup of orthodox science. Some of these have published direct suggestions—albeit, merely *as* suggestions—of an exactly similar nature. Most outstanding among such is, in my opinion, Dr. Jacques Vallee, who holds degrees in mathematics and astronomy and has done research in the fields of artificial satellites, and microwave and radar technology. He is an expert in computer technology and was a consultant on NASA's "Mars Map" project as well as a research assistant at the MacDonald Observatory.

In his most recent book, entitled *Passport to Magonia,* he puts forward *his* suggestion on page 152.[254] This is, moreover, the first that I have ever heard of that makes sense to me, and not only on practical grounds but on technological ones to boot. Its basis is that at least some of the UAOs both could be and might be projections. In other words, as Vallee expressed himself, these things are of the nature of that which we now call holograms. These are "structures" put together as sort of photographs of objects which you can walk around and view from all angles and see just how the object would look (and *does* look) from all those angles.[255]

However, Dr. Vallee went further by suggesting that some OINTs long ago developed mechanical means of projecting not just an image (tridimensionally) but an actual solid object itself, and then devised methods for withdrawing these, either instantly or in other ways, back into their space-time continuum. If we have developed the hologram, there is not the slightest reason why we cannot in time—and probably a comparatively short time—also find out how to project solids. After all, we got one-line "projection" in radio; then two-dimensional in television; and three-dimensional in these holograms. Then, of course, there is the apocryphal story of the cat sent through a coaxial cable by a bunch of RCA engineers twenty years ago! Apocryphal it may be, but imagination always precedes hypotheses, and then the resultant theories finally get tested—and the damnedest things often come out of this procedure and combined exercises.

The reason that I personally am so enthralled, and delighted I may say, with Vallee's suggestion is that he tells in his book how he came to it. This is precisely what I have been pondering for some thirty years now, and is as follows. How is it, I have always wondered, that UAOs throughout the ages are reported to have appeared in just those forms that were at least partly understandable to those to whom they appeared? Discounting allegory, and making every allowance for subsequent garbling, Ezekiel's thing was a wheel and Elijah's a fiery chariot, which (as the Aramaic version has it) "belched fire from its arse." The things alleged to have come down from the sky and to have picked up cattle and so forth in our Midwest at the end of the last century were described as vast airships, and from them men with beards who talked with midwestern accents were said to have descended. The British see flying chamber-pots; the Swedes, flying boxcars; natives of New Guinea, hovering airplanes piloted by little chaps who wave at them; and, as Vallee tells us, an Italian technician sees complicated radio equipment through the portholes of a UAO that landed near him in North Africa. Be it noted also that Dr. Villela saw a submarine come charging up out of the Antarctic ice.

The same may be said about the occupants of UAOs as alleged. The Irish see little green men; the northern Italians, tall blue men ("true" blue-bloods?); the Latin Americans are attacked by horrible little hairy dwarfs, apparently made of metal against which machetes and knives shatter; peaceable and loving but disturbed North Americans meet gorgeous blondes sitting on rocks in the woods who admonish them to ban the bomb; and so on and on. Being a biologist, I have often wondered why I haven't seen a bug-eyed monster, but alas, all I have seen have been hundreds of maneuvering green lights in the Caribbean when admittedly I was enjoined to look for just such signaling devices employed by German intelligence fellows during W.W. II; a couple of really horrid red things over Pennsylvania, but again, be it noted, in company with an electronics engineer; a really preposterous and enormous white sort of egg that sailed over my house in the presence of five witnesses, and this time two of them aeronautical engineers; and a really monumental disk, in company with my wife, when I was potentially bird-watching. And it is this last that really gets me.

If you really dig back to the dawn of history in search of this UAO business, you will soon spot this altogether too pat correlation between what many people say they saw and what they might be expected to comprehend. On the other hand, come these damned DISKS. There are no *natural,* discoidal, aerial objects, and there never have been, as far as we know. What is more, try as we may, and after all the gab by modern engineers, *we* have not been able to develop a satisfactory discoidal machine that flies. So where did late paleolithic man, the ancient Dravidian Indians, the Sumerians, the ancient Egyptians, the Romans, and all the others on down to post-World-War-II North Americans get the idea of aerial discoidal planes? Could it, as Dr. Vallee suggests, be that some OINTs project what they want each of us to see, either to convince us of something of which they wish us to be convinced or to throw us for a loop; but that, at the same time, *they* themselves just keep popping in and out in their own devices, which happen to be discoidal? Think this one over.

So we are left with two very wide-open questions. The first is, What *are* OINTs? And the second is, Just *where* are they?

Now that we know that there is an invisible world around us, and since we have seen that ours need not be, and almost certainly is not, the only universe either in space or in time, OINTs could, of course, be anywhere. As to what they may be, who is to say? Merely asking this question is to beg it. There may be an infinity of different types of them and they could change type, or form, or anything else, at any time. They could be just as "solid" as we are, in their own way, corporeally speaking, or they could be just as ephemeral as our "thoughts." They could be among us or even actually *in* us; and, alternatively, *we* may be OINTs ourselves! Yet, there does seem to be a pattern, and for my part there is one feature that has emerged from all that I have read on and experienced of this business, and this is very startling, though, if you come to consider it calmly, it is by no means as balmy as it might at first appear. This is simply that the OINTs are, at least from our present point of view and as of this date, *incredibly and abysmally stupid.* How can I say this?

Consider for a moment what is happening to us. We have "invented" devices that we call computers. Some of these, such as those, for instance, developed by Drs. John C. Loehlin of the University of Texas, Kenneth M. Colby of Stanford, and the Gullahorns of Michigan, are now already not only "thinking" but developing personalities and showing characteristics such as we call emotions. Meantime, the business workhorse computers continue to churn out expense accounts and make irreparable mistakes in charge accounts. Still others assess the desirability of bombing Cuba or of giving aid and comfort to either one of our major potential enemies. And all along the line nobody, from heads of state to the people who assemble these idiotic machines, and least of all those who program them, really has the foggiest notion how or why they work. There is no single human alive who could design and build and set in motion even the simplest of such devices any more than there is one who could produce a hydrogen bomb. In fact, the more complex our technology becomes, the more stupid we become. Soon machines will be teaching the next generation of our species, and it will take but one buffoon to transpose one zero for a 1 and forty thousand kids could grow up believing that horses always *pushed* carts instead of pulling them. Might it not be that at least some OINTs are so far ahead of our present status that they have completely lost control of themselves and just plain given up *thinking,* just as we appear to have given up *instinct* in favor of thinking when we stumbled on technology? Take poltergeists, for instance. They are obviously some kind of OINTs because they (as the engineers say) "do work." Thus, they must be entities. However, the "work" they do is, at least according to the record, 100 percent stupid, mischievous, and for the most part both illogical and insane. Having invented an invisibility machine and been taught by a computer how to live forever, let us say, on free ions, what have they got left to do?

Finally, to sum up, therefore, we should point out that while UAOs have been reported from inner space, from the atmosphere, and from the hydrosphere, and even from inside the solid lithosphere below us; and while all manner of beasties, both seen and unseen and in various guises, from the horrible and bestial to the gorgeous and humanoid, have been reported to have come out of them, the whole lot should probably best be regarded merely as another universality. That they may be endlessly varied would seem to be an eminently sensible concept, and that some of them live in the sea is no more balmy a notion than that some of them live in the sky, in inner space, or on other solid bodies in outer space. Given that much technical command, they could live anywhere or everywhere, and move about instantly, or faster, anywhere throughout space and/or time.

That they are for the most part overcivilized and quite mad is, in my opinion, an open-ended question but quite probable. Perhaps we will never be able to cope with them until we, too, all go quite mad, and it looks as of now as if we were doing our level best to achieve this presumably enviable estate.

APPENDIX A Missing Persons and Other Things on Land

I often wonder just how many people know that both people and things have been and still are being reported as vanishing on land. Speaking first of man-made constructions of from modest to large size, let me start off with a case that is totally explicable within our current terms of reference. It was a clear case of piracy.

A friend of mine had a lovely house with a three-car garage and a little guest cottage behind this. The buildings stood about half a mile back from a dirt road. This road, which stretched for some ten miles between two major highways, formed the access to a score of beautiful old farmsteads and half a dozen houses of modern construction. My friend was a businessman in New York City and used this lovely place not only as a summer residence—it was only about fifty miles from New York—but for weekends, as he had to do most of his work out of office hours and in peace and quiet. Unhappily he was then divorced, which caused him much distress; so, having no children, he took leave of absence from his company and went to Europe for an extended vacation. When he returned he picked up his mail at his office and his apartment in New York, and then drove straight home. When he got there, his home was no longer there. All that was left was the concrete ground floor with a large hole in it, and all the wood shingles from the roof of the main house, garage, and cottage were neatly bundled and stacked up by the driveway.

Completely dumfounded and confounded, he drove to his nearest neighbor, and something like the following interchange took place:

"What happened to my house?"

"Well, as it said in the local paper, you moved it to your place in Maine." (My friend had land there).

"But I didn't. Why didn't you tell somebody?"

"Well, that's what we heard and then all them trailer trucks and heavy equipment coming up the road day after day . . . We just naturally thought . . ."

The whole house, plus its contents, and even the heating and other service machinery, which had been hauled out through the large, ragged hole in the concrete floor, had *vanished,* and not one iota of it has ever been found since. What is more, the main building was partly constructed of country stone! If anything like this had happened at sea, everybody, even the owners of the construction, would have just shrugged. It might well have been attributed to piracy as this incident might be classed, though it was likewise a cut-and-dried case of theft.

But when a large barn vanishes overnight without sound or fury, in the middle of a suburban road with houses on both sides and all along the opposite side of the road, matters become somewhat more complicated.[256] No wind or other meteorological disturbance was reported by any of the neighbors that night, and nobody reported anything else unusual in the area, yet the barn was gone completely next day but for a few pieces of wood and some junk that had been stored in the back of it. If this report is true, what are we to make of it?

There is another way in which things can vanish. This is in tornadoes. Tornadoes, more often called twisters when over the sea, have tremendous drawing power, taking huge masts with all the rigging clean out of large sailing vessels. It is naturally assumed that this junk is subsequently dropped into the sea. On land no such easy explanation is permissible, especially in open country; yet there is case after case of things going up but never being recorded as coming down. This, if it ever becomes a substantiated fact, could account for the so-called vanishing of airplanes over both land and water, and of smaller surface vessels, but we can hardly conceive of it being the means of elimination of large vessels or of subs. Nor can we fall back upon it as the agency which apparently plucks humans from ships without damaging the ship, and which leaves dogs, cats, canaries, and other pets unharmed. Which brings me to the second aspect of these disappearances—to wit, that of people.

If you take the list of vanishings (in Chapter 8) alone and add up only those which give figures for the number of people aboard, you will find that we have 1,299 in this area alone. If we had figures for the others, this would run into the thousands, and we must realize that this is only a very slim sampling of all the cases that have been reported. How many more have never been reported?

Then add the crews and passengers of the planes and (possibly) of of some of the subs. The total looks like being staggering. However, it is as nothing compared to the recorded disappearances on land. The New York City Bureau of Missing Persons listed 12,764 reports in 1968; 12,961 in 1967; 11,776 in 1966; 10,880 in 1965; and 11,003 in 1964, making a grand total of 59,385. Of these, 57,688 were positively accounted for.[257] This leaves 1,697 cases marked "pending." And, be it noted, their definition of a missing person does *not* include runaway husbands, absconding bookkeepers, or anyone with what they term an obvious reason for disappearing; they are very specific about this. Their Press Relations Officer states that only a "minute percentage" are never found. This statement is understandable from a PR man, but let's examine the figures. Pending cases that are solved are included in the figure for the number of missing persons located during the next year (or years). The original total of pending cases listed here was 1,702, which suggests that thus far they have found only five of these! Considering the number of cadavers that the police and others do eventually find, the unaccounted-for would seem to be extraordinarily high even for a population of 8 million—remember, we are talking about New York *City* alone. The "minute percentage" seems to be 0.2 percent; by extrapolation, about 60,000 people vanish every year in the United States. So what of all the rest of the world?

Of course, this business is considerably muddied by the almost periodic cases involving prominent persons such as Ambrose Bierce,[258] Judge Crater,[259] and others of that standing, but it must be borne in mind that these cases get very special attention from investigative authorities and thus, if finally unexplained, add very considerably to the mystery. And what is most intriguing is that they, like the missing crews of ships, would appear to constitute cases of selectivity, so that we are forced once again to go back to Charles Fort's remark about the number of missing people called Ambrose, "was somebody collecting Ambroses?"[260] I have often wondered how many Millers in the United States, and Garcias in Mexico are on the "Lost Forever" list; and I would sorely like to be vouchsafed the time to try to find out the names of all the missing crews of these surface ships, with descriptions of them and their backgrounds, in order to see if anything of significance, from a statistical point of view, might emerge.

APPENDIX B The Ancient
Indian Vimanas

There is a tremendous volume of published material in almost all western languages on a subject that somewhere along the line and about a century ago was tabbed "the Ancient Writings." About 99 percent of this is not only drivel but pure fabrication. It has become the bible of the mystics, pseudoscientists, and crackpots and it—or specific parts of it, such as "The Tibetan Mysteries," the "Atlantean Texts," and so forth—are now quoted as a sort of gospel. However, if you ask any Orientalist, historian, or librarian in any of the great museums of the world, you will encounter a wry smile. No such works have ever been known to exist outside the imaginations of the mystics. Nonetheless, there are some truly ancient and authenticated texts, notably of Indian origin, which is to say from various parts of that great subcontinent, and handed down from various of its cultures from various dates.

It is, moreover, from these authenticated texts, mostly in poetic form, that some truly astonishing concepts have been derived. Poetic they may be; and nothing more than myth, legend, or folklore may they purport to record; but they make statements that are more than just surprising. Several are, what is more, couched in perfectly straightforward terms and are, time and time again, stated to be not legendary but technological, and thus called *Manusa*. These are said by the writers to explain how certain devices were constructed for aerial flight, but not *how* to so construct them because the inventors and the establishment did not want such things to be mass-produced and get into the hands of any other than the rulers, commonly called "kings" and "princes." What is more, among the *non*-technical works devoted to the more poetic stories, and known as *Daiva,* there would appear to be more than ample suggestion, if not evidence, that such airships could be and were put to the most gruesome and devastating use in wartime.

These texts make most fascinating reading, but being unable to read the originals or copies of them in the language in which they were written, I appealed to friends who were either Orientals themselves or students of Oriental literature. Among these was the late Dr. Ranjee Shahani, who at the time of his death was Professor of English Literature at Seton Hall University. Dr. Shahani had published considerably on these texts, and I derive most of the following from his works. At the same time, I quote certain passages as published (in translated form) by the British author, Desmond Leslie,[261] by kind permission of the author and publishers. From these sources we are told that:

In the *Manusa*, the most elaborate details for building (such aerial machines) are set down. The *Samarangana Sutradhara* says that they were made of light material, with a strong well-shaped body. Iron, copper, and lead were used in their construction. They could fly to great distances and were propelled by air. This text, according to Leslie, devotes 230 stanzas to the building of these machines, and their uses in peace and war. This author then goes on to state that this same text says:

"Strong and durable must the body be made, like a great flying bird, of light material. Inside it one must place the *Mercury-engine* with its iron heating apparatus beneath. By means of the *power latent in the mercury* which sets the driving *whirlwind* in motion, a man sitting inside may travel a great distance in the sky in a most marvellous manner.

"Similarly by using the prescribed processes one can build a vimana as large as the temple of the God-in-motion. Four strong *mercury* containers must be built into the interior structure. When these have been heated by controlled fire from iron containers, the vimana develops thunder-power through the mercury. And at once it becomes like a pearl in the sky.

"Moreover, if this iron engine with properly welded joints be filled with mercury, and the fire be conducted to the upper part, it develops power with the roar of a lion."

Leslie and several others who at least tried to take a serious view of these odd statements subsequently indulged in some perfectly valid speculations as to just what the significance of mercury might be. These are both sensible and permissible but lead off into matters that do not concern us here. Needless to say, they did not encompass the basic observation that a circular dish of mercury revolves in a contrary manner to a naked flame circulated below it, and that it gathers speed until it exceeds the speed of revolution of said flame. I fancy that Mr. Leslie will be enchanted with this new observation.

Here is the projection of energy by an exceedingly simple process. Should the ancients have stumbled across this process—though how in the dickens they might have done so is almost beyond comprehension—they might well have followed up the lead and ended up by finding out how to tap and channel such energy. Take this lead far enough and one can suggest the development of an "engine" employing it and being put to use to do (as the engineers say) work.

Desmond Leslies's theme is that this was one type of engine developed for aerial flight, and he extrapolates therefrom to the suggestion that it may have been developed far enough for space travel, and that something on this principle powers some UFOs. Our interest here is, however, in the formation and performance of vortices, concerning which I would ask you to refer to Appendix C.

APPENDIX C Herr Theodor Schwenk on Vortices

Vortices, or in more popular parlance whirlpools, constitute a subject of considerable complexity. They are individual entities being born due to a particular set of circumstances, having a life span that, given precise knowledge of enough factors, is predictable, and eventually dying through slow disintegration or accident. They form in gases—including, of course, air—liquids of all kinds, and even in solids when they are in a plastic state. The vortex as a structure lies at the very core of existence, as in the atom and apparently beyond down to the behavior of quanta.

The origin of vortices, their structure, and their behavior constitute a somewhat complex subject calling for mental visualization of three-dimensional movement. They are whirligigs, the centers of which have been pulled either downward or upward, and mostly downward in the case of air and water. As a geometric form they permeate the whole of life as well as mere matter. The best exposition of vortices, and one that is couched in terms that are understandable to anybody, may be found in a book entitled *Sensitive Chaos*, by Theodor Schwenk.[262] Therein there is a passage on p. 39 which succinctly describes the causes of vortices as follows: "Wherever any qualitative differences in a flowing medium come together, these isolated formations (vortices) occur. Such differences may be: slow and fast; solid and liquid; liquid and gaseous. We could extend the list: warm and cold; denser and more tenuous; heavy and light (for instance, salt water and fresh); viscous and fluid; alkaline and acid. . . . At the surfaces of contact there is always a tendency for one layer to roll in upon the other. In short, wherever the finest differentiations are present the water acts as a delicate 'sense organ' which as it were perceives the differentiations and then in a rhythmical process causes them to even out and to merge."

It should be noted that in vortices in a liquid such as water, objects are sucked inward and downward, whereas in a gas such as air they go upward and outward, as in tornadoes. Our Vile Vortices would appear to coincide with larger vortices in the surface layers of the oceans, but we are not presuming to suggest that these ever form gigantic maelstroms that have a hole going down the middle into which ships could be sunk. Rather, the alleged action of the VVs would seem to be in the atmosphere above these vast, comparatively placid whirligigs. In this medium, things would be sucked up and then tossed out over the upper rim of the vortex. Considering the power of tornadoes or twisters over the sea, it is just conceivable that lighter planes might be so whirled upward and tossed far away where search parties would never think of looking for them. However, the idea is neither proven nor altogether tenable from a purely physical point of view. While the VVs do appear to be associated with natural vortices, the mysterious effects that have been described as occurring within them do not seem to be purely mechanical, and we have to investigate a number of other factors.

In the same book named above, there is another most pertinent passage which applies to the centers of vortices and which provides a very neat and simple explanation of what is called suction-pressure. This states:

"Imagine we have some kind of filled space—we will call it A and place a plus sign in front of it $(+A)$. Now we can make the space emptier and emptier, whereby A gets smaller and smaller; but there is still something in the space, therefore we still use the $+$ sign. We can imagine that it could be possible to create a space which is entirely empty of air, although this is not possible under earthly conditions because a space can only be made approximately empty. Were it possible, however, to make a space entirely void, it would contain nothing but space. Let us call it nought; the space has zero contents. Now we can do with the space as you can do with your purse. When you have filled it you can take out more and more, until at last there is nothing left in it. If then you still want to go on spending money, you cannot take out any more, but you can incur debts. But if you have made debts there is less than nothing in your purse. This, then, is how you can imagine the space—not only empty, but one might say sucked out, filled with less than nothing $(-A)$."

Just how you borrow against a nothingness, vacuum, or space I leave to the cosmologists; but I am wondering if this is not where anti-matter, counter-matter, and things like Gravity II, might not come in. Vortices generate great energies the origin of which has not yet been sufficiently explained. From, in what, and from what fields are they generated? Do purely mechanical vortices stimulate others in other fields such as the electromagnetic, magnetic, gravitic, and other?

ate	Place	Into	Out of	On, In, or Over	Involved or Official Confirmation	Time
4 Oct. 1948	Bear Creek, Harbor, N.Y.	Lake Ontario			Involved	1:15 A.M.
948	Canada	"remote lake"				
6 Aug. 1952	Watkins Glen, N.Y.	Seneca lake			Involved	
7 Sept. 1955	Purdy, N.Y.		Titicus Reservoir			early A.M.
9 Oct. 1956	Tobyhanna, Pa.	Harvey Lake				afternoon
8 Mar. 1957	Ciudad Bolivar, Venezuela	Orinoco River				
June 1957	New Orleans, La.	Mississippi River				
8 Apr. 1958	Elyria, Ohio	Lake Erie				7:20 P.M.
24 May 1958	Grand Bend, Ontario	Lake Huron			Yes	1 A.M.
13 Oct. 1958	Wayne Co., N.Y.	Lake Ontario			Involved	2 A.M.
15 July 1960	New York City			East River	Yes	3 A.M.
26 July 1960	Niagara Falls			Niagara River	Involved	
14 Oct. 1961	Two Harbors, Mich.	Lake Superior	Lake Superior		Involved	5 P.M.
25 May 1962	Kent, Washington	Lake Meridian				10:30 P.M.
19 July 1962	Asheboro, N.C.	unnamed creek				
28 Aug. 1962	Concord, N.C.	Twin Lake				
15 Sept. 1962	Edgewater, N.J.	Oradell Reservoir	Oradell Reservoir		Involved	7:55 P.M.
2 Dec. 1962	Akron, Ohio to Syracuse, N.Y.	Lake Erie			Involved	8:45 P.M.
2 Dec. 1963	Dunkirk, N.Y.	Lake Erie				
22 Apr. 1963	Chicago, Ill.	Lake Michigan				
31 Oct. 1963	Iguape, Brazil	Peropava River			Involved	
27 Jan. 1964	Oshkosh, Wis.	Lake Winnebago			Yes	10-11 P.M.
14 Feb. 1964	Michigan and Indiana	Lake Michigan			Yes	
13 Apr. 1964	Walthamstow, England	River Lea				
27 Aug. 1964	Klamath Falls, Oregon			on Klamath Lake		
9 Sept. 1964	Radford, Va.	New River			Yes	noon
10 Oct. 1964	Port Colborne, Ont.	Lake Erie			Involved	6 P.M.

General Description	Behavior	Witnesses	Reference
"fiery ball"; "burning plane"	Going at terrific speed; moving up and down	Two adults	94
spherical object	No details	?	95
"flying saucer"—no description	Dove into lake; splashed water 8-10 feet high	Three adults	96
luminous sphere, size of basketball	Rose 1 foot; fell back into water with loud splash; then two bluish globes appeared in water, took off into mind (see text)	Two adults	97
silvery "cigar"	Seen over Tobyhanna; then disappeared into lake	Four adults	98
"bright object"; seen by children	Object fell into water; then light became very strong	Four children	99
"blue streak"; broke in pieces (?)	[Only one witness reported its breaking in two]	Many	100
"Fiery object" with two "horns"	Sparks like molten metal from front and sides;	"Hundreds"	101
"red flare"	Arched into sky, leaving trail of red light; then plunged	Provincial Police	102
"Fiery object"; "burning plane"	"Crashed"	One adult	103
"Oil-tanker Alkaid holed by UAO	Nothing seen; dragging operations revealed nothing	[Coast Guard; Army Engineers]	104
Unidentified light on river	Light moved about a mile along the river for 2 hours	Police; Fire Dept.	105
Object the size of an ore carrier	Skidded into water; bobbed on surface; then took off to SE	One adult; object on water —three adults	106
Flaming plane with a "loud roaring sound"	"Plunged" in; explosion heard	Unknown	107
No description	Whizzed through treetops; settled in creek, accompanied by sound of bubbles	Two adults	108
Oblong object	No details	Unknown	109
Oval object	Landed, submerged a few seconds, took off silently	Three boys; one man heard splash	110
light-bulb shaped object; bright	Coursed its way eastward, angling off toward the north, and "arched" its way into the lake	Residents of twelve cities	111
"glowing object"	"Passed through the sky and plunged into the lake"	Unknown; Coast Guard search	112
"glowing white ball of flame"; "bolide"	Not described	Many	113
disc	"writhed and struggled" in the air; hit a palm tree; fell into river; water "boiled"	One child and two adults	114
fiery object; possible burning plane	"Fell" into lake	Police and others	115
flaming object; possible meteor	Fell from NE; "faster than a flare, slower than a meteor"	Several adults	116
silver "cigar," 9 feet long	Crashed into river; left scar in concrete edge of towpath; tore down telephone wires	Several adults	117
flares on lake	Lights like flares seen over and on lake; no further details	Unknown	118
"Plane on fire"	Fell, trailing flame and smoke 30-40 feet; appeared that something flew off the side before it crashed	Several adults	119
crash heard; nothing seen	No details known	Several	120

Date	Place	Into	Out of	On, In, or Over	Authorities Involved or Official Confirmation	Time
7 Nov. 1964	Michigan	Lake Michigan				1:38 A.M
14 Jan. 1965	Elsinore, Calif.			Over Lake Elsinore		
21 Jan. 1965	Michigan and Illinois	Lake Michigan				5.40 P.M.
25 Jan. 1965	Fredericksburg, Va.			Over Rappa- hannock River		8 P.M.
12 Feb. 1965	Kenora, Ont., Canada	unnamed lake				8:30 P.M
22 Mar. 1965	Seattle, Wash.		Lake Washington			P.M.
4 Aug. 1965	Duluth, Minn.	St. Louis Bay			Yes	
5 Sept. 1965	Marquette, Mich.	Lake Superior			Yes	
6 Sept. 1965	Mexico City	Lake Texcoco				
30 Oct. 1965	Quebec Prov., Canada	St. Maurice River				5:15 P.M
4 Nov. 1965	Middletown, Ohio	Great Miami River	Great Miami River			P.M.
27 Nov. 1955	Racine, Wis.	Lake Michigan				
9 Dec. 1965	Ohio and Pennsylvania	Lake Erie				P.M.
23 Dec. 1965	Klamath Falls, Ore.	Klamath Lake				6:30 A.M
14 Mar. 1966	Chicago, Ill.	Lake Michigan			Yes	9 P.M.
23 June 1966	Menindee, Australia					noon
3 June 1967	Ontario, Canada		Lake Kipissing	out of or off Lake Kipissing		
1967	New Brunswick, Canada	Trout Brook Lake				
11 Sept. 1967	Vermilion, Ohio	Lake Erie			Yes	
17 Oct. 1967	Shillong, India	unnamed river (& out again)			Involved	
5 Apr. 1968	Malung & Serna, Sweden	unnamed lakes			Yes	
20 May 1968	Littleton, N.H.			On Moore Lake		2 A.M.
24 Nov. 1968	Vermilion, Ohio	Lake Erie				P.M.
1968	Peru	Lake Titicaca				

General Description	Behavior	Witnesses	Reference
Flash of light; "bolide"	No details	Unknown	121
Brilliant lights hovering over lake	Moved erratically in pattern; hovered; bright for 5 minutes, dim for 3—cycle; after 1 hour rose and disappeared to east	Many	122
"Possible meteorites"	"appeared to explode and fall"; other accounts do not mention explosion	Many, including police	123
"Frozen pie plate" bobbing up and down	Bobbed slowly up and down over center of river; in view 10 minutes	Many	124
Orange-yellow object with green "tail"	In view 1 minute; appeared to fall straight down	Several	125
Brilliant red fireball	Went straight up	Unknown	126
"An object"	"Splashed down"	Coast Guard	127
"Fireball"	"Plunged" into lake about 10 miles offshore	Coast Guard and others	128
"A saucer"	Landed in one of several lake-sized pools in otherwise dried-up lake bed	Many	129
"Aluminum boat" upside down, 22' in diameter; flame-spurting motor in back	Landed in river; submerged; water changed to dark brown; current disappeared, then flowed in opposite direction	Many	130
Bright flashing light in and out	Stationary flashing light sped off and landed in river, then took off again in a deep red glow	One adult	131
Brilliant small light grew to large size	Appeared to separate before it disappeared	Many	132
"Fireball"	"Dropped into lake"	Apparently thousands	133
"Fireball"	"Dropped into lake"	Unknown	134
"Fireball"	Moved from east to west and disappeared into lake; too fast for any other observations	Air traffic control observer	135
Splash heard; no description of object seen taking off	Object not visible on lake surface; then seen climbing diagonally; "disappeared in seconds"	Four adults	136
Green & white lights	"rose from the water with a whoosh and sped off"	One adult	137
"Small UFO 3 feet in diameter"	Traveled across like in "spinning fashion, spraying water 7-8 feet high; noisy; zipped into bushes; back and submerged	One, no age given	138
Yellow object; "possible meteor"	Visible about 12 seconds; or 30 seconds; may have split in two or may have been two objects	Several	139
Not described	At 500 feet when first seen; swooped down, damaged vegetation; "sucked and churned the water," finally sped off	Many	140
Not seen or found	Holes in ice on lakes, 700 sq. yds. in extent through ice 3 feet thick	Unknown	141
Whitish mound 2 ft. wide, 1 ft. above water; two "red glowing eyes"	Red glow seen; all night noises stopped; glow moved toward wharf, "charged" witnesses; glow prevaded wharf area	Three	142
"Plane crash"; "fireball"	"Plane" skidded along water until flames disappeared; no sound; smell of diesel oil (?)	Three persons (including two boys)	143
No details	General reference to objects "diving" into lake	Local population	144

REFERENCES

1. Hyde, Ed, "U.F.O.'s—at 450 Fathoms!" *Man's Illustrated,* March 1966.
2. Caidin, Martin, *Hydrospace,* New York: E. P. Dutton, 1964.
3. Sanderson, Ivan T., *Uninvited Visitors,* New York: Cowles Communications, Inc., 1967.
4. Condon, Dr. Edward U. (as Project Director), *Scientific Study of Unidentified Flying Objects,* New York: Bantam Books, 1969.
5. Saunders, Dr. David R., and Harkins, R. Roger, *UFOs? YES!,* New York: New American Library, 1969.
6. Bloecher, Ted, *Report on the UFO Wave of 1947,* Washington, D.C.: NICAP (reprint), 1969; Edwards, Frank, *Flying Saucers, Serious Business,* New York: Lyle Stuart, Inc., 1966; Fuller, John G., *Incident at Exeter,* New York: Putnam, 1966; Lore, Gordon I. R., Jr., and Deneault, Harold H., Jr., *Mysteries of the Skies; UFOs in Perspective,* Englewood Cliffs, N.J.: Prentice-Hall, 1968; Lorenzen, Coral E., *The Great Flying Saucer Hoax,* New York: William-Frederick Press, 1962; Ruppelt, Edward J., *The Report on Unidentified Flying Objects,* Garden City, N.Y.: Doubleday, 1956; Stanton, L. Jerome, *Flying Saucers: Hoax or Reality?* New York: Belmont Books, 1966; *Symposium on Unidentified Flying Objects:* Hearings before the Committee on Science and Astronautics, U.S. House of Representatives, July 29, 1968, Washington, D.C.: U.S. Government Printing Office, 1968; Vallee, Jacques, *Passport to Magonia,* Chicago: Henry Regnery Co., 1969; Vallee, Jacques, and Janina, *Challenge to Science: The UFO Enigma,* Chicago: Henry Regnery Co., 1966; Young, Mort, *UFO: Top Secret,* New York: Essandess Special Editions [Simon & Schuster], 1967. Recommended journals are *Flying Saucer Review,* of London, and the *A.P.R.O. Bul-*

letin. For an extensive bibliography, see Catoe, Lynn E., *UFOs and Related Subjects: An Annotated Bibliography,* Washington, D.C.: U.S. Government Printing Office, 1969.

7. Sanderson, Ivan T., *Animal Treasure,* New York: Viking Press, 1937, p. 251.
8. Creighton, Gordon, taped radio interview for Westinghouse, 1966.
9. Ford, Art, speech before Engineering Society of Detroit, 23 September 1966, published in *Satellite Research Bulletin;* personal communications, etc.
10. "Army Team Carried Away in Hotel Abduction Test," *Chicago-Sun Times,* 6 July 1969.
11. *Zodiac,* staff magazine of Cable and Wireless, Ltd., October 1923: *Daily Mail,* 22 August, 1923; *Evening Standard,* 28 August 1923.
12. Caidin, Martin, *Hydrospace,* New York: E. P. Dutton, 1964; Hyde, Ed, "U.F.O.'s—At 450 Fathoms!" *Man's Illustrated,* March 1966; and others.
13. *The Guinness Book of Records,* London: Guinness Superlatives, Limited, 1967, p. 162.
14. *Ibid.,* p. 232.
15. *Flying Saucer Review,* Vol. 12, No. 5, p. 32. (*Note:* Hereafter *Flying Saucer Review* will be abbreviated as *FSR.*)
16. Report by Oscar A. Galindez in *FSR,* Vol. 14, No. 2, p. 22.
17. Heyerdahl, Thor, *Kon-Tiki,* New York: Garden City Books, 1953, p. 120.
18. Ramos, Bernardo, "Inscripçoes e Tradiçoes da America pre-historica," 1932.
19. Heyerdahl, Thor, private communication.
20. Gearhart, Livingston, "Bombed by Meteors," *Fate* Magazine, March 1965, p. 80, quoting *The New York Times,* 5 November 1906.
21. *Ibid.*
22. Fort, Charles, *The Books of Charles Fort,* (edited by Tiffany Thayer), New York: Henry Holt & Co., 1941 and subsequently, p. 274. (*Note:* Hereafter abbreviated simply as Fort.)
23. Flammarion, *Thunder and Lightning,* p. 68.
24. *American Meteorological Journal,* 12 November 1887.
25. Gaddis, Vincent, *Invisible Horizons,* Philadelphia: Chilton Books, 1965, pp. 84-85.
26. *Monthly Weather Review,* 1887, quoted in *FSR,* Vol. 4, No. 5, p. 30.
27. *UFO Investigator,* Vol. IV, No. 5, March 1968.

28. "U.F.O.'s—At 450 Fathoms!" *Man's Illustrated,* March 1966.
29. Gaimar, Geoffrey, *Lestorie des Engles solum la Translacion Maistre Geffrei Gaimar,* 12th-century MS.
30. Greg, R. P., "A Catalogue of Meteorites and Fireballs, from A.D. 2 to A.D. 1860," in *Report of British Association,* 1860, pp. 48-107.
31. Fort, p. 276.
32. Vallee, Jacques, *Anatomy of a Phenomenon,* Chicago: Henry Regnery Co., 1965, pp. 14, 21.
33. *UFO Investigator,* Vol. IV, No. 5 (March 1968), p. 4.
34. Wilkins, Harold T., *Flying Saucers on the Attack,* New York: Citadel Press, 1954, p. 77.
35. *Naval Aviation News,* February 1951; *Fate Magazine,* October 1951, p. 7.
36. Dated but otherwise unidentified news clipping.
37. Cape Town, South Africa, *Sunday Times,* n.d.
38. *Fate Magazine,* March 1954, p. 9.
39. *Ibid.,* March 1955, p. 18.
40. *Ibid.*
41. *Ibid.,* Feb. 1955, p. 11.
42. *Ibid.,* April 1958, p. 114.
43. *UFO Investigator,* Vol. IV, No. 5, March 1968.
44. Norman, Samuel, "Recent UFOs Over Japan," *Fate,* June 1956, pp. 22-24.
45. *The A.P.R.O. Bulletin,* January 1964.
46. *FSR: World Roundup of UFO Sightings and Events,* New York: Citadel Press, 1958, p. 147.
47. Port Chester, N.Y., *Item,* 22 June 1957.
48. *South Pacific Post,* Port Moresby, Papua, New Guinea, 25 August 1957; quoted in *FSR,* Vol. 4, No. 4, p. 7.
49. *FSR,* Vol. 3, No. 6, p. 9.
50. *Evening Okayama News,* 21 November 1957.
51. Vallee, Jacques, *Anatomy of a Phenomenon,* Chicago: Henry Regnery Co., 1965, p. 141.
52. UPI; St. Petersburg, Fla. *Times,* 12 February 1960.
53. Seattle *Times,* 9 March 1960.
54. *FSR,* Vol. 7, No. 3, p. 22.
55. *FSR,* Vol. 8, No. 2, pp. 25-26.
56. *London Daily Mail,* 7 July 1961.
57. Dated but otherwise unidentified news clipping.
58. *Honolulu Advertiser,* 13 March 1963.
59. *Northern Echo,* 23 November 1963, quoted in *FSR,* Vol. 10, No. 2, p. 23.

60. Seattle *Post-Intelligencer,* 21 August 1964.
61. *Liverpool Echo,* 15 December 1964, quoted in *FSR,* Vol. 11, No. 2, p. 26.
62. *Seaside* [Oregon] *Signal,* 12 January 1965.
63. *Monterey Peninsula Herald,* 30 January 1965.
64. *FSR,* Vol. 11, No. 3, p. 27.
65. UPI, in Los Angeles *Herald Examiner,* 4 August 1965; San Francisco *Examiner,* 5 August 1965.
66. *Melbourne Age,* 30 August 1965.
67. San Pedro *News Pilot,* 3 December 1965.
68. *The A.P.R.O. Bulletin,* May-June 1968.
69. *The UFO Investigator,* Vol. IV, No. 5, March 1968.
70. *Ibid.*
71. *The A.P.R.O. Bulletin,* May-June 1968.
72. Yarmouth, Nova Scotia, *Light Herald,* 12 October 1967; Halifax, N.S., *Chronicle Herald,* 6 October 1967.
73. A.P., 18 March 1958.
74. *FSR,* Vol. 6, No. 3, pp. 14-15; Vol. 10, No. 4, p. 13.
75. *The A.P.R.O. Bulletin,* May 1961, p. 6.
76. *Fate Magazine,* December 1961, p. 27.
77. *Ibid.,* October 1962, p. 10.
78. *FSR,* Vol. 8, No. 6, p. 23.
79. *Buffalo Evening News, Long Island Press, etc.,* A.P. report, 10 April, 1963.
80. *Boston Globe,* 10 August 1963, UPI report.
81. *The A.P.R.O. Bulletin,* May 1964.
82. *Saucer News,* June 1964, p. 18.
83. *FSR,* Vol. 11, No. 3, p. 36.
84. *Taranaki Herald* (New Plymouth, N.Z.), 25 May 1966.
85. *FSR,* Vol. 12, No. 4, p. 29, reprinted from *Spaceview,* No. 47, Feb./March 1966.
86. *Ibid.*
87. *Ibid.*
88. *Ibid.*
89. *Ibid.,* pp. 29-30.
90. *Los Angeles Times,* 6 July 1965.
91. Stiff, Robert A., "A Tragic Sighting in Argentina," in Steiger, Brad, and Writenour, Joan, *The Allende Letters,* Universal Pub. Co., 1968.
92. AP, Miami, 27 September 1966.
93. *Annual Register,* 1767; *Chronicle,* pp. 127-128.
94. Rochester, N.Y., *Democrat & Chronicle,* 14 October 1948.
95. *Fate,* September 1960, p. 48.

96. Buffalo, N.Y., *Evening News,* 26 August 1952.
97. CSI [Civilian Saucer Intelligence] Publication #20 (News Letter No. 8), 25 July 1957, p. 21.
98. Stroudsburg, Pa., *Daily Record,* 14 November 1956.
99. *Netherlands UFO Bulletin # 5.*
100. New Orleans *Times Picayune,* 2 June 1957; CSI Files.
101. Confidential NICAP *Bulletin,* 9 July 1958.
102. Sarnia (Ontario) *Observer,* 24 May 1958.
103. Rochester, N.Y., *Democrat & Chronicle,* 13 October 1958.
104. *Fate,* November 1960, pp. 11-12.
105. Buffalo, N.Y. *Courier Express,* 27 July 1960.
106. *The A.P.R.O. Bulletin,* November 1961, p. 3.
107. KVI-Radio newscast, 10:30 P.M., 25 May 1962.
108. *Saucer News,* September 1962, p. 24.
109. Augusta, Ga., *Chronicle,* 30 August 1962.
110. Hackensack, N.J., *Record,* 17 September 1962.
111. Conneaut, Ohio, *News Herald,* 3 December 1962.
112. *The A.P.R.O. Bulletin,* September 1964, p. 6.
113. Chicago *Tribune,* 22 April 1963.
114. *The A.P.R.O. Bulletin,* January 1964, p. 1; *Fate,* May 1964, pp. 62-65.
115. Oshkosh *Northwestern,* 28 January 1964.
116. Benton Harbor *News Palladium,* 15 February 1964; St. Joseph, Mich., *Herald Press,* 15 February 1964.
117. *FSR,* Vol. 10, No. 4, p. 21.
118. Klamath Falls *Herald and News,* 27 August 1964.
119. Roanoke, Va., *Times,* 10 September 1964, 12 September 1964; *Saucer News,* December 1964, p. 25.
120. Toronto *Daily Star,* 10 October 1964.
121. Grand Rapids, Mich. *Press,* 7 November 1964.
122. Lake Elsinore *Valley Sun,* 21 January 1965.
123. Benton Harbor *News Palladium,* 22 January 1965; also Chicago *Tribune* and Manitowoc *Herald,* same date.
124. Fredericksburg *Free Lance Star,* 26 January 1965.
125. Kenora, Ontario, *Miner & News,* 19 February 1965.
126. Report from NICAP Subcommittee, Washington State.
127. Rochester, Minn., *Bulletin,* 5 August 1965.
128. Seattle *Post-Intelligencer* (UPI), 7 September 1965.
129. *Los Angeles Times,* 6 September 1965.
130. Shawingan Falls *Standard,* 3 November 1965.
131. Middletown, Ohio, *Journal* and Dayton *Journal Herald,* 13 November 1965.
132. Racine, Wis., *Journal Times,* 28 November 1965.

133. Elyria, Ohio, *Telegram* and Canton, Ohio, *Repository,* 10 December 1965.
134. Klamath Falls *Herald News,* 24 December 1965.
135. Detroit *News,* 14 March 1966.
136. Broken Hill, N.S.W., Australia, *Barrier Truth,* 23 June 1966.
137. *The UFO Investigator,* Vol. IV, No. 5, March 1968.
138. *Ibid.,* No. 6, May-June 1968.
139. Elyria, Ohio *Chronicle-Telegram,* 11 September 1967.
140. *FSR,* Vol. 14, No. 1, p. iii.
141. *Ibid.,* No. 4. pp. 34-35.
142. Wolkomir, Richard, "The Glowing 'Thing' in Moore Lake," *Fate,* November 1968, pp. 32-36.
143. *Cleveland Plain Dealer,* 25 November 1968; *FSIC Bulletin,* December 1968, p. 2.
144. *Spacelink,* Vol. 5, No. 4, p. 13.
145. CSI Publication #20 (News Letter No. 8), 25 July 1957, p. 21.
146. 1964 news clipping, column by Alan Jay, newspaper not identified.
147. Lorenzen, Coral and Jim, *Flying Saucer Occupants,* New York: Signet Books, 1967; *UFOs over the Americas,* New York: Signet Books, 1968; *UFO: The Whole Story,* New York: Signet Books, 1969.
148. *The A.P.R.O. Bulletin,* January 1964, p. 1; *Fate,* May 1964, pp. 62-65.
149. Heinlein, Robert A., *The Moon Is a Harsh Mistress,* New York: G. P. Putnam's Sons, 1966.
150. Hunt, Inez, and Draper, Winetta, *Lightning in His Hand: Nikola Tesla, 1856–1943,* Denver, Colo., Sage Books, 1964.
151. *Ibid.*
152. Catalogue of *El Museo del Oro,* Bogotá, Colombia: Banco de la República, 1948.
153. "Fantastic Flying Sub," *Popular Mechanics,* September 1967, pp. 114-115.
154. See articles on hydrodynamics and on submarines in any standard encyclopaedia.
155. *The Guinness Book of Records,* London: Guinness Superlatives, Limited, 1967, p. 232.
156. *Nature,* April 1875.
157. Fort, p. 278.
158. *Notice to Mariners,* U.S.H.O., No. 38 (N.S.), 22 September 1962.
159. Bodler, Cmdr. J. R., "Unexplained Phenomenon in the Sea,"

U.S. Naval Institute Proceedings, January 1952; reprinted in *Fate,* as "Wheel of Light in the Sea," September 1952.

160. Fort, pp. 276-77.
161. *Ibid.,* p. 277.
162. *Ibid.,* pp. 272, 275, 276.
163. *Illustrated London News,* 14 October 1961.
164. Minto, Wallace L., "What Lights the Mystery 'Wheels'?" *Fate,* July 1964, p. 53.
165. Fort, p. 278.
166. *Ibid.,* p. 277.
167. *Ibid.,* p. 279.
168. *Ibid.,* p. 277.
169. *Ibid.,* p. 275-76.
170. *Ibid.,* pp. 276-77.
171. *Ibid.,* p. 277.
172. *Ibid.,* p. 278.
173. *Ibid.,* p. 278.
174. Bodler, Cmdr. J. R., *op. cit.* (ref. 159).
175. *Notice to Mariners,* U.S.H.O., No. 38 (N.S.), 22 September 1962.
176. "Some Australian Sightings" (taken from Department of Air files), bylined John Hallows, unidentified Australian newspaper (probably Victoria).
177. Gaddis, Vincent H., "The Deadly Bermuda Triangle," *Argosy,* February 1964.
178. Pyle, Ernie, "Plane Just Vanished," undated clipping from *New York World-Telegram,* by wireless from "A forward airdrome in French North Africa."
179. *Fate,* August 1955, p. 16.
180. Gaddis, Vincent, *Invisible Horizons,* Philadelphia: Chilton Books, 1965, pp. 175-80. (*Note:* Hereafter abbreviated as Gaddis.)
181. Gaddis, p. 187; Fort, p. 635; London *Times,* 6 November 1840.
182. Gaddis, p. 188.
183. New York *Standard,* February 1963 (day date missing).
184. Godwin, John, *This Baffling World,* New York: Hart Publishing Co., 1968, p. 240.
185. *Ibid.*
186. New York *Standard,* February 1963 (day date missing).
187. Gaddis, pp. 131-145; Fort, p. 634.
188. Gaddis, p. 188; Fort, p. 642; New York *Standard,* February 1963.
189. Gaddis, p. 116.

190. Godwin, John, *op. cit.,* p. 240.
191. Gaddis, pp. 188-89.
192. Fort, pp. 635-36.
193. New York *Standard,* February 1963 (day date missing).
194. Gaddis, p. 189; Godwin, John, *op. cit.,* p. 242.
195. Gaddis, p. 189.
196. Godwin, John, *op. cit.,* p. 242.
197. Gaddis, p. 187.
198. *Ibid.,* p. 197.
199. *Ibid.,* p. 188.
200. *Ibid.,* p. 188.
201. *Ibid.,* pp. 184-85.
202. Letter to Editor, *American Legion Magazine,* June 1962.
203. Gaddis, pp. 175-180.
204. *Doubt,* No. 16, 1946, p. 239.
205. Gaddis, p. 181.
206. *Ibid.,* p. 181.
207. *Ibid.,* p. 181.
208. *Ibid.,* p. 182-83.
209. *Ibid.,* p. 186.
210. *Ibid.,* p. 186.
211. *Ibid.,* p. 186.
212. *Ibid.,* p. 186.
213. *Ibid.,* p. 187.
214. *Ibid.,* p. 186.
215. Long Beach *Press-Telegram,* 16 April 1960.
216. Gaddis, p. 174.
217. Godwin, John, *op. cit.,* pp. 250-51.
218. Gaddis, p. 173.
219. *Ibid.,* p. 174.
220. *Ibid.,* p. 173-74.
221. Gaddis, Vincent, personal communication, n.d.
222. *Ibid.*
223. *Ibid.*
224. Personal communication, 30 July 1968 (name on file).
225. AP dispatch, 18 October 1968.
226. Reuters dispatch, 12 July 1969; London *Sunday Times,* 13 July 1969.
227. Gaddis, pp. 146-49, 151-60; Fiji *Times and Herald,* 19 November 1955; *Life,* 12 December 1955; Maugham, Robin, *Argosy,* June 1962.
228. Gaddis, 131-145; Gould, Rupert T., *The Stargazer Talks,* London: Geoffrey Bles, 1944; Wilkins, H. T., *New Light on the Mary Celeste,* Girard, Kansas: Haldeman-Julius Publica-

tions, 1947; Snow, Edward R., and Lockhart, J. G., *Mysteries of the Sea: A Book of Strange Tales,* New York: Frederick A. Stokes, n.d.

229. Gaddis, pp. 114, 115, 143; Snow, Edward R., *Mysteries and Adventures Along the Atlantic Coast,* New York: Dodd, Mead, 1948.

230. Gaddis, p. 114; Washington, D.C. *Times-Herald,* 11 February 1953; *Fate,* June 1953.

231. Gaddis, pp. 110-111; Jessup, Morris K., *The Case for the UFO,* New York: Citadel Press, 1955; Edwards, Frank, *Strangest of All,* New York: Lyle Stuart, 1956; *Fate,* June 1953.

232. Gaddis, p. 116; Gould, Rupert T., *The Stargazer Talks,* London: Geoffrey Bles, 1944.

233. Gaddis, pp. 116-117.

234. Miller, R. DeWitt, *Forgotten Mysteries,* Chicago: Cloud, Inc., 1947; *Coronet,* December 1952; Edwards, Frank, *Strangest of All,* New York: Lyle Stuart, 1956.

235. Sanderson, Ivan T., *More "Things,"* New York: Pyramid Publications, 1969, pp. 153-165.

236. Personal communication, name on file.

237. Bisque, Ramon E., and Rouse, George E., "Geoid and Magnetic Field Anomalies; Their Relationship to the Core-Mantle Interface," paper presented at Sea-Floor Spreading Session of the American Geophysical Union annual meeting, Washington, D.C., April 11, 1968; Bisque, Ramon E., and Rouse, George E., "Geoid and Magnetic Field Anomalies; Their Relationship to the Core-Mantle Interface," *The Mines Magazine,* May 1968, pp. 20-22. See also: Small, William E., "'Giant Step' Toward a Unifying Theory of Geophysics?" *Scientific Research,* June 10, 1968, pp. 39-40; "Geophysics: A Mining Bonanza," *Industrial Research,* June 1968; *Science News,* 30 March 1968, p. 301.

238. Carstoiu, John, "The Two Gravitational Fields and Gravitational Waves Propogation," *Proceedings* of the National Academy of Sciences (in press).

239. Sanderson, Ivan T., "The Spreading Mystery of the Bermuda Triangle," *Argosy,* August 1968.

240. Carstoiu, John, *op. cit.*

241. Weber, Joseph, "Evidence for Discovery of Gravitational Radiation," *Physical Review Letters,* Vol. 22, No. 24, pp. 1320-24 (16 June 1969); Davis, Harold L., "Gravity Pulses Confirmed—But Where Do They Come From?" *Scientific Research,* 4 August 1969, pp. 23-24.

242. Schubert, Gerald, and Whitehead, J. A., *Science,* 3 January 1969.

243. It is impossible to list all references in this field, but see index to *Science* for numerous articles; see also our reference 237; and Curtis, George D., "An Electromagnetic Radiation Pattern Over the Ocean," *Undersea Technology,* August 1964, p. 29.

244. Article by John Tunstall, London *Times,* 14 July 1969.

245. National Geographic Society maps: Atlantic Ocean Floor, June 1968; Indian Ocean Floor, October 1967; Pacific Ocean Floor, October 1969.

246. *Goode's World Atlas,* 10th ed., Chicago: Rand McNally & Company, 1957, p. 161.

247. *Ibid.*

248. *Hammond World Atlas,* New Perspective Edition, Maplewood, N.J.: Hammond Incorporated, 1967.

249. James, Trevor, *They Live in the Sky,* Los Angeles, Calif.: New Age Publishing Co., 1958.

250. Ford, Barbara, "Safe City: Apartment Living Inside a Mountain," *Science Digest,* August 1969, pp. 16-19.

251. Sanderson, Ivan T., *Animal Treasure,* New York: Viking Press, 1937, p. 251.

252. Cochran, Andrew A., "Life and the Wave Properties of Matter," *Dialectica,* International Review of Philosophy of Knowledge, *19,* No. 3-4, 15. 9-15. 12., 1965, pp. 290-312; "Mind, Matter and Quanta," *Main Currents in Modern Thought,* Vol. 22, No. 4, March-April 1966.

253. Jung, C. G., *Flying Saucers, A Modern Myth of Things Seen in the Skies,* New York: Harcourt, Brace and Company, 1959.

254. Chicago: Henry Regnery Company, 1969.

255. Herriott, Donald R., "Applications of Laser Light," *Scientific American,* Vol. 219, No. 3, September 1968, p. 141.

256. *Fate,* August 1955, p. 16.

257. Annual Reports, Bureau of Missing Persons, City of New York.

258. Fort, p. 684.

259. Churchill, Allen, *They Never Came Back,* New York: Ace Books, pp. 56-85.

260. Fort, p. 847.

261. Leslie, Desmond, and Adamski, George, *Flying Saucers Have Landed,* New York: The British Book Centre, 1953, pp. 90-94.

262. London: Rudolph Steiner Press, 1965.

INDEX

LOST CITIES

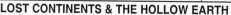

TECHNOLOGY OF THE GODS
The Incredible Sciences of the Ancients
by David Hatcher Childress

Popular *Lost Cities* author David Hatcher Childress takes us into the amazing world of ancient technology, from computers in antiquity to the "flying machines of the gods." Childress looks at the technology that was allegedly used in Atlantis and the theory that the Great Pyramid of Egypt was originally a gigantic power station. He examines tales of ancient flight and the technology that it involved; how the ancients used electricity; megalithic building techniques; the use of crystal lenses and the fire from the gods; evidence of various high tech weapons in the past, including atomic weapons; ancient metallurgy and heavy machinery; the role of modern inventors such as Nikola Tesla in bringing ancient technology back into modern use; impossible artifacts; and more.
356 PAGES. 6x9 PAPERBACK. ILLUSTRATED. BIBLIOGRAPHY. $16.95. CODE: TGOD

VIMANA AIRCRAFT OF ANCIENT INDIA & ATLANTIS
by David Hatcher Childress, introduction by Ivan T. Sanderson

Did the ancients have the technology of flight? In this incredible volume on ancient India, authentic Indian texts such as the *Ramayana* and the *Mahabharata* are used to prove that ancient aircraft were in use more than four thousand years ago. Included in this book is the entire Fourth Century BC manuscript *Vimaanika Shastra* by the ancient author Maharishi Bharadwaaja, translated into English by the Mysore Sanskrit professor G.R. Josyer. Also included are chapters on Atlantean technology, the incredible Rama Empire of India and the devastating wars that destroyed it. Also an entire chapter on mercury vortex propulsion and mercury gyros, the power source described in the ancient Indian texts. Not to be missed by those interested in ancient civilizations or the UFO enigma.
334 PAGES. 6x9 PAPERBACK. RARE PHOTOGRAPHS, MAPS AND DRAWINGS. $15.95. CODE: VAA

LOST CONTINENTS & THE HOLLOW EARTH
I Remember Lemuria and the Shaver Mystery
by David Hatcher Childress & Richard Shaver

Lost Continents & the Hollow Earth is Childress' thorough examination of the early hollow earth stories of Richard Shaver and the fascination that fringe fantasy subjects such as lost continents and the hollow earth have had for the American public. Shaver's rare 1948 book *I Remember Lemuria* is reprinted in its entirety, and the book is packed with illustrations from Ray Palmer's *Amazing Stories* magazine of the 1940s. Palmer and Shaver told of tunnels running through the earth—tunnels inhabited by the Deros and Teros, humanoids from an ancient spacefaring race that had inhabited the earth, eventually going underground, hundreds of thousands of years ago. Childress discusses the famous hollow earth books and delves deep into whatever reality may be behind the stories of tunnels in the earth. Operation High Jump to Antarctica in 1947 and Admiral Byrd's bizarre statements, tunnel systems in South America and Tibet, the underground world of Agartha, the belief of UFOs coming from the South Pole, more.
344 PAGES. 6x9 PAPERBACK. ILLUSTRATED. $16.95. CODE: LCHE

A HITCHHIKER'S GUIDE TO ARMAGEDDON
by David Hatcher Childress

With wit and humor, popular Lost Cities author David Hatcher Childress takes us around the world and back in his trippy finalé to the Lost Cities series. He's off on an adventure in search of the apocalypse and end times. Childress hits the road from the fortress of Megiddo, the legendary citadel in northern Israel where Armageddon is prophesied to start. Hitchhiking around the world, Childress takes us from one adventure to another, to ancient cities in the deserts and the legends of worlds before our own. Childress muses on the rise and fall of civilizations, and the forces that have shaped mankind over the millennia, including wars, invasions and cataclysms. He discusses the ancient Armageddons of the past, and chronicles recent Middle East developments and their ominous undertones. In the meantime, he becomes a cargo cult god on a remote island off New Guinea, gets dragged into the Kennedy Assassination by one of the "conspirators," investigates a strange power operating out of the Altai Mountains of Mongolia, and discovers how the Knights Templar and their off-shoots have driven the world toward an epic battle centered around Jerusalem and the Middle East.
320 PAGES. 6x9 PAPERBACK. ILLUSTRATED. BIBLIOGRAPHY. INDEX. $16.95. CODE: HGA

THE LAND OF OSIRIS
An Introduction to Khemitology
by Stephen S. Mehler

Was there an advanced prehistoric civilization in ancient Egypt? Were they the people who built the great pyramids and carved the Great Sphinx? Did the pyramids serve as energy devices and not as tombs for kings? Mehler has uncovered an indigenous oral tradition that still exists in Egypt, and has been fortunate to have studied with a living master of this tradition, Abd'El Hakim Awyan. Mehler has also been given permission to present these teachings to the Western world, teachings that unfold a whole new understanding of ancient Egypt and have only been presented heretofore in fragments by other researchers. Chapters include: Egyptology and Its Paradigms; Khemitology—New Paradigms; Asgat Nefer—The Harmony of Water; Khemit and the Myth of Atlantis; The Extraterrestrial Question; more.
272 PAGES. 6x9 PAPERBACK. ILLUSTRATED. COLOR SECTION. BIBLIOGRAPHY. $18.95. CODE: LOOS

IN QUEST OF LOST WORLDS
Journey to Mysterious Algeria, Ethiopia & the Yucatan
by Count Byron Khun de Prorok

Finally, a reprint of Count Byron de Prorok's classic archeology/adventure book first published in 1936 by E.P. Dutton & Co. in New York. In this exciting and well illustrated book, de Prorok takes us into the deep Sahara of forbidden Algeria, to unknown Ethiopia, and to the many prehistoric ruins of the Yucatan. Includes: Tin Hinan, Legendary Queen of the Tuaregs; The mysterious A'Haggar Range of southern Algeria; Jupiter, Ammon and Tripolitania; The "Talking Dune"; The Land of the Garamantes; Mexico and the Poison Trail; Seeking Atlantis—Chichen Itza; Shadowed by the "Little People"—the Lacandon Pygmie Maya; Ancient Pyramids of the Usamasinta and Piedras Negras in Guatemala; In Search of King Solomon's Mines & the Land of Ophir; Ancient Emerald Mines of Ethiopia. Also included in this book are 24 pages of special illustrations of the famous—and strange—wall paintings of the Ahaggar from the rare book *The Search for the Tassili Frescoes* by Henri Lhote (1959). A visual treat of a remote area of the world that is even today forbidden to outsiders!
324 PAGES. 6x9 PAPERBACK. ILLUSTRATED. $16.95. CODE: IQLW

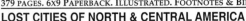

ANTI-GRAVITY

THE FREE-ENERGY DEVICE HANDBOOK
A Compilation of Patents and Reports
by David Hatcher Childress

A large-format compilation of various patents, papers, descriptions and diagrams concerning free-energy devices and systems. *The Free-Energy Device Handbook* is a visual tool for experimenters and researchers into magnetic motors and other "over-unity" devices. With chapters on the Adams Motor, the Hans Coler Generator, cold fusion, superconductors, "N" machines, space-energy generators, Nikola Tesla, T. Townsend Brown, and the latest in free-energy devices. Packed with photos, technical diagrams, patents and fascinating information, this book belongs on every science shelf. With energy and profit being a major political reason for fighting various wars, free-energy devices, if ever allowed to be mass distributed to consumers, could change the world! Get your copy now before the Department of Energy bans this book!
292 PAGES. 8X10 PAPERBACK. ILLUSTRATED. BIBLIOGRAPHY. $16.95. CODE: FEH

THE ANTI-GRAVITY HANDBOOK
edited by David Hatcher Childress, with Nikola Tesla, T.B. Paulicki,
Bruce Cathie, Albert Einstein and others

The new expanded compilation of material on Anti-Gravity, Free Energy, Flying Saucer Propulsion, UFOs, Suppressed Technology, NASA Cover-ups and more. Highly illustrated with patents, technical illustrations and photos. This revised and expanded edition has more material, including photos of Area 51, Nevada, the government's secret testing facility. This classic on weird science is back in a 90s format!
• How to build a flying saucer.
•Arthur C. Clarke on Anti-Gravity.
• Crystals and their role in levitation.
• Secret government research and development.
• Nikola Tesla on how anti-gravity airships could
   draw power from the atmosphere.
• Bruce Cathie's Anti-Gravity Equation.
• NASA, the Moon and Anti-Gravity.
253 PAGES. 7X10 PAPERBACK. BIBLIOGRAPHY/INDEX/APPENDIX. HIGHLY ILLUSTRATED. $16.95.
CODE: AGH

ANTI–GRAVITY & THE WORLD GRID

Is the earth surrounded by an intricate electromagnetic grid network offering free energy? This compilation of material on ley lines and world power points contains chapters on the geography, mathematics, and light harmonics of the earth grid. Learn the purpose of ley lines and ancient megalithic structures located on the grid. Discover how the grid made the Philadelphia Experiment possible. Explore the Coral Castle and many other mysteries, including acoustic levitation, Tesla Shields and scalar wave weaponry. Browse through the section on anti-gravity patents, and research resources.
274 PAGES. 7X10 PAPERBACK. ILLUSTRATED. $14.95. CODE: AGW

ANTI–GRAVITY & THE UNIFIED FIELD
edited by David Hatcher Childress

Is Einstein's Unified Field Theory the answer to all of our energy problems? Explored in this compilation of material is how gravity, electricity and magnetism manifest from a unified field around us. Why artificial gravity is possible; secrets of UFO propulsion; free energy; Nikola Tesla and anti-gravity airships of the 20s and 30s; flying saucers as superconducting whirls of plasma; anti-mass generators; vortex propulsion; suppressed technology; government cover-ups; gravitational pulse drive; spacecraft & more.
240 PAGES. 7X10 PAPERBACK. ILLUSTRATED. $14.95. CODE: AGU

ETHER TECHNOLOGY
A Rational Approach to Gravity Control
by Rho Sigma

This classic book on anti-gravity and free energy is back in print and back in stock. Written by a well-known American scientist under the pseudonym of "Rho Sigma," this book delves into international efforts at gravity control and discoid craft propulsion. Before the Quantum Field, there was "Ether." This small, but informative book has chapters on John Searle and "Searle discs;" T. Townsend Brown and his work on anti-gravity and ether-vortex turbines. Includes a forward by former NASA astronaut Edgar Mitchell.
108 PAGES. 6X9 PAPERBACK. ILLUSTRATED. $12.95. CODE: ETT

TAPPING THE ZERO POINT ENERGY
Free Energy & Anti-Gravity in Today's Physics
by Moray B. King

King explains how free energy and anti-gravity are possible. The theories of the zero point energy maintain there are tremendous fluctuations of electrical field energy imbedded within the fabric of space. This book tells how, in the 1930s, inventor T. Henry Moray could produce a fifty kilowatt "free energy" machine; how an electrified plasma vortex creates anti-gravity; how the Pons/Fleischmann "cold fusion" experiment could produce tremendous heat without fusion; and how certain experiments might produce a gravitational anomaly.
190 PAGES. 5X8 PAPERBACK. ILLUSTRATED. $12.95. CODE: TAP

ANTI-GRAVITY

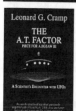

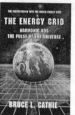

STRANGE SCIENCE

UNDERGROUND BASES & TUNNELS
What is the Government Trying to Hide?
by Richard Sauder, Ph.D.

Working from government documents and corporate records, Sauder has compiled an impressive book that digs below the surface of the military's super-secret underground! Go behind the scenes into little-known corners of the public record and discover how corporate America has worked hand-in-glove with the Pentagon for decades, dreaming about, planning, and actually constructing, secret underground bases. This book includes chapters on the locations of the bases, the tunneling technology, various military designs for underground bases, nuclear testing & underground bases, abductions, needles & implants, military involvement in "alien" cattle mutilations, more. 50 page photo & map insert.

201 PAGES. 6X9 PAPERBACK. ILLUSTRATED. $15.95. CODE: UGB

UNDERWATER & UNDERGROUND BASES
Surprising Facts the Government Does Not Want You to Know
by Richard Sauder

Dr. Sauder lays out the amazing evidence and government paper trail for the construction of huge, manned bases offshore, in mid-ocean, and deep beneath the sea floor! Bases big enough to secretly dock submarines! Official United States Navy documents, and other hard evidence, raise many questions about what really lies 20,000 leagues beneath the sea. Many UFOs have been seen coming and going from the world's oceans, seas and lakes, implying the existence of secret underwater bases. Dr. Sauder also adds to his incredible database of underground bases onshore. New, breakthrough material reveals the existence of additional clandestine underground facilities as well as the surprising location of one of the CIA's own underground bases. Plus, new information on tunneling and cutting-edge, high speed rail magnetic-levitation (MagLev) technology.

264 PAGES. 6X9 PAPERBACK. ILLUSTRATED. BIBLIOGRAPHY. INDEX. $16.95. CODE: UUB

REICH OF THE BLACK SUN
Nazi Secret Weapons and the Cold War Allied Legend
by Joseph P. Farrell

Why were the Allies worried about an atom bomb attack by the Germans in 1944? Why did the Soviets threaten to use poison gas against the Germans? Why did Hitler in 1945 insist that holding Prague could win the war for the Third Reich? Why did US General George Patton's Third Army race for the Skoda works at Pilsen in Czechoslovakia instead of Berlin? Why did the US Army not test the uranium atom bomb it dropped on Hiroshima? Why did the Luftwaffe fly a non-stop round trip mission to within twenty miles of New York City in 1944? *Reich of the Black Sun* takes the reader on a scientific-historical journey in order to answer these questions. Arguing that Nazi Germany actually won the race for the atom bomb in late 1944, *Reich of the Black Sun* then goes on to explore the even more secretive research the Nazis were conducting into the occult, alternative physics and new energy sources. The book concludes with a fresh look at the "Nazi Legend" of the UFO mystery by examining the Roswell Majestic-12 documents and the Kecksburg crash in the light of parallels with some of the super-secret black projects being run by the SS.

352 PAGES. 6X9 PAPERBACK. ILLUSTRATED. BIBLIOGRAPHY. $16.95. CODE: ROBS

QUEST FOR ZERO-POINT ENERGY
Engineering Principles for "Free Energy"
by Moray B. King

King expands, with diagrams, on how free energy and anti-gravity are possible. The theories of zero point energy maintain there are tremendous fluctuations of electrical field energy embedded within the fabric of space. King explains the following topics: Tapping the Zero-Point Energy as an Energy Source; Fundamentals of a Zero-Point Energy Technology; Vacuum Energy Vortices; The Super Tube; Charge Clusters: The Basis of Zero-Point Energy Inventions; Vortex Filaments, Torsion Fields and the Zero-Point Energy; Transforming the Planet with a Zero-Point Energy Experiment; Dual Vortex Forms: The Key to a Large Zero-Point Energy Coherence. Packed with diagrams, patents and photos. With power shortages now a daily reality in many parts of the world, this book offers a fresh approach very rarely mentioned in the mainstream media.

224 PAGES. 6X9 PAPERBACK. ILLUSTRATED. $14.95. CODE: QZPE

HITLER'S FLYING SAUCERS
A Guide to German Flying Discs of the Second World War
by Henry Stevens

Learn why the Schriever-Habermohl project was actually two projects and read the written statement of a German test pilot who actually flew one of these saucers; about the Leduc engine, the key to Dr. Miethe's saucer designs; how U.S. government officials kept the truth about foo fighters hidden for almost sixty years and how they were finally forced to "come clean" about the foo fighter's German origin. Learn of the Peenemuende saucer project and how it was slated to "go atomic." Read the testimony of a German eyewitness who saw "magnetic discs." Read the U.S. government's own reports on German field propulsion saucers. Read how the post-war German KM-2 field propulsion "rocket" worked. Learn details of the work of Karl Schappeller and Viktor Schauberger. Learn how their ideas figure in the quest to build field propulsion flying discs. Find out what happened to this technology after the war. Find out how the Canadians got saucer technology directly from the SS. Find out about the surviving "Third Power" of former Nazis. Learn of the U.S. government's methods of UFO deception and how they used the German "Sonderbueroll" as the model for Project Blue Book.

388 PAGES. 6X9 PAPERBACK. ILLUSTRATED. INDEX. $18.95. CODE: HFS

THE TIME TRAVEL HANDBOOK
A Manual of Practical Teleportation & Time Travel
edited by David Hatcher Childress

In the tradition of *The Anti-Gravity Handbook* and *The Free-Energy Device Handbook*, science and UFO author David Hatcher Childress takes us into the weird world of time travel and teleportation. Not just a whacked-out look at science fiction, this book is an authoritative chronicling of real-life time travel experiments, teleportation devices and more. *The Time Travel Handbook* takes the reader beyond the government experiments and deep into the uncharted territory of early time travellers such as Nikola Tesla and Guglielmo Marconi and their alleged time travel experiments, as well as the Wilson Brothers of EMI and their connection to the Philadelphia Experiment—the U.S. Navy's forays into invisibility, time travel, and teleportation. Childress looks into the claims of time travelling individuals, and investigates the unusual claim that the pyramids on Mars were built in the future and sent back in time. A highly visual, large format book, with patents, photos and schematics. Be the first on your block to build your own time travel device!

316 PAGES. 7X10 PAPERBACK. ILLUSTRATED. $16.95. CODE: TTH

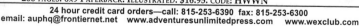

CONSPIRACY & HISTORY

SECRETS OF THE HOLY LANCE
The Spear of Destiny in History & Legend
by Jerry E. Smith and George Piccard

As Jesus Christ hung on the cross a Roman centurion pieced the Savior's side with his spear. A legend has arisen that "whosoever possesses this Holy Lance and understands the powers it serves, holds in his hand the destiny of the world for good or evil." *Secrets of the Holy Lance* traces the Spear from its possession by Constantine, Rome's first Christian Caesar, to Charlemagne's claim that with it he ruled the Holy Roman Empire by Divine Right, and on through two thousand years of kings and emperors, until it came within Hitler's grasp—and beyond! Did it rest for a while in Antarctic ice? Is it now hidden in Europe, awaiting the next person to claim its awesome power? Neither debunking nor worshiping, *Secrets of the Holy Lance* seeks to pierce the veil of myth and mystery around the Spear. Mere belief that it was infused with magic by virtue of its shedding the Savior's blood has made men kings. But what if it's more? What are "the powers it serves"?

312 PAGES. 6x9 PAPERBACK. ILLUSTRATED. BIBLIOGRAPHY. $16.95. CODE: SOHL

MIND CONTROL AND UFOS
Casebook on Alternative 3
by Jim Keith

Drawing on his diverse research and a wide variety of sources, Jim Keith delves into the bizarre story behind *Alternative 3*, including mind control programs, underground bases not only on the Earth but also on the Moon and Mars, the real origin of the UFO problem, the mysterious deaths of Marconi Electronics employees in Britain during the 1980s, top scientists around the world kidnapped to work at the secret government space bases, the Russian-American superpower arms race of the 50s, 60s and 70s as a massive hoax, and other startling arenas.

248 PAGES. 6x9 PAPERBACK. ILLUSTRATED. $14.95. CODE: MCUF

THE ENERGY MACHINE OF T. HENRY MORAY
by Moray B. King

In the 1920s T. Henry Moray invented a "free energy" device that reportedly output 50 kilowatts of electricity. It could not be explained by standard science at that time. The electricity exhibited a strange "cold current" characteristic where thin wires could conduct appreciable power without heating. Moray suffered ruthless suppression, and in 1939 the device was destroyed. Frontier science lecturer and author Moray B. King explains the invention with today's science. Modern physics recognizes that the vacuum contains tremendous energy called the zero-point energy. A way to coherently activate it appears surprisingly simple: first create a glow plasma or corona, then abruptly pulse it. Other inventors have discovered this approach (sometimes unwittingly) to create novel energy devices, and they too were suppressed. The common pattern of their technologies clarified the fundamental operating principle. King hopes to inspire engineers and inventors so that a new energy source can become available to mankind.

192 PAGES. 6x8 PAPERBACK. ILLUSTRATED. REFERENCES. $14.95. CODE: EMHM

DIG HERE!
Lost Mines & Buried Treasure of the Southwest
by Thomas Penfield, introduction by David Hatcher Childress

The most amazing book on lost treasure ever written, giving the locations of well over 100 fabulous fortunes waiting to be found in the ore-rich Southwest! For the first time lost treasure stories of the Southwest are stripped bare of their legends and lies! Each treasure account is preceded by the approximate location, estimated total value and authentication. Reading sources for each a count are also included so you can do additional research on the intriguing facts and lore of these treasures. *Dig Here!* is a veritable gold mine itself, overflowing with fascinating lore, spellbinding backgrounds, driving Western drama—and exciting, reliable facts! Chapters include: Treasure of Tumacacori; Lost Mine of the Tonto Apaches; Lost Dutchman Mine; Treasure of the Cursed Cerro Colorado; Black Princess Lost Mine; Lost Treasure of Montezuma's Head; Aztec Montezuma's Treasure; Treasure of Montezuma's Well; Montezuma's Treasure at Casa Grande; Lost Adams Diggings; Treasure of Skeleton Canyon; Lost Mine of the Silver Stairway; Geronimo's Lost Gold Mine; The Mysterious Treasure of Karl Steinheimer; more.

228 PAGES. 6x9 PAPERBACK. ILLUSTRATED. BIBLIOGRAPHY. INDEX. $14.95. CODE: DIGH

THE CHILDREN OF THE SUN
A Study of the Egyptian Settlement of the Pacific
by W.J. Perry

A reprint of the groundbreaking work of Professor W.J. Perry, an early diffusionist who believed that civilization spread throughout the world via transoceanic voyaging—an idea that most historians still fail to accept, even in the face of mounting evidence. First published in 1923, this classic presents the fascinating evidence that envoys of the ancient Sun Kingdoms of Egypt and India travelled into Indonesia and the Pacific circa 1500 BC, spreading their sophisticated culture. Perry traces the expansion of megalithic building from its origin in Egypt through Indonesia and across the Pacific all the way to the Americas. These early mariners searched for gold, obsidian, and pearls in their incredible explorations from island to island—they were the Children of the Sun! Includes: The Coming of the Warriors; Rulers and Commoners: The Sky World; The Indo-Egyptian Alliance of Builders; The Oceania-Indonesian Alliance of Explorers; more.

554 PAGES. 6x9 PAPERBACK. ILLUSTRATED. BIBLIOGRAPHY. INDEX. $18.95. CODE: CSUN

DIG HERE!

Lost Mines & Buried Treasure of the Southwest

Thomas Penfield

UFOS, PSI AND SPIRITUAL EVOLUTION
A Journey through the Evolution of Interstellar Travel
by Christopher Humphries, Ph.D.

The modern era of UFOs began in May, 1947, one year and eight months after Hiroshima. This is no coincidence, and suggests there are beings in the universe with the ability to jump hundreds of light years in an instant. That is teleportation, a power of the mind. UFOs sometimes float along close to the ground, in complete silence. That is levitation, another power of the mind. If it weren't for levitation and teleportation, star travel would not be possible at all, since physics rules out star travel by technology. So if we want to go to the stars, it is the mind and spirit we must study, not technology. The mind must be a dark matter object, since it is invisible and intangible and can freely pass through solid objects. A disembodied mind can see the de Broglie vibrations (the basis of quantum mechanics) radiated by both dark and ordinary matter during near-death or out-of-body experiences. Levitation requires warping the geodesics of space-time. The latest theory in physics is String Theory, which requires six extra spatial dimensions. The mind warps those higher geodesics to produce teleportation. We are a primitive and violent species. Our universities lack any sciences of mind, spirit or civilization. If we want to go to the stars, the first thing we must do is "grow up." That is the real Journey.

274 PAGES. 6x9 PAPERBACK. ILLUSTRATED. REFERENCES. $16.95. CODE: UPSE

24 hour credit card orders—call: 815-253-6390 fax: 815-253-6300
email: auphq@frontiernet.net   www.adventuresunlimitedpress.com   www.wexclub.com

CONSPIRACY & HISTORY

LIQUID CONSPIRACY
JFK, LSD, the CIA, Area 51 & UFOs
by George Piccard

Underground author George Piccard on the politics of LSD, mind control, and Kennedy's involvement with Area 51 and UFOs. Reveals JFK's LSD experiences with Mary Pinchot-Meyer. The plot thickens with an ever expanding web of CIA involvement, from underground bases with UFOs seen by JFK and Marilyn Monroe (among others) to a vaster conspiracy that affects every government agency from NASA to the Justice Department. This may have been the reason that Marilyn Monroe and actress-columnist Dorothy Kilgallen were both murdered. Focusing on the bizarre side of history, *Liquid Conspiracy* takes the reader on a psychedelic tour de force. This is your government on drugs!
264 PAGES. 6x9 PAPERBACK. ILLUSTRATED. $14.95. CODE: LIQC

INSIDE THE GEMSTONE FILE
Howard Hughes, Onassis & JFK
by Kenn Thomas & David Hatcher Childress

Steamshovel Press editor Thomas takes on the Gemstone File in this run-up and run-down of the most famous underground document ever circulated. Photocopied and distributed for over 20 years, the Gemstone File is the story of Bruce Roberts, the inventor of the synthetic ruby widely used in laser technology today, and his relationship with the Howard Hughes Company and ultimately with Aristotle Onassis, the Mafia, and the CIA. Hughes kidnapped and held a drugged-up prisoner for 10 years; Onassis and his role in the Kennedy Assassination; how the Mafia ran corporate America in the 1960s; the death of Onassis' son in the crash of a small private plane in Greece; Onassis as Ian Fleming's archvillain Ernst Stavro Blofeld; more.
320 PAGES. 6x9 PAPERBACK. ILLUSTRATED. $16.00. CODE: IGF

SAUCERS OF THE ILLUMINATI
by Jim Keith, foreword by Kenn Thomas

Seeking the truth behind stories of alien invasion, secret underground bases, and the secret plans of the New World Order, *Saucers of the Illuminati* offers groundbreaking research, uncovering clues to the nature of UFOs and to forces even more sinister: the secret cabal behind planetary control! Includes mind control, saucer abductions, the MJ-12 documents, cattle mutilations, government anti-gravity testing, the Sirius Connection, science fiction author Philip K. Dick and his efforts to expose the Illuminati, plus more from veteran conspiracy and UFO author Keith. Conspiracy expert Keith's final book on UFOs and the highly secret group that manufactures them and uses them for their own purposes: the control and manipulation of the population of planet Earth.
148 PAGES. 6x9 PAPERBACK. ILLUSTRATED. $12.95. CODE: SOIL

THE ARCH CONSPIRATOR
Essays and Actions
by Len Bracken

Veteran conspiracy author Len Bracken's witty essays and articles lead us down the dark corridors of conspiracy, politics, murder and mayhem. In 12 chapters Bracken takes us through a maze of interwoven tales from the Russian Conspiracy to his interview with Costa Rican novelist Joaquin Gutierrez and his Psychogeographic Map into the Third Millennium. Other chapters in the book are A General Theory of Civil War; The New-Catiline Conspiracy for the Cancellation of Debt; Anti-Labor Day; 1997 with selected Aphorisms Against Work; Solar Economics; and more. Bracken's work has appeared in such pop-conspiracy publications as *Paranoia, Steamshovel Press* and the *Village Voice*. Len Bracken lives in Arlington, Virginia and haunts the back alleys of Washington D.C., keeping an eye on the predators who run our country.
256 PAGES. 6x9 PAPERBACK. ILLUSTRATED. BIBLIOGRAPHY. $14.95. CODE: ACON.

MIND CONTROL, WORLD CONTROL
by Jim Keith

Veteran author and investigator Jim Keith uncovers a surprising amount of information on the technology, experimentation and implementation of mind control. Various chapters in this shocking book are on early CIA experiments such as Project Artichoke and Project R.H.I.C.-EDOM, the methodology and technology of implants, mind control assassins and couriers, various famous Mind Control victims such as Sirhan Sirhan and Candy Jones. Also featured in this book are chapters on how mind control technology may be linked to some UFO activity and "UFO abductions."
256 PAGES. 6x9 PAPERBACK. ILLUSTRATED. FOOTNOTES. $14.95. CODE: MCWC

NASA, NAZIS & JFK:
The Torbitt Document & the JFK Assassination
introduction by Kenn Thomas

This book emphasizes the links between "Operation Paper Clip" Nazi scientists working for NASA, the assassination of JFK, and the secret Nevada air base Area 51. The Torbitt Document also talks about the roles played in the assassination by Division Five of the FBI, the Defense Industrial Security Command (DISC), the Las Vegas mob, and the shadow corporate entities Permindex and Centro-Mondiale Commerciale. The Torbitt Document claims that the same players planned the 1962 assassination attempt on Charles de Gaul, who ultimately pulled out of NATO because he traced the "Assassination Cabal" to Permindex in Switzerland and to NATO headquarters in Brussels. The Torbitt Document paints a dark picture of NASA, the military industrial complex, and the connections to Mercury, Nevada which headquarters the "secret space program."
258 PAGES. 5x8. PAPERBACK. ILLUSTRATED. $16.00. CODE: NNJ

MIND CONTROL, OSWALD & JFK:
Were We Controlled?
introduction by Kenn Thomas

Steamshovel Press editor Kenn Thomas examines the little-known book *Were We Controlled?*, first published in 1968. The book's author, the mysterious Lincoln Lawrence, maintained that Lee Harvey Oswald was a special agent who was a mind control subject, having received an implant in 1960 at a Russian hospital. Thomas examines the evidence for implant technology and the role it could have played in the Kennedy Assassination. Thomas also looks at the mind control aspects of the RFK assassination and details the history of implant technology. A growing number of people are interested in CIA experiments and its "Silent Weapons for Quiet Wars." Looks at the case that the reporter Damon Runyon, Jr. was murdered because of this book.
256 PAGES. 6x9 PAPERBACK. ILLUSTRATED. NOTES. $16.00. CODE: MCOJ

24 hour credit card orders—call: 815-253-6390 fax: 815-253-6300
email: auphq@frontiernet.net   www.adventuresunlimitedpress.com   www.wexclub.com

HISTORY—CONSPIRACY

POPULAR PARANOIA
The Best of Steamshovel Press
edited by Kenn Thomas
The anthology exposes the biologocal warfare origins of AIDS; the Nazi/Nation of Islam link; the cult of Elizabeth Clare Prophet; the Oklahoma City bombing writings of the late Jim Keith, as well as an article on Keith's own strange death; the conspiratorial mind of John Judge; Marion Pettie and the shadowy Finders group in Washington, DC; demonic iconography; the death of Princess Diana, its connection to the Octopus and the Saudi aerospace contracts; spies among the Rajneeshis; scholarship on the historic Illuminati; and many other parapolitical topics. The book also includes the Steamshovel's last-ever interviews with the great Beat writers Allen Ginsberg and William S. Burroughs, and neuronaut Timothy Leary, and new views of the master Beat, Neal Cassady and Jack Kerouac's science fiction.
308 PAGES. 8X10 PAPERBACK. ILLUSTRATED. $19.95. CODE: POPA

THE ORION PROPHECY
Egyptian and Mayan Prophecies on the Cataclysm of 2012
by Patrick Geryl and Gino Ratinckx
In the year 2012 the Earth awaits a super catastrophe: its magnetic field will reverse in one go. Phenomenal earthquakes and tidal waves will completely destroy our civilization. Europe and North America will shift thousands of kilometers northwards into polar climes. Nearly everyone will perish in the apocalyptic happenings. These dire predictions stem from the Mayans and Egyptians—descendants of the legendary Atlantis. The Atlanteans had highly evolved astronomical knowledge and were able to exactly predict the previous world-wide flood in 9792 BC. They built tens of thousands of boats and escaped to South America and Egypt. In the year 2012 Venus, Orion and several others stars will take the same 'code-positions' as in 9792 BC! For thousands of years historical sources have told of a forgotten time capsule of ancient wisdom located in a labyrinth of secret chambers filled with artifacts and documents from the previous flood. We desperately need this information now—and this book gives one possible location.
324 PAGES. 6X9 PAPERBACK. ILLUSTRATED. BIBLIOGRAPHY. $16.95. CODE: ORP

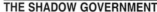

THE SHADOW GOVERNMENT
9-11 and State Terror
by Len Bracken, introduction by Kenn Thomas
Bracken presents the alarming yet convincing theory that nation-states engage in or allow terror to be visited upon their citizens. It is not just liberation movements and radical groups that deploy terroristic tactics for offensive ends. States use terror defensively to directly intimidate their citizens and to indirectly attack themselves or harm their citizens under a false flag. Their motives? To provide pretexts for war or for increased police powers or both. This stratagem of indirectly using terrorism has been executed by statesmen in various ways but tends to involve the pretense of blind eyes, misdirection, and cover-ups that give statesmen plausible deniability. Lusitiania, Pearl Harbor, October Surprise, the first World Trade Center bombing, the Oklahoma City bombing and other well-known incidents suggest that terrorism is often and successfully used by states in an indirectly defensive way to take the offensive against enemies at home and abroad. Was 9-11 such an indirect defensive attack?
288 PAGES. 6X9 PAPERBACK. ILLUSTRATED. $16.00. CODE: SGOV

MASS CONTROL
Engineering Human Consciousness
by Jim Keith
Conspiracy expert Keith's final book on mind control, Project Monarch, and mass manipulation presents chilling evidence that we are indeed spinning a Matrix. Keith describes the New Man, whose conception of reality is a dance of electronic images fired into his forebrain, a gossamer construction of his masters, designed so that he will not—under any circumstances—perceive the actual. His happiness is delivered to him through a tube or an electronic connection. His God lurks behind an electronic curtain; when the curtain is pulled away we find the CIA sorcerer, the media manipulator... Chapters on the CIA, Tavistock, Jolly West and the Violence Center, Guerrilla Mindwar, Brice Taylor, other recent "victims," more.
256 PAGES. 6X9 PAPERBACK. ILLUSTRATED. INDEX. $16.95. CODE: MASC

WAKE UP DOWN THERE!
The Excluded Middle Anthology
by Greg Bishop
The great American tradition of dropout culture makes it over the millennium mark with a collection of the best from The Excluded Middle, the critically acclaimed underground zine of UFOs, the paranormal, conspiracies, psychedelia, and spirit. Contributions from Robert Anton Wilson, Ivan Stang, Martin Kottmeyer, John Shirley, Scott Corrales, Adam Gorightly and Robert Sterling; and interviews with James Moseley, Karla Turner, Bill Moore, Kenn Thomas, Richard Boylan, Dean Radin, Joe McMoneagle, and the mysterious Ira Einhorn (an Excluded Middle exclusive). Includes full versions of interviews and extra material not found in the newsstand versions.
420 PAGES. 8X11 PAPERBACK. ILLUSTRATED. $25.00. CODE: WUDT

DARK MOON
Apollo and the Whistleblowers
by Mary Bennett and David Percy
•Was Neil Armstrong really the first man on the Moon?
•Did you know a second craft was going to the Moon at the same time as Apollo 11?
•Do you know that potentially lethal radiation is prevalent throughout deep space?
•Do you know there are serious discrepancies in the account of the Apollo 13 'accident'?
•Did you know that 'live' color TV from the Moon was not actually live at all?
•Did you know that the Lunar Surface Camera had no viewfinder?
•Do you know that lighting was used in the Apollo photographs—yet no lighting equipment was taken to the Moon?
All these questions, and more, are discussed in great detail by British researchers Bennett and Percy in Dark Moon, the definitive book (nearly 600 pages) on the possible faking of the Apollo Moon missions. Bennett and Percy delve into every possible aspect of this beguiling theory, one that rocks the very foundation of our beliefs concerning NASA and the space program. Tons of NASA photos analyzed for possible deceptions.
568 PAGES. 6X9 PAPERBACK. ILLUSTRATED. BIBLIOGRAPHY. INDEX. $25.00. CODE: DMO

WAKE UP DOWN THERE!

The
EXCLUDED MIDDLE
Anthology

24 hour credit card orders—call: 815-253-6390 fax: 815-253-6300
email: auphq@frontiernet.net   www.adventuresunlimitedpress.com   www.wexclub.com